S0-BLE-575

KNOWING
AND
BEING

James Richard Mensch

KNOWING
AND
BEING

B
831.2
.M46
1996
West

A Postmodern Reversal

The Pennsylvania State University Press
University Park, Pennsylvania

James Richard Mensch is Professor of Philosophy at Saint Francis Xavier University in Antigonish, Nova Scotia, Canada. He is the author of *The Question of Being in Husserl's Logical Investigations* (Martinus Nijhoff Press, 1981), *Intersubjectivity and Transcendental Idealism* (SUNY Press, 1988), *The Beginning of the Gospel of St. John: Philosophical Perspectives* (Peter Lang Publishers, 1992), and *After Modernity: Husserlian Reflections on a Philosophical Tradition* (SUNY Press, 1996).

Library of Congress Cataloging-in-Publication Data

Mensch, James R.
    Knowing and being : a postmodern reversal / James Richard Mensch.
        p.   cm.
    Includes bibliographical references and index.
    ISBN 0-271-01554-3 (cloth : alk. paper)
    ISBN 0-271-01555-1 (paper : alk. paper)
    1. Postmodernism.   2. Subjectivity.   3. Object (Philosophy)
4. Knowledge, Theory of.   I. Title.
B831.2.M46   1996
149'.9—dc20   95-40442
                                                                  CIP

Copyright © 1996 The Pennsylvania State University
All rights reserved
Printed in the United States of America
Published by The Pennsylvania State University Press,
University Park, PA 16802-1003

It is the policy of The Pennsylvania State University Press to use acid-free paper for the first printing of all clothbound books. Publications on uncoated stock satisfy the minimum requirements of American National Standard for Information Sciences—Permanence of Paper for Printed Library Materials, ANSI Z39.48-1992.

Contents

Acknowledgment

I wish to thank Professor Samuel Ijsseling, the director of the Husserl Archives in Louvain, Belgium, for the generous access provided me to the Nachlass.

*This book is dedicated to
Jennifer Mensch, daughter and friend.*

Introduction

We seem to be at the end of an age. We are no longer moderns, but rather "postmoderns." "Postmodernism" has become a catchall phrase for everything from fashion styles to novels. Its very multiplicity of meanings points to the pluralism that has spread across our culture. In the arts, every style is acceptable, from abstract expressionism to photorealism. Traditional harmonies reappear in music, often alongside the most severe atonalities. Architects, who popularized the term "postmodernism" some thirty years ago, feel free to use an often bewildering variety of styles. Even in philosophy, where once a rigid dogmatism reigned, "doing philosophy" is no longer limited to a set of particular problems or methodologies. Here, too, postmodernism implies pluralism with its corresponding lack of determining norms.[1] The postmodern period is thus postnormative. By contrast, the modern period was preeminently normative. In philosophy, its birth was marked by Descartes's *Rules for the Direction of the Mind*, which prescribed a set of norms for correct thinking. Since then, it has produced rules for practically everything. From the Kantian conditions for the possibility of experience, to the Marxian laws of dialectical materialism, to our century's various guides on everything from sexuality to accounting, modernity has been intent on declaring *in advance* how things must be.

---

1. As Joseph Natoli and Linda Hutcheon observe, this lack of determining norms applies to the concept of postmodernism itself when we take it as a cultural movement: "Postmodernism has provoked precious little agreement on anything from the reasons for its existence to its definition, let alone on the evaluation of its effects" ("Introduction," in *A Postmodern Reader,* p. xi).

The collapse of modernity is, then, the collapse of this attempt. It is the exhaustion of its central project, which is the attempt to draw such norms through an appeal to subjectivity. Rather than providing a single standard, subjectivity itself has been pluralized. Competing views of what it is, drawn from economics, popular psychology, sociology, and so forth, flood the marketplace with clashing norms. As a consequence, the attempt to draw norms from the subject undermines itself. With every conflict regarding the subject, the evidence grows that the problem does not lie in some particular derivation, but rather in the project itself, in the very attempt to explain the world in terms of subjective performance.

This problem was actually implicit at the very start of the project. Philosophical modernity has some unlikely sources. Its immediate impulses came from reports on cannibals and dreams. Montaigne in his essay, "Of Cannibals," finds the virtues of cannibals no less admirable than those of 16th century France. A similar, but much more penetrating relativism is advanced by Cervantes' *Don Quixote*. With its confusions regarding its supposed author, its stories framing stories, the book systematically undermines the boundary between reality and fiction. The Don claims that his delusions are real, ascribing all contrary evidence to enchanters. The inability of his auditors to counter his argument exposes the bankruptcy of contemporary claims regarding reality and illusion.

Modernity in philosophy begins with Descartes's response to this in his *Meditations on First Philosophy*. In the first Meditation, he considers the possibilities that everything we now sense and experience is actually a dream and that "an evil spirit, not less clever and deceitful than powerful" prevents us from realizing this (*Meditations*, p. 22). To banish this enchanter, Descartes searches for something absolutely certain, something he cannot doubt. He finds it in the "I" or subject of the "I think." Even if we doubt every object of this subject's thought, we cannot doubt the subject itself. It becomes the *ens certissimum*, the being whose certainty is such that it can stand as a norm, a standard against which to judge all other claims to knowledge. This norm is mediated through the concepts of clarity and distinctness. To the point that our perceptions and thoughts of other objects approach the clarity and distinctness of our grasp of the subject, we can be equally certain of the reality of their objects.

This positioning of the subject or self as normative has worked for hundreds of years. In fact, in a broad sense, modernity *is* this appeal to subjectivity. Descartes's argument, however, for all its apparent force, has a fateful contradiction. The subject to which he appeals is not an object like other objects. It is a subject who thinks objects, who doubts or perceives them as the case may be. Descartes argues that all objects of attention can be doubted; what cannot be doubted is the attending itself. Qua attending, however, the subject is not an object, but rather that which directs itself to objects. As such, Descartes's attempt to turn it into a "thinking thing"— an entity whose perception can stand as a norm for the perception of other objects—is highly problematical. To the point that we cannot doubt it, it escapes any characterization that could give it some objective content.

This becomes apparent when we consider the self's unity. Descartes argues that the self that cannot be doubted is also the self that cannot be grasped by the imagination, since it is not an extended body. Bodies are divisible. The attending self or mind, by contrast, is a thoroughgoing unity. As he puts it in the sixth Meditation, "It is one and the same mind which as a complete unit wills, perceives, and understands." Since I cannot say I am a different mind when I will or understand or sense, as I often perform these activities simultaneously, these activities do not point to different "parts" of myself (*Meditations*, VI; p. 81). In fact, as later philosophers were to conclude, insofar as I persist as I pass from one form of mental activity to another, I cannot be identified with any of them. Not only am I nonextended, I am also neither my sensing nor my willing nor my understanding, but only a sort of empty unity of apperception underlying these and all other conscious states. How can such a unity serve as a fixed "Archimedean point" for the Cartesian endeavor? If we cannot assign it definite content, how can we claim to know it "clearly and distinctly"?

This difficulty is not confined to Descartes; it also affects the Kantian attempt to base certainty on the self, that is, to see the self as "the transcendental ground of the necessary lawfulness of appearances composing an experience" (*Kritik der reinen Vernunft*, A 127). For Kant, the self is such a ground through its syntheses (B 130). Synthesis is its action of connecting perception with perception so that, through their ordering, we have an extended experience of some object—an object that shows itself as one and the same in the different perceptions. Given that the syntheses yield the experience of an object, judgments that embody their rules naturally apply to this object. "A priori" certainty (certainty "before" the experience) naturally attaches to them. In Kant's words, it is inherent in our "assuming that the object must conform to our knowledge," the conditions of such knowledge being those of synthesis (B xvi). Can we have such certainty about the synthesizing subject? We could, if it, itself, were a result of such synthesis, that is, if it were a unity that appeared through a multitude of connected perceptions. It, however, is not such. The subject is what connects the perceptions. It is, so to speak, the uncombined combiner. Thus, when we regard it, "nothing multiple is given" (B 135). Like Descartes's mind or self, it is a "thoroughgoing identity" (A 116). It must be. If it were not, if it were multiple, it would not be the ground but rather the result of combination (or synthesis).

For Kant, the appearing of an entity is the result of the subject's combination of perceptions. This, however, implies that the subject, taken as what "first makes possible the concept of combination" (and, hence, of appearing), cannot appear (B 131). Since it is uncombined, it is, in Kant's words, a "noumenal" as opposed to a phenomenal subject. Once again the Cartesian problem reappears. To make the subject normative is to make it disappear. For Kant, the normativity of the subject is based upon its action of synthesizing perceptions, that is, on "combination" understood as "an act of its selfhood" (B 130). The rules of synthesis yield the norms. Yet the very reasoning that makes the subject normative positions it as an uncombined, noumenal unity. As the "transcendental ground" of the lawfulness of experience, it escapes all positive characterization.

Our text will go into this difficulty in some detail. As we shall see, this problem reappears again and again as Descartes's successors attempt to make subjectivity normative. The history of modernity is the story of the subject's disappearance under the weight of the requirements placed on it. The reason for this is that at an ultimate, foundational level—the level where the subject could be encountered as a ground—it turns transparent. Rather than being any definite thing, it appears as an openness to the world. Aristotle was the first to have observed this. As he expresses it, "before mind thinks," that is, before it grasps an object, "it has no actual existence" (*De Anima* 429a24). It is "potentially identical with the objects of its thought," indeed, this potentiality is its openness. But, he adds, it "is actually nothing until it thinks" (429b31). This means that it has no inherent content, that all such content is derived from the objects it thinks. This is why the attempt to grasp it as an object is bound to fail. Objects have definite content. A subject, however, has content only in its temporary identity with what is not itself, that is, what it is transparent or open to. The result is the special seductive quality displayed by the subject. Infinitely adaptable, it appears, in its content, to support every possible analysis, every possible normative structure—from the Kantian to the Freudian. Inherently, however, it is the last place we should look for such normative structures. It manifests norms because it is open to them. It takes them on as a result of its being shaped by its environment. Its very openness to norms, thus, signifies its lack of any inherent normative structures or laws. Instead of being a ground of the world, the subject is grounded by it. Rather than being something that in its singularity yields universal norms, subjectivity is pluralized by the situations it finds itself in.

The reversal this implies can best be put in terms of temporalization. As Kant observed, all "our representations . . . are subject to time, the formal condition of inner sense. Time is that in which they must be ordered, connected and brought into relation" (*Kritik der reinen Vernunft,* A 99). On the level of "inner sense," the sense by which we grasp subjective processes, we are, formally regarded, simply a series of temporal relations. This insight allows us to see why the subject cannot have any inherent content. Time per se exhibits every sort of content, since it lacks any content of its own. Its moments are empty containers—or rather, place-holders—of possible contents. In fact, it is this very lack of inherent, distinguishing content which undercuts the notion of discrete moments. It is a correlative of the continuity of time. Granting this openness of time, if the subject is a field of temporal relations, any content it has must come from its objects. Its being as such a field *is,* in other words, *its openness* to what is not itself.

It is possible to draw a radical conclusion from the above, one that Kant did not make. If we really hold that subjectivity is temporality, then the implication is that it has as many forms as time has. This means we can speak of subjectivity as sheer nowness, as temporal flowing, as the form of objective synthesis, as our being-there in and through other persons, and even as the unidirectional flow of objective causality (the flow that allows us to suppose that our own inner relations are subject to causal laws). Each corresponds to a different situation of the subject—or, what is the same—an openness to a different type of object. When I grasp a mathematical relation (when at the moment of insight I am no longer conditioned by the before and after of time), then I exhibit the first form of subjectivity. I exhibit a very different form when playing as a member of a musical ensemble. Not only does Kant not draw this conclusion, he is forced to vitiate the insight upon which it is based. He does this because his focus is on normativity. The subject's normativity rests on its synthetic function. This function, however, is also a temporalization. Thus, for Kant, the subject makes extended experience possible by inserting experience into the before and after of time. Such "before" and "after" are what the subject adds to the experience. The norms that rest on this ordering can never be violated by experience. They are "a priori." Yet since time in its before and after is the subject's product, the subject itself—that is, the active, synthesizing subject—cannot really be a field of temporal relations.

The action of temporalizing situates it as prior to time. In itself—*an sich*—it is the noumenal, nontemporally appearing self.

To take advantage of the insight which identifies the openness of the subject with that of time, we must reverse this relationship between the subject and experience. The subject does not "time" experience, experience "times" the subject. Understanding subjectivity as temporality, we can then say that the different forms of subjectivity are set by the different forms of experience. The subject's allowing itself to be set (or "timed") by them is its openness. It is an openness that reveals, rather than conceals, one that lets the world be what it actually is. Such "letting be" is not to be conceived in the Heideggerian sense of letting the world reveal itself through *our* projects, goals, or criteria for being. "Letting be" here means letting the world temporalize itself in and through an apprehending subject. This subject times the world, not by being the origin of time, but by letting itself be timed by it. In the process, it lets the world be by letting the world set the laws of its appearing.

The details of this process will be the subject of several chapters. Chapter 5, for example, suggests how the process can be instantiated in machines. Rather than by going into its mechanics, the purposes of this introduction will be better served by giving the process's premise. Ontologically, this is a reversal of the fundamental presupposition of modernity. From Descartes onward, modernity presupposes the dependence of being on time. It takes being as being-temporally-present. What is now is what exists, and what exists is what occupies the present moment in time. If we grant this, then the process of temporalization constitutes the very *presence* which is, according to modernity, the *being* of an entity.[2] Closely related to this premise is what we shall call the "epistemological paradigm." This is the view that takes knowing as a subjective performance and takes its standards as determinative of the being that is known. This determination of being by knowing follows immediately once we equate being with temporal presence and see this subjective performance as involving temporalization. If to know is to temporalize, that is, to insert experience into the before and after of time, it is also to generate the temporal presence of the known. If being equals such presence, knowing generates the being of the known. Kant, of course, attempts to avoid this conclusion. Yet it haunts him, as it haunts most of his successors. A sign of its presence is given by the difficulties that attend it. They center around the subjective performances which are implicitly taken as determining being. What is

2. See Martin Heidegger, *Sein und Zeit,* p. 25.

their ontological status? If we do take being as temporal presence, then they seem to be positioned as *before* "being" in this defined sense. As responsible for temporalization, such performances are not just noumenal. They become ontologically a kind of *Ab-grund,* a nongrounded ground that is both ultimate and an "abyss."[3] It is not just that such subjectivity cannot appear in the field it makes possible through its activities. The difficulty is that it cannot account for itself in any of the ontological categories that trace their roots to it.[4] To the point that such categories are universal, they exclude the subjectivity that is their basis. Their universal validity implies, then, the invalidity of their basis. Such self-referential inconsistency, both in the logical and ontological sense, is, as we shall see, the characteristic sign of modernity, one that points back to its fundamental premise.

To avoid it, we have to reverse this premise. Concretely, this means working out a paradigm that bases time on being. As already indicated, this will involve us in the assertion that there are as many forms of time—of subjectivity as an openness—as there are forms of being. It will necessitate the further assertion that rather than being ontologically ground-less, the subject in its activities or performances is grounded by the world in which it functions. Such grounding places what can be called the "weight of normativity" on the world. Yet it does so in a way that fundamentally changes the sense of normativity. In its customary sense, normativity implies a distinction between reality and "mere" appearance—the real being what conforms to some norm, the illusory being everything else. For example, if we take the norm as being definitely describable in mathematical terms, then what cannot be numbered, that is, what is inherently ambiguous, cannot be taken as real. By contrast, the reversal, which seeks to ground the subject in the world, is not a shift in norms or a revision of what is to count as real and what is not. Rather, it twists out of this division by dissipating the notion of a normative ground.[5]

This "twisting out" involves the plurality of contexts making up the

---

3. Heidegger writes, "Kant's recoil from the ground which he himself revealed, namely the [performances of the] transcendental imagination, is . . . that movement of philosophical thought which . . . places us before the abyss [Abgrund] of metaphysics" (*Kant and the Problem of Metaphysics,* §38; p. 222).

4. Jacques Derrida generalizes this difficulty in terms of "center" and "structure." In his words: "The center . . . governs the structure, while escaping structurality." It is responsible for the structure, and yet escapes its characterization ("Structure, Sign, and Play in the Discourse of the Human Sciences," p. 224). The difficulty, he argues, is inherent in all metaphysical, foundational discourse. See ibid., p. 225.

5. Cf. Martin Heidegger, "Will to Power as Art," §24, in *Nietzsche,* I, 200ff.

world. It points to the being of the subject as a being-situated by such contexts. The same holds for the subject's actions, especially those in which it attempts to situate itself and others. The fact that every subject is both agent and patient—both actor and acted upon—indicates that the "ground" here is not some ultimate, singular foundation. It is rather the world understood as a self-determining plurality of individual activities and actions. To accept this is, in fact, to dissipate the notion of a "ground"—at least insofar as it is defined by the modern project of seeking an axiomatic foundation for what is to count as "real." In a situation of individuals determining environments determining individuals, there is no first cause, no ultimate determinant or even manageable system of determinants of the real. Where each action is both ground and grounded, the notion of a ground is robbed of its foundational character. Embracing the circle of such determination is, then, to abandon any claim to the metaphysics of ultimate grounds or causes which characterizes the modern project.[6] It is, as a consequence, to escape the distinctions between reality and mere appearance which are based upon them. To twist successfully out of these distinctions is to accomplish the reversal; it is to cross the line from the modern to the postmodern.

An introduction is, of course, only a promissory note. To redeem it, we shall have to work its thoughts out, that is, actually think them through as a response to modernity. The danger of such thinking is to become entrapped by the presuppositions of modernity. We cannot, for example, escape the distinction between reality and mere appearance without reversing the epistemological paradigm. This, however, demands that we think the priority of being over knowing. The difficulty of this thought is that we cannot see how we can speak about being before we know how far our statements actually describe it. Talk about being presupposes its knowability. But to secure this presupposition, a science of knowing, one with a secure foundation in the knowing subject, seems required. With this, we slip back into modernity. We become simply another of Descartes's successors. It is precisely to avoid this that we shall turn to a premodern paradigm—specifically that of Aristotle—to try to think through what is involved in making being prior to knowing. Our consideration of Aristotle (in Chapter 4) is no more to be viewed as a "return" to an earlier way of

6. If we assume that "metaphysics has always understood being as a *Grund* or foundation," this dissipation of the notion of a ground can, in Vattimo's sense, be called a "*Verwindung* of metaphysics." It is a *Verwindung* (a recovery from) rather than an overcoming, since the notion of ground, rather than being negated, is rendered harmless (Gianni Vattimo, *The End of Modernity*, p. 40).

thinking than Nietzsche's reflections on Greek tragedy or Heidegger's on the pre-Socratics or, for that matter, the Renaissance's reflections on the ancient world. In each case, we have an example of reflections on an ancient culture being used to overturn one's own. In our case, the reflections I advance on Aristotle's concepts of knowing and being serve to break out of the prejudices of modernity. It is only as such that they guide the subsequent chapters' project to grasp the overturning which is postmodernism. Thus, their goal is not some prime mover or universal mind—a νοῦς—that is always thinking. It is rather a situating of subjectivity that makes sense of its pluralization.

1

Cartesian Meditations

Descartes and the Problem of Knowledge

§1. *Descartes's Insight.* No better figure can be called on to characterize modernity than Descartes. He is at once its foremost exemplar and its chief founder. He initiated not just modern philosophy, but, with Galileo, modern science as well. It is chiefly to his genius that we owe the conceptual framework that allows us to mathematize nature. By teaching us how to apply numbers to things he made modern science possible. To see how this very success leads us into philosophical difficulties, I want to briefly note its elements.

The problem of mathematizing nature is not at all apparent to us today. We live in a world that conceptually, and often to a large degree physically, has been shaped by modern science and technology. It is already a numerable world with its exact dimensions, shapes, and angles. Everywhere we see the products of our technologies. To escape this, we have to take a walk in the country. Going beyond the farmlands and woodlots that serve the city, we need to seek out a place where we can see a piece of undisturbed wilderness. Regarding it, we can begin to grasp the ancient view that "beneath the circle of the moon," the application of mathematics to nature was not possible at all. Above the moon, the planets may trace out regular, mathematically describable orbits. As the Egyptian mathematician Ptolemy showed, with the help of circles turning on circles, we can reduce any apparent irregularities in the planetary motions to a combination involving strict mathematical regularities. But here below, as is apparent in the view of any wilderness, we find only a confused tangle of forms. There are no straight lines, circles, ellipses, or any easily describable mathematical forms. The motions we see—birds darting through the trees, ambling brooks, the eddying clouds of a departing storm—seem to the highest degree irregular. Intermittent and variable, they follow no recognizable shape or curve. All periodicity, all repetition which could be placed in recurring cycles seems equally lacking.

How do we mathematize such a nature? Following Galileo, it was the genius of Descartes to make a division in what we "see." On the one hand, we have the immediate objects of our five senses: the colors, odors, tastes, sounds, and tactile qualities of the bodies we encounter. On the other, we have the extensions, the shapes (considered as a "limitations" of these extensions), the relative positions and the changes in these positions, that is, the motions, of these bodies. We also have their duration and number (*Meditations*, III; p. 41). As is obvious, we "see" these two sets of qualities quite differently. The first set is immediately apprehended, the second requires some action on the part of our understanding. Thus, to grasp a number, we must count. Some form of counting is also required if we are to apprehend duration as a specific quantity. Five days, five hours, five minutes, for example, are all grasped by counting periods of circular motion, whether it be the motion of the sun or watch hand. To count we have to abstract, we have to consider different individuals—for example, apples, people, whatever—only in their quality of being one. The ability to abstract is also present in the grasp of the other elements of the set. Thus we must abstract from color to consider extension as such. Similarly, we must attend only to the relative location of a body to grasp its position, whereas to apprehend its motion as motion, we must abstract again to focus on the change in its position. For an understanding of the quantity of motion, this change of position must itself be quantified and considered in relation to a quantity of duration. This brings us to a second difference between the two sets. The first set of qualities is not easily quantifiable, but the second is. Thus, it seems impossible to apply numbers to odors or colors so as to say that one is so many times the other. All sense of an extensive (as opposed to an intensive) scale seems to be lacking. We can, however, say that one shape, for example, that of a circle, is twice the size of another, or speak of numerical multiples of duration, extension, and motion. Here it seems that the very process of abstraction by which we proceed from the first to the second set renders the second quantifiable.

Given that the second set is quantifiable, Descartes's solution to our question becomes clear. The mathematization of nature can proceed if we can reduce its immediately sensible qualities, its colors, odors, sounds, tastes, and textures, to the second, easily numerable set. Thus, if we can reduce color to motion, translating it into the frequency and amplitude of light waves, we can quantify it. The same holds for sound, though here the motion is of the pressure ridges in the air. Molecular counts will do for odors and tastes, while texture can be numbered in terms of differences in the positions of material particles and the elasticity (or lack thereof) that the particles manifest in their interrelations. The point of this is not the details of this account. They tend to change with each advance of science. Descartes's founding genius lay rather in articulating a double intuition. He saw, first of all, that changes in the immediately sensible qualities of an object correspond to changes in the numerable qualities grasped through acts of our understanding. He then saw that this correspondence can be interpreted as a correspondence between perception and thing. In his words, "From the fact that I perceive different kinds of colors, odors, tastes, sounds, heat, hardness and so on, I very readily conclude that in the objects from which these various sense perceptions proceed there are some corresponding variations" (*Meditations,* VI; p. 77). To a change in sound, for example, there corresponds a change in the frequency of the sound wave. Of course, the change in the sound wave is actually quite different from the change in heard sound, which is experienced as a change in pitch. As Descartes admits, "These variations are not really similar to the perceptions" (ibid.). Yet even though what we experience is different from the reality, we can still get at it through a level of abstraction (that of mathematization) which captures the corresponding variations.

A good way to understand this solution is in terms of the doubt whose resolution motivates the writing of the *Meditations.* It may be, Descartes speculates in the first Meditation, that an evil, all powerful god has created him such that he always errs. To those who doubt the necessity of postulating such a god, he replies: "To whatever degree less powerful they consider the author to whom they attribute my origin, in that degree it will be more probable that I am so imperfect that I am always mistaken" (*Meditations,* I; p. 21). As he puts the same point in the sixth Meditation, the origin of his doubt was that "pretending not to know the author of my being, I saw nothing to make it impossible that I was so constructed by nature that I should be mistaken even in the things which seem to me most true" (p. 73). Thus, it seems most true "that in an object which is hot there is some quality similar to my idea of heat; that in a white, or black, or green object there is the same whiteness, or blackness, or greenness which I perceive; that in a bitter or sweet object there is the same taste or the same flavor, and so on for the other senses" (p. 77). Yet none of this is, in fact, the case. Were he differently constructed, that is, constructed after the pattern of some other animal, a different set of perceptions would occur. Both cannot lay claim to displaying the inherent qualities of the object. In fact, as he indicates, his sensuous perceptions are not given to him to provide accurate information about the inherent qualities of objects. Their purpose is survival rather than truth. They are given, he writes, "only to indicate to my mind which objects are useful or harmful" (p. 79). As such, the information they provide is strictly relative to his particular nature. They tell him what to seek or avoid in order to maintain his bodily integrity. Given that different animals have different survival needs, what their senses indicate will naturally differ. To a different bodily construction there will thus correspond a different set of perceptions serving a different set of needs.

We need not enter into a discussion of evolutionary biology to see the skeptical implications of these thoughts. On one level, Descartes doubts that he has been created by nature just right, that is, with just the mental and perceptual structures which allow him to apprehend the objects of the world as they are in themselves. On another level, his concluding discussions on how illness and bodily disorders affect perceptions undercut the whole notion of being rightly constructed (see pp. 79–84). As they indicate, on the level of immediate, sensuous perception, we always apprehend the world relative to our particular physical makeup. Seen in this context, the mathematization of nature can be regarded as an attempt to escape from our situatedness. Even though the sensuous qualities of nature, its colors, odors, sounds, and so on, are subjectively relative, we can, by attending to the numerable aspects of what we perceive, reach a level which puts us in contact with what is "out there." In other words, what is numerable transcends the particular perception and applies to the reality. Descartes puts this in terms of clarity and distinctness. What is numerable is "clear and distinct," and "everything which we conceive very clearly and very distinctly is wholly true"—that is, applies directly to the reality (*Meditations,* III; p. 34. See also V, p. 32). To take an example, when we regard the impact of two hard bodies, among the things we can number are their masses and the velocities. When we do measure these, we find, as Descartes discovered, that momentum is conserved, that is, that the product of mass and velocity of the bodies is the same before and after the impact. Because of its clarity, we can assert that this relation holds for reality itself. Because of this, we can ascribe it to all the interactions of the particles of nature. Its clarity, thus, allows us to move from an empirical base of a few crucial experiments to assertions assumed to hold for the whole of nature.

§2. *Premises and Problems.*   The immediate and enduring success of the Cartesian endeavor has tended to discourage the questioning of its premises. The enormous predictive power of mathematical physics is often taken as a proof of its assumptions about reality. Yet there are limits to its success, and these become apparent when we examine its basis. To begin with, the assumption that mathematics provides an access to reality assumes that reality is inherently mathematizable. Its elements—and this not just on the gross level, but rather throughout its structure, ranging from the very large to the very small—are assumed to be numerable. Their changing positions and durations are assumed to be mathematically expressible.[1] Numerability is here thought of in terms of things' being in space and time. Because they are in space and time, they have numerable positions and durations. This is the point of the grid that Descartes introduced when he founded analytical geometry. The grid allows us to assign a pair of numerical coordinates to every point on it. A figure, for example, drawn on the grid becomes associated with a set of coordinates identifying each of its points. The equation specifying the numerical relation between the coordinates becomes, then, the equation for the figure. From a Cartesian perspective, it *is* the figure. The figure is just the equation determining the positions of a set of points on the grid. By way of contrast, we may note that, for the ancient Euclidian geometry, figures were positionless. *What* they were, as specified by their definitions, was considered apart from *where* they were, the question of position playing no part in the demonstration of their properties.[2] Now, to consider the figure as a function relating the points on the grid is to make the grid a grounding condition for the figure. The figure exists by being locatable on the grid. The

1. For an extended discussion of the presumptions and problems involved in the original Galilean project of mathematizing nature, see Edmund Husserl's *Die Krisis der europäischen Wissenschaften und die transzendentale Phänomenologie,* §9.

2. The best account of the differences between ancient and modern mathematics is still Jacob Klein's *Greek Mathematical Thought and the Origin of Algebra.* Klein was a student of Husserl.

points that make up the figure have their identity as numerical coordinates, and the figure itself achieves its being as the equation specifying their relation. Thus the figure becomes numerable, and numerability is thought of in terms of the grid's spatial positions.

This transformation of ancient mathematics is matched by an equivalent transformation of nature. Once we add a time line to the grid, we can identify each event with the numerical coordinates giving its position and time. The way is thus open to the mathematical description of nature. Implicit in this account is the assumption that nothing can exist without being in space and time, while these can continue even as the things within them come and go. In the pre-Cartesian view, a thing's being was chiefly a matter of its form—that is, of *what* it was as specified by its definition. As we shall see when we come to discuss Aristotle's account, an object's *where* and *when* were considered accidental rather than essential to its being. Here, however, space and time become the grounding conditions of the objects within them. The mathematical account of something according to its spatial-temporal relations is thus transformed from a description to an ontological explanation. It claims to explain why the thing is as it is. Behind this claim is the fact that, by virtue of the grid, we can grasp nature as a numerable field, that is, grasp it clearly and distinctly. Transcending the particularity of our immediate sense perceptions, we thus can come into contact with its reality. We can grasp it as it is in itself. For this, however, to be possible, the "in itself," that is, the very being, must be just what is locatable within the grid. It must be numerable, and numerability must be thought of in terms of spatial-temporal positions.

The limitations of this view appear when we attempt to place ourselves within it. How are we to explain knowing, taken as a subject-object relation, in terms of the grid? Certainly, we can assign a definite position to the subject and another to the object, but then the question of knowing becomes one of transcendence. It concerns our ability to transcend our "here" and to reach the object, which appears to be "there" at a physical remove. Can we really reach it to "get" it as it is in itself? At least at the level of the senses, this is not at all apparent. How do we match what is within us with what is without? As Descartes notes: "The principal and most common error which can be encountered here consists in judging that the ideas [sense perceptions] which are in myself are similar to, or conformable to, things outside myself" (*Meditations*, III; p. 36). Our reaching the object depends, of course, on its reaching us. Can it, through its influence on its environment reach our sensory organs? Given that it physically remains there, we seem to be driven to talk of its likeness reaching us. In Descartes's words, I have to assert "that this alien entity sends to me and imposes upon me its likeness" (p. 37). Given that I encounter the object through a number of different senses, the conception seems to be that of the object reassembling itself from my multiple and differing perceptions so as to produce in my brain a replica or likeness of itself. With the talk of images versus originals we encounter our first difficulty. How can we know that the image so produced is like the original? Do we have to again traverse the distance between ourselves and the object to compare image and object? If we do, then how can we tell whether this second attempt at transcendence with *its* resulting image is successful? The verification of this image seems to require a third effort, which requires a fourth for its confirmation, and so on indefinitely.[3]

A second difficulty appears when we attempt to use the grid to explain what we mean by "object" and "replica." What is real in terms of the grid are mathematically describable spatial-temporal processes. In terms of such, we can ask whether the image is the electric currents coursing through our synapses. Is it also the chemical processes that accompany these? Perhaps it is the pattern of the changing molecular arrangements which occur during the perceptual process. Once we pursue this line of thought, we face the question of the sense in which the physical replica or image could be made "like" the original. The original is itself a collection of mathematically describable, space-filling processes, some of which set up parallel processes by impinging on our own sensory organs. Yet, as noted, what we sense is at least in part relative to our sensory apparatus. Let us put this in terms of the fact that the two sets of processes (the original and its subjective replica) are here thought of as linked through the law of causality. This states that caused events are determined by the material makeup of the interacting bodies and the spatial-temporal relations existing between them. A change in any one of these changes the event. If the event is the production of the replica of the object, then the law makes this relative to (among other factors) the particular material structure of the perceiving organism. Different organisms—say, a cat, a parrot, and a man—have different structures and, hence, different replicas of the original within their heads. Thus, the very idea of grasping with the senses the object as it is "in itself" collapses once we make causality the link between the object and ourselves. As long as perception requires an

3. Ludwig Wittgenstein describes a parallel situation of a person "looking for an object in a room. He opens a drawer and doesn't see it there; then he closes it again, waits, and opens it once more to see if perhaps it isn't there now, and keeps on like that" (*On Certainty*, §315; p. 40). This attitude makes sense if each look can be verified only by the next.

embodied perceiver, the object that is grasped will be relative to the structure of this embodiment.

The grid, of course, appears as a solution to this difficulty. It allows the mathematical description of nature, and the point of such description is to reach a level of abstraction which transcends our embodiment. Does mathematics in fact provide this level? Is it independent of the peculiarities of our nature? The numerable elements of our experience are reached through abstraction. As such they require the faculty of understanding. How can we claim that such a faculty is not, like the senses, relative to the nature of our embodiment? It is interesting to note in this context that when Descartes begins to doubt, he does not limit himself to the objects of sense perception. He writes: "How can I be sure but that . . . I am always mistaken when I add two and three or count the sides of a square, or when I judge of something else even easier" (*Meditations*, I; p. 20). If we cannot be sure in these cases of exemplary clarity and distinctness, then the clarity and distinctness are not sure signs of being. This indicates that the understanding itself may be relative to the peculiarities of our embodiment. If it is, then I cannot say with Descartes, that "everything which I conceive clearly and distinctly as occurring in [corporeal objects]—that is to say, everything, generally speaking, which is discussed in pure mathematics or geometry—does in truth occur in them" (*Meditations*, VI; p. 76).

Descartes's response to this doubt is well known. He finds himself in the remarkable situation of having to prove God's existence before he can be certain of the existence of even a single, external object. His proof is designed to show that God is not a deceiver. Thus Descartes first demonstrates God's existence as a most perfect being and then goes on to show that all attempts to deceive are the result of some imperfection. It, therefore, follows that a perfect God cannot deceive. In particular, He cannot have given Descartes a deceptive nature. As he states the conclusion: "From the fact that God is not a deceiver, it necessarily follows that in this matter [that of correct employment of the senses and the understanding] I am not deceived" (*Meditations*, VI; p. 85). This argument, it should be stressed, is not just intended to banish the specter of God as an evil genius, that is, as a spirit personally intent on deceiving us. It is also intended, in Descartes's mind at least, to cancel the thought of a deceptive nature. The key point here is contained in his assertion: "All that nature teaches me contains some truth. For by nature, considered in general, I now understand nothing else but God himself, or else the order and system that God has established for created things" (p. 76). If we do equate God and nature, then the argument that God is not a deceiver directly applies to nature. If we take God as nature's creator, the argument still applies to nature. In particular, it still applies to Descartes's nature, defined by him as "nothing else but the arrangement or assemblage of all that God has given me" (ibid.).

The proof for the existence of God is long and complex, taking up most of the third and fifth Meditations. Yet quite apart from its details, many of which are borrowed from late Scholastic philosophy, it suffers from an overwhelming flaw. In its complex reasoning, it assumes what it wishes to prove. In particular, it presupposes God's existence as the guarantor of our nature. Thus if such a God exists, Descartes can trust his understanding. He can trust the arguments he uses to prove God. If, however, there is no God, or if, as equated to nature, He is indifferent to error, this trust has no basis. Although Descartes's arguments may be clear and distinct, clarity and distinctness may not be the sign that we are in touch with reality. Thus, once we give up the guarantee of a nondeceptive God (or nature), our understanding may be regarded as similar to our senses. Its purpose may be survival rather than truth. To advance beyond our previous remarks on this score, let us recall the Darwinian thesis of natural selection, a selection that is driven by the struggle for existence. According to this view, each creature along with its faculties is a product of an evolutionary line of development, one whose purpose is survival rather than epistemological correctness. Each species (humans included) thus apprehends the world in the way that allows it a particular advantage in its struggle for survival. This implies that there are as many "worlds"—as many possible apprehensions of the world—as there are ecological niches. As for the world "in itself," which supposedly contains all of these, we can posit this, not as an empirical (observed) reality, but only as a kind of logical necessity. Yet even this becomes questionable once we say that logic itself is a biologically grounded process; for this implies that "even logic alters with the structure of the brain."[4] So regarded, it has a value only as a particular, biologically contingent strategy for survival.

Reflecting on the above, we can say that its inability to account for the

---

4. Cited by Husserl in his *Logische Untersuchungen* (Tübingen, 1968), I/147, n. 1. As Husserl asks in considering the implications of the theory of evolution: "Do not the logical forms and laws express a contingent characteristic of the human species, a characteristic which could be different and, in the course of its future development, will probably be different?" (*Die Idee der Phänomenologie,* Hua II, 21). Gunter Stent raises the same issues in his article, "Limits to the Scientific Understanding of Man," p. 1054. For Nietzsche, the answer is clear: "It is improbable that our 'knowledge' should extend further than is strictly necessary for the preservation of life" (*Will to Power,* §494; p. 272). This means that "the way of knowing and of knowledge is itself already part of the conditions of existence." Their change is its change (§496, pp. 272–73).

fact of knowing gives a certain incoherence to the entire Cartesian project. On the one hand, we have a science, mathematical physics, whose success at predicting and explaining events has swept away all doubts about its premises. On the other, once we apply such premises to the knowing that engenders it, to scientists themselves in their grasp of the world, we seem to involve ourselves (and science as well) in a self-undermining skepticism. In a curious turn of events, relativizing mathematics and logic relativizes reason itself, including the very processes of reason, of argument and proof, which are used to show the relativity of reason. The incoherence we face is thus similar to that of the familiar liar's paradox. When someone declares he is lying, then, if he is indeed lying, he is telling the truth; but if he is telling the truth, he is *not* lying. Thus, in declaring that he *is lying,* he is *not* telling the truth. As is obvious, we can go around this circle as long as we like. Paradoxes such as these exhibit self-referential inconsistency. The statement of their thesis when applied to itself undercuts itself. As the logician Frederic Fitch noted, skeptical theories, in making a universal claim, fall into such inconsistency. On the one hand, a theory that casts doubt on reason (and, hence, on all theories as rational constructs) casts doubt on its own validity. On the other hand, if it is really valid, it *wrongly* casts doubt on itself in casting doubt on all theories. In Fitch's words, ". . . if it is valid, it is self-referentially inconsistent and, hence, not valid at all."[5]

§3. *The Missing Element.* Having said this, we haven't said anything about the source of this incoherence. A fair guess, however, is that something crucial is missing in the Cartesian account. For John Locke, the missing element is the lack of any relation between the numerable qualities of our experience, the "size, figure, or motion of any particles," and the fact of perception. Calling these the "primary qualities of bodies," he asserts that we are not "able to discover any connection betwixt these primary qualities of bodies and the sensations that are produced by them." We can grasp how a change in "the size, figure, and motion of one body should cause a change in the size, figure and motion of another body." But such a change is not itself a perception. What is lacking is even the idea of a connection. In Locke's words, "We are so far from knowing what figure, size or motion of parts produce a yellow colour, a sweet taste, or a sharp

5. See Frederic B. Fitch, "Self-Reference in Philosophy," in I. Copi and J. Gould, eds., *Contemporary Readings in Logical Theory,* pp. 156–57. Husserl's refutation of psychologism in his *Logische Untersuchungen* employs the same reasoning. His strategy is to show that it is inconsistent when it attempts to explain itself as a theory. For an account of this, see James Mensch, *The Question of Being in Husserl's Logical Investigations,* pp. 27–33.

sound, that we can by no means conceive how *any* size, figure, or motion of any particles, can possibly produce in us the idea of any colour, taste, or sound whatsoever: there is no conceivable connection between the one and other" (*An Essay Concerning Human Understanding,* bk. 4, chap. 3, §13; 2:151). A good way to see this is to note that if we do limit ourselves to the processes describable in terms of the Cartesian grid, it is as sensible to say that the retina of the eye "perceives" a color as to say that the optic nerve perceives it as to say that certain cells in the brain at the end of this nerve perceive it as to say that other cells affected by these cells are the perceivers. Limited to the notion of space-filling processes setting up other space-filling processes, we seem condemned to posit a whole series of perceivers behind perceivers. Within the categories allowed by the grid, we have no reason to assert that one rather than the other is *the* perceiver.

Leibniz makes the same point in his analogy of the mill. Perceptions, he writes,

> are inexplicable by mechanical causes, that is to say, by figures and motions. Supposing that there were a machine whose structure produced thought, sensation, and perception, we could conceive of it as increased in size with the same proportions until one was able to enter into its interior, as he would into a mill. Now, on going into it he would find only pieces working upon one another, but never would he find anything to explain Perception. (*Monadology,* §17; p. 254)

The point here has nothing to do with size. We are not engaged here in a kind of false analogy which asserts that, were we to enter, for example, into the molecular structure of water, we would find particle working on particle, but nothing whatever of wetness. If by wetness we mean the fluidity of water as well as its ability to penetrate other materials, such properties can be explained on the molecular level by pointing to the looseness of the intermolecular bonding. The order of explanation is simply that of linking physical properties on one spatial level (one level of size) with those on another. But Leibniz's claim, which repeats that of Locke, does not concern size but rather being. His underlying claim is that perception, taken as an actually experienced, psychological event, has a being that cannot be captured by the categories of the grid.

Granting this, the missing element is nothing less than consciousness itself. The conscious, knowing subject cannot be thought in terms of the grid. The categories by which the grid gives intelligibility to the extended world fail to capture the subject. This conclusion, it is to be noted, is already implicit in Descartes's dualism. Turning the method of doubt on himself, the only thing he finds which he cannot doubt is the doubting "self." This, however, is a reduced "self." It is not the self with a social position. It is not even the self having a "face, hands, arms, and all this mechanism composed of bone and flesh and members" (*Meditations,* II; p. 25). It is, rather, the self that doubts whether any of this pertains to it, the self which, at least in the initial stages of its doubt, assumes "that I have no senses . . . that body, shape, extension, motion and location are merely inventions of my mind" (p. 23). Reduced, then, to what Descartes can be certain of, the self becomes only a "thinking thing." "Thought," he asserts, "is an attribute that belongs to me; it *alone* is inseparable from my nature (*Meditations,* II; p. 26, emphasis added; see also VI, p. 74). Thought, here, is a generic term. It includes doubting, understanding, affirming, denying, willing, imagining, and sensing—in short, all the elements we designate by consciousness (II, p. 27). What it does not include are the *correlates* to these actions. Given that God may be a deceiver; or if God equals nature, that nature itself may be deceptive, all the objects the self can attend to can be doubted. What cannot be doubted is simply the attending itself. In other words, the self that remains is actually not an object, but rather that which directs itself to objects.

If my essence consists solely in such attending—"thinking" in the broad sense in which Descartes defines it—I must, he argues, be completely non-extended. Given that bodily extension is one of the things I can doubt, it follows "that I am entirely and truly distinct from my [extended] body." Indeed, reduced to what I can be certain of, it seems that "I can be or exist without [this body]" (*Meditations,* VI; p. 74). The distinction between mind and body is deceptively simple: "The body, from its nature, is always divisible and the mind is completely indivisible" (p. 81). As Descartes explains, "It is one and same mind which as a complete unit wills, perceives, and understands and so forth. But just the contrary is the case with corporeal or extended objects" (ibid.). The latter cannot be imagined as *not* being divisible into parts. Since, on the contrary, I cannot say I am a different mind when I will or understand or perceive, since I often perform these activities simultaneously, I cannot be divided and, hence, cannot be taken as extended. In fact, as later philosophers were to point out, insofar as I persist as I pass from one form of mental activity to another, I cannot be identified with any of them. Not only am I nonextended, I am also not my sensing or my willing or my understanding, but only a sort of unity of attending underlying these and all other conscious states.

With this we come to the classic mind-body problem: how can this non-extended subject interact with the body? As we have seen, the external, corporeal world is granted existence only to the point that it is the object of clear and distinct perceptions. For this, it must be conceived in terms of the grid, which means, primarily in terms of extension. This holds even with regard to our own flesh. "I have," Descartes writes, "a distinct idea of a body—insofar as it is only an extended being which does not think." Yet, as we have just noted, I also "have a clear and distinct idea of myself insofar as I am only a thinking and not an extended being" (*Meditations* VI; p. 74). Given this, the two are "distinct." But with this distinction comes the question of how to mediate between them. In "The Passions of the Soul," Descartes proposes that the soul communicates to "the machine of the body" by means of a "little gland," the pineal. Moving it, it moves the body (Article XXXIV, *Philosophical Works of Descartes,* 1:347). Yet, given that between the extended and the nonextended there can be no point of physical contact, this obviously won't do. If we reduce mind and body to what we can be certain of, it is possible to arrive at extension as that which distinguishes bodies from minds. But the price we pay is the apparent lack of any mediating category. It is this lack which makes Locke affirm that there is no "conceivable connection" between perception and physical processes. Without it, as Leibniz's analogy of the mill suggests, the subject, the actual person constructing science, is simply absent on the physical level he investigates.

The Notion of the Normative Subject

This absence of the subject, this inability to relate it to the world in which it functions, recalls, in modern terms, an ancient difficulty. The ancient world, too, sought for certainty. It also had its norms for what counted as knowledge. The perceived failure of its philosophy, particularly its Platonic variant, was that of relating such norms (the ideas or εἴδη) to the physical world. In the premodern period, the difficulty appears as the failure to solve the problem of the universals—that is, how to relate the universal, atemporal species (or ideas) to particular realities. The failure to solve this problem led to the nominalism and relativism that set the climate for Descartes's search for certainty. As we shall see, his solution revives, yet transforms, the ancient conception of normativity. What we may call the weight of normativity shifts from the ideas to the subject. With this, the problem of the universals reappears as that of the subject's relation to the world. The result is that the otherworldliness of the Platonic norms is matched by a similar otherworldliness of the normative subject. Cartesian dualism is, thus, both a repetition and a repositioning of an ancient problem. To see this, we must first briefly examine the problem of the universals in its original Platonic form.

§1. *The Platonic Background.* For Plato, the normative function of the ideas is based upon their actuality. They are supremely actual because they embody in the highest degree what it means to be. This is self-identity. As he writes: "The very essence of to be" (the αὐτὴ ἡ οὐσία τοῦ εἶναι) is to be "always in the same manner in relation to the same things." This is to be "unchanging" and, thus, to remain the same with oneself. The ideas, "beauty itself, equality itself, and every itself" are called "being" (τὸ ὄν) because they "do not admit of any change whatsoever" (*Phaedo* 78d). The insight here can be expressed in terms of an analysis of what change means. Change is always change of something—that is, of an underlying self-identity. This means that a real loss of self-identity is not change, but rather annihilation pure and simple. Now, the presence of self-identity not only makes possible the persistent being in time of the individual, it also makes possible the predication of an idea of this individual. Suppose, through time-lapse photography, we were to view a person proceeding from a newborn baby to extreme old age. Plato would assert that it is the presence of some self-identical element that allows us to predicate the same idea of "human" of this changing individual. When the person dies, this is no longer possible. What answers to the concept "human" is no longer there. We can express this in terms of the Parmenidean assertion that "the same thing exists for both thinking and being" [τὸ γὰρ αὐτὸ νοεῖν ἔστιν τε καὶ εἶναι—Fragment 3]. For Plato, self-identity is required for both being and for being thought. What is not self-identical can neither be nor be thought.

A number of important consequences for the normativity of the ideas follow from this reasoning. The first is that the ability to recognize being and the ability to predicate an idea of a thing always occur together. They must, since both are based on the apprehension of an underlying self-identity. Given that predicating an idea of a thing is the same as recognizing that that thing is intelligible, "being" and "intelligibility" have to be understood as coextensive terms. One cannot ascribe the one without ascribing the other; whatever has a share in being must also have a share in intelligibility. In Greek, "participation" (μετέχειν) means "having a share in." Participation here is to be understood as participation in both being and intelligibility. We can put this in terms of the Platonic doctrine that a thing is intelligible by virtue of participating in its idea. The idea itself is the conceptual expression of the self-identity that Plato calls the essence of "to be." Thus one can also say that a thing has being by virtue of its participating in its idea—that is, participating in the self-identity that the idea expresses in terms of an unchanging concept.

This functional equivalence of being and intelligibility is at the basis of the ontological normativity of the ideas. It implies that to the point that we grasp the ideas we are in contact with being. Both ideas and being are based on self-identity. Thus from a Platonic perspective, I can trust my perceptions to the extent that they reveal the underlying self-identities present in the ideas. To the point that the ideas also appear in conversation, it too becomes an access to reality. This is why Plato has Socrates engaging in conversations with the most diverse sorts of people. The dialectic that ensues has as its purpose the sifting of talk for ideas, i.e., seeing the ideas through (*dia*) the words (*logoi*).

In each case, the operative doctrine is that, for a thing to be, it must conform to its idea. It is this doctrine which allows us to give the ideas a normative function, that is, to assert that to the extent that we are in contact with them, we are not deceived, but rather touch reality. The difficulty with this, as Plato himself points out, concerns the meaning of this conformity. Does the thing conform to its idea when it is "like" it? This implies that the idea is like the thing. If we grant this, a number of difficulties appear. The first follows from the fact that we grasp the likeness of things by grasping their ideas. Thus we see that members of a species are "like" each other by grasping what is the same in all of them. The apprehension of this identity is a grasp of the idea, the one in many, uniting them. As Plato has Parmenides ask the young Socrates in the following exchange, "And when two things are alike, must they not partake in the same idea? They must. And will not that of which the two partake, and which makes them alike, be the idea itself? Certainly" (*Parmenides* 132e). If this is true, then to apprehend the similarity between the idea and the thing, we must grasp a second idea embracing these. If this new idea is "like" the first two, the apprehension of their similarity requires a third idea. To grasp the latter's likeness, we require a fourth idea, and so on indefinitely. As Plato summarizes the argument: "The idea cannot be like the individual, or the individual like the idea; for if they are alike, some further idea of likeness will always be coming to light, and if they be like anything else, another and new ideas will always be arising, if the idea resembles that which partakes of it" (133a).

We thus face the Platonic version of the replica reality regress we noted above. Descartes's problem was how he could know whether the replica or image in his head was like the reality supposedly producing it. As we said, a comparison of the two through a new perception, would produce a new perceptual image, but to verify this image's likeness to its original would require a new comparison with a new image and so on indefinitely. The same sort of regress occurs when we strive to verify the similarity between thing and idea. Once again the difficulty points to the fact that very different types of entities are involved, the difference being such that it undermines all talk of likeness. For Descartes's successors, the difference was between perception and its assumed material causes. For Plato, it is a matter of two different types of self-identity. A thing has a material, numerical identity. By virtue of its bodily being, we can point to it and say "this one." An idea, however, has specific unity or identity. It is a one in many. Given the general correlation between being and intelligibility, this distinction must mirror itself in predication. In fact, we cannot predicate of the idea what we predicate of the things standing under it. Thus we cannot say that the idea of greatness is itself a great or large idea. Neither is the idea of smallness a small idea or, to take Frege's example, the idea of black cloth either black or made of cloth.[6] Were we to make such assumptions, then as Plato notes, participation would mean literally having material portions, with all the absurdities this involves (*Parmenides* 131d). Yet if we cannot predicate of the ideas what we predicate of the things, how do we come to know them? Assuming there is no resemblance, then, as Plato says about the ideas, "their essence is determined by a relation among themselves, and has nothing to do with the resemblances, or whatever they are to be termed, which are in our sphere" (133c–d). Beginning as we do with what is in our sphere, "none of the ideas are known to us" (134b).

With this we have the collapse of the notion of self-identity as a standard

6. For Frege, the general conclusion here is that the properties of objects specified by concepts are not themselves properties of these concepts. When we think a concept by means of its definition, we, thus, do not think of any actual objects that have the properties specified by this concept. In Frege's words, "Whether such objects exist is not immediately known by means of their definitions. . . . Neither has the concept defined got this property, nor is a definition a guarantee that the concept is realized" (*Translations from the Philosophical Writings of Gottlob Frege*, p. 145). Given this, we cannot say that being in touch with the concept puts us in touch with the reality. The concept, in other words, loses its normative function.

of being. The notion of participation also disappears. This follows, since participation demands a *single* notion of being, one common to both the thing and its idea. A thing could not possess its being by virtue of its participation in its idea if both thing and idea did not exist by virtue of the same essence (the same ουσία) of *to be*. This, for Plato, is the self-identity which images, things, mathematical objects, and ideas supposedly possess to an increasing degree. In other words, self-identity or self-sameness is what allows us to take Plato's divided line and see it as a hierarchy of beings with ideas at the top—this, because it supposedly gives us a single standard by which we can measure different levels of being. But the problem here is that we cannot predicate of the ideas what we predicate of the things. This implies that there are two different types of self-identity understood as the quality of being one. As Plato points out, an idea cannot be shared or "participated" in by being divided. It is indivisibly one. Yet an individual's unity can be split. It can be materially divided, be "greater" or "smaller," qualities not available to an idea. Thus, although an idea cannot be larger or smaller, a thing can (131d).

The medieval question of the universals works endlessly on the terms of this debate. Its real issue is actually about being. It is: How can the unity of the idea or species be present in a multitude of individuals or, conversely, how can single individuals share in the unity of the species. Both the realists and nominalists agree that "to be" means to be self-identical and interpret this as being "one." They disagree, however, on what this last means. If it means being one thing (one material reality), then the ideas which have only specific unity are not. They are nothing but "common names" produced by habit, circles of association, historical, sociological processes—the list is endless. An illegitimate child who is not acknowledged puts many men under suspicion of paternity. If we reverse this and say that "to be" means to be a specific unity, then the same fate befalls individual things. "What" a thing is, its form or species grasped as a conceptual unit, is what is. In itself, in its own individual, bodily unity, the thing is not. Both solutions are obviously one-sided. Our senses convince us that there are individual things, while our specifically human mental life requires the grasp of conceptual unities. The difficulty is that the attempt to invest either side with a normative function—this is, to make ideas standards or, through empiricism, to draw all knowledge from things— makes the other side incomprehensible.[7]

7. For an account of how medieval philosophy attempted to solve this question, see James Mensch, "Between Plato and Descartes—The Mediaeval Transformation in the Ontological Status of the Ideas," pp. 40–47.

§2. *Cartesian Normativity.* Two figures symbolize the resultant schizo-phrenic age in which modernity is born. The first is Montaigne, the nominalist sceptic. In his essay "On Cannibals," he declares that "we have no other criterion of truth and reason than the example and pattern of the opinions and customs of the country wherein we live" (*Selected Essays,* pp. 77–78). After praising the virtues of the cannibals and finding them in no wit inferior to those of sixteenth-century France, he laughingly concludes: "But hold on! They don't wear breeches" (p. 89). Pants, rather than any conception of morality, make Europe superior. A similar relativism is advanced from the other side by Cervantes' *Don Quixote,* the international best-seller of the seventeenth century. For the Don, it is not things but rather his ideas of them which have the force of reality. Any evidence to the contrary is explained by the "enchanters [who] have persecuted, are persecuting, and will continue to persecute me" (*Don Quixote,* p. 722). Evil and all-powerful, they make it impossible to decide on what precisely is real, what is a dream and what not. On one level, the whole book can be considered as a meditation on the impregnability of the Don's argument. It is not too much to say that such enchanters reappear in the form of Descartes's supposition that God may be an evil genius, one personally bent on deceiving him.

The Cartesian response to this has already been indicated. It is an attempt to reestablish normativity through subjectivity. Thus, in the first instance Descartes banishes the specter of the evil genius by pointing to his own subjectivity as something which cannot be doubted. So regarded, the subject becomes the *ens certissimum,* the being whose certainty is such that it can stand as a norm, a standard against which to judge all other claims to knowledge. This norm is mediated through the concepts of clarity and distinctness. As Descartes writes, "In this first conclusion [that I exist] there is nothing else which assures me of its truth, but the clear and distinct perception of what I affirm" (*Meditations,* III; p. 34). Of course, as he admits, clarity and distinctness would not be sure signs of being "if it should ever happen that something which I conceived just as clearly and distinctly should prove false." Against this, he makes a move crucial to modernity. He takes it "as a general principle that everything which we conceive very clearly and very distinctly is wholly true" (ibid.). In other words, to the point that our perceptions and thoughts of other objects approach the clarity and distinctness of our grasp of the subject, to that point we can be equally certain of the reality of their objects.

Clarity and distinctness are "subjective" concepts, that is, they characterize the subjective grasp of reality. To take them as norms is thus to attempt to reestablish normativity through subjectivity. The best way to put this is in terms of knowing and being. For the ancient world in general and for Plato in particular, being was prior to knowing. Standards for knowing were given by the ideas, which through their self-identity represented being to the highest degree. Thus the success of knowing was judged by its grasp of being, which was interpreted as the self-identity manifested by the ideas. As we said, it was assumed that to the point that we are in contact with the self-identity present in the ideas, we are not deceived, but rather touch reality. For Descartes, however, the reverse is the case. It is standards of knowing, in particular those of clarity and distinctness, which determine those of being. In other words, epistemology, the science of knowing, takes precedence over metaphysics. It sets the standards for what can be. What can be is what can be clearly and distinctly grasped. Whatever eludes such apprehension does not exist. Crucial to this position is the assumption that not even God can avoid it. Thus the benevolent God, whose existence Descartes proves, acts in accordance with our standards of knowing. This, for example, is what allows Descartes to assert: "Since I know that all the things I conceive clearly and distinctly can be produced by God exactly as I conceive them, it is sufficient that I can clearly and distinctly conceive one thing apart from another to be certain that the one is distinct from the other" (*Meditations,* VI; pp. 73–74). In fact, as he earlier affirms, having shown "that He is not a deceiver, I can infer as a consequence that everything which I conceive clearly and distinctly is necessarily true" (*Meditations,* V; p. 67). This definition of God as nondeceptive is, to state the obvious, a definition in terms of the categories of knowing. As we noted, the proof for God also employs such categories—in particular, those of clarity and distinctness. To the point that the God it proves is not bound by these, the proof of his existence loses its persuasive force. We, thus, have the circularity we mentioned above: the God so proved must create according to such categories. Only then can I be assured of the latter's unrestricted normativity and, hence, be assured of the validity of the proof.

   The binding of God by the rules of human knowing is a sure sign that we have entered the modern age. Since even God must obey them, subjective standards of knowing become universal. Every possible being becomes correlated to the subjective processes of knowing. The processes, in fact, determine what can count as a being. What cannot come to presence through them cannot be. If we accept this, then the fact that such subjective processes seem to be immediately available, that is, lie open to our direct inspection, promises a field of fruitful inquiry. From Locke and

Hume to Husserl and continuing on to the present day, enquiries into human understanding have been pursued not just for their epistemological but also for their ontological significance. To the point that such studies yield universal rules, that is, rules which apply to knowing as such, they uncover the modern equivalents of the Platonic ideas. For Plato a thing exists to the extent that it participates in its idea. The idea contains the standard of its being. For the modern, the thing is to the point that it can come to presence. The standards for its being are those rules for its coming to presence which are revealed by an analysis of the actions by which we know it.

Descartes initiates this attempt to do metaphysics through epistemology by analyzing his grasp of a piece of beeswax. Originally hard, cold, emitting a sound when rapped, and perfumed by a distinctive floral odor, the wax loses all these qualities as it is brought close to the fire. Admitting that it is one and the same entity, two conclusions follow. The first is that the wax is "neither that sweetness of honey, nor that pleasant odor of flowers, nor that whiteness, nor that shape, nor that sound, but only a body"—in short, only extended matter which assumed first one configuration and now assumes another (*Meditations,* II; p. 30). The second is that the reality of the wax is not grasped by the senses. Its apprehension is "solely an inspection by the mind, which can be imperfect and confused as it was formerly, or clear and distinct as it is at present" (ibid., pp. 30–1). According to this analysis, knowing involves turning from the senses to an inspection by the mind. Such an inspection achieves its clarity and distinctness when it reduces the directly sensible qualities of the object to their quantifiable analogues, these being chiefly the configurations of extension. Granting this, the rules for an object's coming to a clear and distinct presence are just those which allow us to reduce its directly sensible qualities to its "primary qualities," that is, to the size, figure, mass, and motion we grasp through this "inspection by the mind." Such rules, particularly as they structure the activities of the modern laboratory, function as norms determining in advance what can count as being.

§3. *The Cartesian Legacy: George Berkeley.* The result of this new normativity is the division of the world into appearance (the directly sensible qualities of things) and true reality (the primary qualities). As with the original, Platonic normativity, the problem arises of how to relate the two. If we could, all would be well. Unfortunately we cannot. We have no idea of the possible connection between a sense perception with its qualia and the primary qualities of matter. It is precisely this ignorance which allows

Berkeley to engage in a series of arguments whose purpose is to reverse the Cartesian normativity of primary over directly perceivable ("secondary") qualities. Since we have no idea of this connection, far from being clear and distinct, the view that matter with its primary qualities *causes* the "secondary" is radically incoherent. Echoing Locke, Berkeley writes that we are "unable to comprehend in what manner body can act upon spirit, or how it is possible it should imprint any idea on the mind." If this is so, we have no reason to posit matter as something characterized by such primary qualities. In fact, the lack of connection signifies that "the production of ideas or sensations in our mind can be no reason why we should suppose [the existence of] matter or corporeal substances" (*Of the Principles of Human Knowledge,* §19; p. 40). Granting this, the primary qualities of bodies, rather than being independent causes of sensuously perceivable qualities, are, in fact, dependent on the latter. In Berkeley's words: "Abstracted from all other [sensuous] qualities," the primary are "inconceivable" (§10, p. 35). Thus we cannot think of extension apart from color, or motion without both. Admitting this, Cartesian science is based on a simple, yet far-reaching category mistake. Basing itself on observed relations *between* experiences, it turns and attempts to make its empirically derived concepts explanatory of experience *per se.* Thus the figure, motion, and extension of bodies do not explain but rather presuppose our actual, given experience of the world. The same can be said for the concept of causality. As an empirical concept, it has its basis in relations of dependency among appearances. Granting this, we cannot use causality to explain what it presupposes, namely, appearance *per se.* This follows, since, according to its basis, the only thing the concept of causality can do is point to a connection between one appearance and another. It is, after all, simply an empirical generalization of the observed relations between what appears.

Berkeley draws a radical conclusion from the inseparability of primary and secondary qualities. It is of interest to us, not in itself, but as another illustration of the modern attempt to draw standards of being from those of knowing. Admitting that the sensuous qualities of objects *exist only in the mind,* that is, only as perceptions, the same holds for the primary ones, "figure, motion, and such like" (§73, pp. 72–73, see also §§9–10). For Descartes, to know is to understand what lies beneath the sensuous appearance. In the Berkelian reversal, to know is to perceive. It is to grasp the sensuously given phenomena rather than any assumed material substrate. Correlatively, to be known is to be perceived. It is to be present as a perception. Drawing his standards of being from knowing, Berkeley draws the obvious inference from this. "To be" is to be perceived. The whole external world has its being as a perception (§3, §88). Its substratum, what supports it, is not anything external. It is not matter with its supposed primary qualities. It is the perceiver (§91).

§4. *The Cartesian Legacy: David Hume.* The same attempt to draw metaphysical conclusions from epistemology is operative in Hume.[8] He begins his celebrated work with the sentence: "All the perceptions of the human mind resolve themselves into two distinct kinds, which I shall call impressions and ideas" (*A Treatise of Human Nature,* bk. 1, part 1, sec. 1; p. 1). "Impressions" are our "sensations, passions and emotions," while "ideas" are "the faint images of these" (ibid.). In the first instance, ideas are just the memory traces of the impressions. Now, if "to be" is to be perceived and all our perceptions resolve themselves into impressions and ideas, being must be limited to these elements. All else must, in other words, be counted as a "fiction." The *Treatise* is remarkable for the rigor with which it carries out this argument. Again and again when considering an ontological claim—for example, the claim of the "self" to be a being—Hume asks, What impression do we have of the supposed being? If there is none, then it gets counted as a fiction.

The same holds for the ancient notion of being, considered as substance. Traditionally, "substance" meant that which is the subject of the various predications, but which cannot, itself, be a predicate. In discourse, it signified that which underlies these predicates as the entity being talked about. In the realm of perception, it stood for that of which we are having perceptions, that which shows itself through them as one and the same and, hence, is distinguished from their multiplicity (see, for example, Plato *Republic* 598a). Given that its notion involves this distinction, it cannot be reduced to perceptions. We must answer in the negative, when asked "whether the idea of *substance* be derived from the impressions of sensation or reflection"—those of reflection being "the passions and emotions" (Hume, *Treatise,* bk. 1, part 1, sec. 6; p. 15). But if this is so, then nothing corresponds to the idea. The idea is a fiction. The only thing we can have in mind, when regarding it is the perceptions themselves, not something underlying them. As Hume states the conclusion: "We have therefore no idea of substance, distinct from that of a collection of particular qualities

8. This, even though as an empiricist he would deny any attempt to do metaphysics. One of the interesting things about basing metaphysics on epistemology is that it allows the metaphysical impulse, the desire to make normative assertions about being, to operate while concealing itself.

[given as contents of the perceptions], nor have we any other meaning when we either talk or reason concerning it" (p. 16). Substance is simply a collection or bundle of what actually counts as being, namely, the perceptions.

The same holds for the notion of a self, understood as the underlying subject which has (rather than is) such perceptions. Once again Hume asks, "from what impression could this idea be derived?" (bk. 1, part 4, sec. 6; p. 251). Given that there cannot be one, nothing corresponds to the idea save those successive perceptions which the self has. As Hume writes: "I may venture to assert of the rest of mankind that they are nothing but a bundle or collection of different perceptions, which succeed each other with an inconceivable rapidity, and are in a perpetual flux and movement" (ibid., p. 252). The point follows when we assert that "to be" is to be known and assume that all we can know are our perceptions rather than any supposed cause of them. As Hume states the assumption: the "ultimate cause" of "the impressions which arise from our senses" is "completely inexplicable." Indeed, it "will always be impossible to decide with certainty, whether they arise immediately from the object, or are produced by the creative power of the mind, or are derived from the author of our being" (bk. 1, part 3, sec. 5; p. 84). What makes this impossible is not just our inability to specify the connection between such sensuous impressions and the supposed primary qualities that pertain to their imagined origins. As already indicated, the very notion of causality proves unsuitable to explain experience. As an empirical concept, it presupposes rather than explains experience. Concretely regarded, it is a concept having to do with the logic of experience, namely, the observed regularities in the experiential flow.

The reduction of being to perception thus reduces the laws of being to those of impressions and ideas. In a word, it reduces them to "psychological" laws. Causal laws undergo a similar reinterpretation. Its point is to explain how the laws of resemblance, contiguity, and association yield the *impression* of necessary connection, which, for Hume, is the *reality* of causality. Once again, his essential premise is at work in the argument. Being must be limited to impressions, since this, in the first instance, is all that we can know. Given this, he has to say "the idea of necessity arises from some impression." This he finds to be nothing else "but that propensity, which custom produces, to pass from an object to the idea of its usual attendants" (bk. 1, Part 3, sec. xiv; p. 165). Since this is "the essence of necessity," and since, according to its essence, such necessity "exists in the mind, not in objects," the laws of necessary connection are the psychological laws that by describing the formation of this "custom," describe the occurring of the impression.

Once again we have a reversal of the Cartesian normative relation. For Descartes, the norms are provided by the quantifiable aspects of perception, that is, its primary qualities. The mathematical laws governing these aspects determine what is real and what is not in the directly sensible world. For Hume, however, it is precisely the qualities of the directly sensible world that provide the norms. The normativity of secondary qualities (of their psychological relations) takes the place of the Cartesian normativity of primary qualities. The laws of psychology replace those of physics. Two items especially indicate this shift. Clarity and distinctness are replaced by the "vividness" of an impression The latter is what indicates that we are in contact with reality. Correspondingly, the ideas are now devalued to "the faint images [of impressions] in thinking and reasoning" (bk. 1, part 1, sec. 1; p. 1). A consequence of this is that "abstract ideas are therefore in themselves individual." They must be if they are only images and if "the image in the mind is only that of a particular object" (sec. 7, p. 20).

As is obvious, we are once again within a schema in which the assertion of the reality of the norm is conjoined with that of the irreality of that for which it is the norm. Since the reality of an idea is its being one in many, its reinterpretation as a particular image is its denial. For Descartes and the scientists who are his successors the sensuous world has the status of mere appearance; what counts as real is the world of primary qualities as reached by the understanding in its grasp of abstract ideas such as extension, time, mass and motion and their mathematical relations. For Berkeley, Hume, and their successors, the opposite is the case: The secondary qualities are real. How does one decide between the two? It might seem that the issue revolves around Berkeley's argument on the inseparability of primary and secondary qualities. If they were separable, they could be grasped through an act of the understanding. What the understanding could grasp (the primary qualities and their causal relations) would (following Descartes) become normative.[9] If they are not, then Berkeley's argument follows, and what is normative are the secondary qualities. At this point all the attempts to do a psychology of arithmetic, from those of the *Treatise* to Husserl's early work, *The Philosophy of Arithmetic,* are in or-

---

9. Since this is not itself an impression or appearance, we can thus dispense with the empiricists' arguments, which dismiss causality as a mere relation between appearances. For the nonempiricist, causality is, rather, a relation between the appearance and what the understanding uncovers as standing behind the appearance.

der. The real issue, however, goes much deeper. It concerns our inability to specify the connection between the norm and that for which it is the norm. Given this, whatever side we choose, we simply interpret the other in a way which denies it.

§5. *The Normativity of the Perceiver.*   We can reinforce this point by noting a further dichotomy. In the last few pages, we have been speaking only in terms of the perceived. Under the assumptions that "to be" is to be known and all we know are our perceptions, the debate concentrates on whether perception is to be taken as sensuous or intellectual. For Descartes, however, the original source of certainty is not the perception but rather the perceiver. The norms of clarity and distinction were in the first instance taken from *its* apprehension. Thus the premise that allows us to say that "to be" is to be perceived also permits the assertion that "to be" is to perceive.[10] This is Leibniz's position. "What is" is the monad considered as a perceiver. Of course, not all monads (or "simple substances") perceive in the same way. Some monads have "more distinct" perceptions as well as the memory of what they have perceived. Some do not. The latter compose what we normally consider as the inanimate world ("Monadology," §§17–21). The difficulty with this position concerns, once again, the question of connection. If "to be" is to perceive, if, in other words, all simple, created substances are perceivers, what is there for them to perceive? How do we relate this concept of being as perceiver to the other half of Descartes's certainties, namely, that "to be" is also to be perceived?

Leibniz's answer is to interpret the perceived in terms of the perceiver. Descartes, we recall, posits the perceiving subject as an indissoluble unity. Renaming this a monad (from the Greek *monos* or unit), Leibniz declares that the monads have "neither extension, nor form, nor divisibility" ("Monadology," §2; p. 251). Completely immaterial, they can have no direct relation to the extended world. This means, as he writes: "The monads have no windows through which anything may come in or go out" (§7; p. 252). As such, they can have no direct influence on each other. The influence is only "ideal." It occurs through the "mediation of God" (§51; p. 262). God is what supplies each monad with its perceptions of all others.[11] He does this "from the beginning of things," supplying each with a set of percep-

10. The premise, of course, is that *to be* is *to be known* or, more generally, it is the premise of the priority of epistemology over metaphysics.

11. It is in terms of such perceptions that the action and passion are distinguished. "Action is attributed to the monad insofar as it has distinct perceptions, and passion or passivity is attributed insofar as it has confused perceptions" ("Monadology," §49; p. 262).

tions that yield *in toto* the best possible world (§§52–58). To take a modern analogy, each monad has a movie running in its head. God runs the projectors. Indeed, he is also the director and producer of the various shows. He has so scripted them that they connect with one another to produce a world with "the greatest possible variety, together with the greatest order which may be." The result, then, is a world with "the greatest possible perfection" (§58).

Whatever we may think of this solution, it is clear that it works out a distinct possibility of Cartesian dualism. Thus, it is after presenting his analogy of the mill that Leibniz declares that each monad or simple substance is inherently a perceiver. Given that perception is a fact and given that it cannot be explained by mechanical means, perception in the sense of perceiving must be an elementary rather than a derived feature of being. As Leibniz draws the conclusion: "It is, accordingly, in the simple substance, and not in the [extended] composite nor in a machine that the Perception is to be sought" (§17). Even God is thought in these terms. He is the great perceiver. In ordering the whole, he "has regard to every part and in particular to each monad" (§60; p. 264). He sees what they see, and he does so clearly and distinctly (ibid.). In a certain sense, we can say that it is because his vision is the "best" that the resultant world is the best possible.

Unfortunately, this interpretation of perception in terms of the perceiver fails to solve the question of the relation of the two. Individual monads (elementary substances or "atoms" of being) are declared to be perceivers; yet instead of explaining what this might mean, the mystery is increased through their identification with an all-seeing God. To be fair to Leibniz, the difficulty here is actually Cartesian. The subject that emerges as a residuum from Descartes's method of doubt is not just completely nonextended and, hence, physically speaking, "windowless." It is, he admits, "that indescribable part of myself which cannot be pictured by the imagination" (*Meditations,* II; p. 28). This follows because it cannot be any of the correlates of the self's actions. It is not something seen, thought of, imagined, willed, and so on. All such correlates can be doubted. What cannot be doubted is the subject of such actions, but such a subject is objectively anonymous. It cannot be characterized or named in terms of any of the objects of its attending.[12] Thus, to the point that we do make it an *ens*

---

12. Husserl explores the same theme in the late manuscripts in his discussions of the "anonymity of the ego." He writes, for example: "The ego which is the counterpart [*gegenüber*] to everything is anonymous. It is not its own counterpart. The house is my counterpart, not vice versa. And yet I can turn my attention to myself. But then this counterpart in which the ego comes forward along with everything which was its counterpart is again split. The

certissimum, that is, a being that can never be doubted, to that point it escapes our grasp. We thus find ourselves in the curious position of asserting the priority of epistemology over ontology on the basis of that which can never be objectively known.

The strangeness of this position becomes apparent once we assert with Berkeley that the whole sensible world has its being as a perception. This means, as we noted, that what supports it is not some external material reality. It is, in Berkeley's words, "those unextended indivisible substances or spirits which act and think and perceive [this world]" (*Principles,* §90; p. 83). Although we call both spirits and perceptions "being," we have here to do with "two kinds entirely distinct and heterogeneous, and which have nothing in common but the name ['being']" (§89; p. 82). Thus, the knowledge we gain from the objective side helps not at all to characterize the subjective side. Space and time, for example, characterize the observed relations between perceptions (or "ideas"). Abstracted from the latter, space and time are nothing at all (§98; §116). Consequently, they cannot characterize spirit regarded as a distinct ontological category.

The same insight is behind Leibniz's assertion that each monad's perceiving is determined "from the beginning of things," that is, from all eternity. This is the only way it can be determined, given that it is not characterizable by time. What we grasp in time is not the subject, but rather its objective correlate. We grasp the perception, not the present perceiver, which, in its unchanging nowness, is not in time.

§6. *Some Difficulties with Empiricism.* An empiricist reaction was probably inevitable in the face of doctrines that place the subject out of time, imply its atemporal determination, and require God's continual intervention to match it to the world. Within a movement, moreover, whose thrust is to base being on knowing, an entity characterized by an absence of what we can know has a precarious position. The result, then, is Hume's denial of the self. Having stated that "the mind is a kind of theater, where several perceptions successively make their appearance; pass, re-pass, glide away, and mingle in an infinite variety of postures and situations," he immediately corrects any impression that the notion of a theater has any ontological content. He writes: "The comparison of the theater must not mis-

---

ego which comes forward as a counterpart and its counterpart [e.g., the house it was perceiving] are both counterparts to me. Forthwith, I—the subject of this new counterpart—am anonymous" (Ms. C 2 I, pp. 3a–b. August 1931). All citations from the C manuscripts follow the original folio pagination. Citations from the other Nachlass manuscripts follow the pagination of the typescripts of the Husserl Archives at Louvain, Belgium.

lead us. They are the successive perceptions only, that constitute the mind" (*Treatise,* bk. 1, part 4, sec. 6; p. 253). Thus taking his standard from the perceived, he denies the existence of a self or subject other than that of a "bundle or collection of different perceptions" (ibid., p. 252).

The conclusion is as problematical as that which it denies. If there is no self, in what do perceptions inhere? Hume, for one, refuses to answer. He states that we have not "the most distant notion of the place, where these scenes are represented, or of the materials, of which it is composed" (ibid., p. 253). Not composed of anything, these perceptions become the irreducible elements of all composition. Both self and world, both the mind and the things it grasps are composed out of them, that is, out of their order and arrangement. For Hume, the laws of such composition are those of resemblance, contiguity, and association of perceptions. William James, Hume's most brilliant successor, adds that the composition involves taking the same experiences twice. Taking the experiences as the possible subjects of memory and imagination, that is, as "transitory, physically inert, with a succession which does not follow a determined order but seems rather to obey emotive fancies," they become components of the bundle of perceptions that compose the self. Taking the very same experiences in another context, that where they "extend in time, enter into relations of physical influence" and so on, the experiences compose the physical world. Originally, however, all we have is a field of experiences. Self and world are simply precipitates of the way we interpret the selfsame experiences. According to how we take them, either "we make of them a field apart which we call the physical world" or "we make of them another field which we call the psychical world" ("The Notion of Consciousness," p. 192). To raise the obvious question here: *who* is making the experience one thing rather than another? The experiences themselves, since they can equally become either, cannot perform this function. But the self that could perform it is supposed to have been eliminated by this function. It is supposed to be the result rather than the cause of its action.

The same point can be made with regard to the notion of causality. From the perspective of the field of elementary experiences, it must be considered a derived or constituted quality. Hume, in fact, bends every effort to show that causality is an effect produced by the resemblance, contiguity, and association of experiences. If it is, however, then these factors bring it about or *cause* it. If we deny their causal agency, then we seem to be at a loss to explain the occurring of the resultant "propensity" to proceed from one idea to another, which, for Hume, is the essence of causality. Yet if we affirm such agency, causality is a premise, not a consequence of our explanation. It is, we may note, no help to bring in the notion of custom or habit, that is, to speak of "that propensity produced by custom," since what is at issue is this production. Indeed, in raising the question, "whose habit," that is, of the subject in which the habit is supposed to inhere, we return to our earlier difficulties regarding the self. Is the self the subject of habits or their result?

§7. *The Failure of Modernity.* The purpose of this chapter is not to resolve but only to raise the difficulties of the Cartesian legacy. As we have seen, they arise from a series of closely related dualisms: those between mind and body, perception and world, perceiver and perception. Dualism is not a feature of any particular standpoint within this legacy. It is not, for example, a quality of Cartesian or Leibnizian rationalism as opposed to the empiricism of a Berkeley, Hume, or James. It is universally present within the modern, Cartesian framework, which assumes the priority of epistemology. More precisely, it is implicit in the normativity that is the point of this priority. Thus, the dualisms we have examined are basically between what we take to be the norm and that for which it is the norm. In each case, the norm seems to disappear under the weight of the requirements placed upon it. Thus the Cartesian normativity of the perceiver becomes absorbed in the perceived, the normativity of primary qualities becomes absorbed in the secondary. Each new norm, however, experiences similar difficulties. Watching this spectacle through reading the history of modern philosophy is rather like observing the microscopic life of a pond. Elements absorb and are absorbed in turn by other elements, this in a ceaseless round.

If the above is correct, the failure of modernity is nothing less than the failure of its central project. This, as we said, was to make subjectivity normative, in broad terms, to make it serve as a substitute for the ideas or forms of ancient philosophy. The forms were to be reinterpreted as rules for bringing objects to presence, while the subject was to be seen as the most certain, the most clear and distinct of the objects we could grasp. In this way, it would serve as a new foundation for knowledge, one whose openness to inspection would be its bulwark against the skepticism of a Montaigne or a Cervantes. Subjectivity, however, was not up to the task. Taken as normative, it fragments into competing norms. The history of modernity in the account we have given is the story of the collapse of these norms. Broadly speaking, it is the story of the disappearance of the subject under the weight of the requirements placed upon it.

The modern period was ushered in by a similar collapse: that of the

Platonic norms in the nominalism and relativism of the early Renaissance. The collapse was caused by the inability to connect norm and "normed," that is, to grasp both under a single category. It is not too much to say that the same inability is at work here. "Ideas and spirit," perceived and perceiver, are as Berkeley points out completely heterogeneous categories. So, for that matter, are body and soul, primary and secondary qualities, or any of a number of the other oppositions that characterize modernity. Its self-confessed inability to relate these implies that we are at its end. We are, as the popular phrase goes, "postmodern." To actually be such, however, would be to escape from the dualisms we have been describing. It would be to identify the cause of the recurrent lack of connection between the norm and the normed, between the true and the apparent world—this, not to establish a new dualism or to embrace an old one, but rather to leave such a framework altogether. The point of the next few chapters is precisely this. As we shall now see, the cause of this failure is nothing less than the paradigm lying at the heart of the modern project.

2

Sins of Omission

The Appeal to Miracles

The collapse of modernity is the collapse of its attempt to supply a replacement for the ideas or forms of ancient philosophy. It is the exhaustion of its central project, which is to reestablish normativity through an appeal to subjectivity. The attempt to explain the world in terms of subjective performances undermines itself. A sign of this is that each explanation leaves something out. There is a gap in its reasoning. A kind of "then the miracle occurs"—a deus ex machina—seems to be needed to reach the required conclusions. This chapter examines some of these gaps to see what they reveal about the nature of this failure. I intend to show that modernity's failure is not that of individual philosophers, not a matter of individuals' having failed to get their arguments right. It is the failure of the premise they all share: that of the priority of knowing over being, that is, of the epistemological paradigm itself. At the heart of the modern project is the assumption that *standards of being are to be drawn from those of knowing, that subjective processes of knowing determine what can count as being.* As we shall see, the gap in the attempts to work this out concerns the being of such knowing, concretely, the being of the subjective processes themselves.

§1. *Cartesian Omissions.* The gap in Descartes's reasoning has already been indicated. Broadly speaking, it is his appeal to God as a guarantor of his reasoning. He writes that while he is attending to some simple mathematical proof, he is not assailed by doubts. But afterwards, "It can easily happen that I doubt its truth, if I do not know that there is a God. For I can persuade myself that I was so made by nature that I could easily make mistakes, even in those matters which I believe I understand with the greatest evidence and certainty" (*Meditations,* V; p. 66). God is required to guarantee his nature, namely, to guarantee that either God (or nature) made him just right. Being rightly made means being endowed with the reasoning processes that can capture the world.

The assumption of the priority of epistemology also implies that such processes possess their own inherent standards for correctness. This follows, since the priority of the knowing relationship is also that of its standards. Not being dependent on anything, the relation must draw its standards from itself, that is, from the evidence provided by its own processes. It cannot, for example, take these standards from some external entity (or feature thereof), since it must, through its standards, itself first decide on the reality of this entity. The Cartesian standards are, of course, those of clarity and distinctness. Descartes's genius was to see that within the reasoning process itself there is an inherent gradation involving these factors. Reasoning is more or less clear. Concepts and evidence are more or less distinct.[1] Now, if we assume the priority of epistemology, we must also assume that what is clearly and distinctly grasped is necessarily true, namely, that the correct employment of reason, according to its own standards, does grasp reality. We thus have to banish the thought that we are "so made by nature" that our inherent standards for knowing are inadequate. To do this, Descartes appeals to God. In his words: "But after having recognized that there is a God, and having recognized at the same time that all things are dependent upon him and that he is not a deceiver, I can

---

1. One can see the difference between primary and secondary qualities in terms of this distinction. Thus we can clearly see how a change in the size, figure, and motion of one body can cause a corresponding change in another body's primary qualities. In fact, we can quantify this relation, achieving thereby a high measure of distinctness (exactitude). Our insight into how a change in the secondary qualities of one body (its color, odor, taste, sound, and texture) could cause a corresponding change in another is, however, far less clear and distinct. In the few cases where we can imagine this, for example, with odors, it is difficult to quantify it. Similarly, it is easier to explain a body's secondary qualities in terms of the primary than the reverse. The whole reductionist strategy of science is based on this. In fact, clarity and distinctness, when applied to the distinction between primary and secondary qualities, mean being capable of fitting in with this strategy.

infer as a consequence that everything which I conceive clearly and distinctly is necessarily true" (ibid., p. 67).

God is thus assumed as the guarantor of the knowing process, in particular of the standards assumed to be inherent in the process. Once we analyze the process into its factors a number of subsidiary assumptions come into view. To begin with, the process involves both subjects and objects. Both must be harmonized if we are to assume that the subject adequately grasps the object. As noted in the previous chapter, this involves a reinterpretation of the conceptions of clarity and distinctness. They become standards, not just for the subjective processes of knowing, but also for being. Thus it is not just my belief that "all things are dependant upon [God]" that convinces me of their adequacy. I must also assume that God is also bound by them. They become standards governing his creative activity. He has created nature such that it is mathematizable (that is, numerable down to its least structures) and hence is graspable according to these standards.

It is easy to see how this assumption is required by the assumed priority of epistemology taken as a science of knowing. If it is prior, epistemology cannot draw its standards from any other science. This would be to interpret the knowing relation in terms of some other relation (e.g., material-causal or historical or sociological), studied by some other science. In such a situation, knowing would be contingent on this other relation. Only when the conditions specified by the latter obtained—for example, when the right material or historical or sociological circumstances were given— would the knowing relation be considered adequate. The difficulty here is obvious. We must assume the knowing relation's adequacy if we are to be certain that we know such external conditions. Thus any interpretation of knowledge in terms of some other factor seems to presuppose from the start the adequacy of epistemological standards. As for the standards themselves, we must assume that they determine what is to count as being. Since they cannot draw their ontological assumptions from any other science, an ontological force must be granted them from the beginning. How are we to do this? What is needed seems to be some ontological premise, one resting on the nature of being; yet the epistemological paradigm, which seeks to make being a conclusion rather than a premise of knowing, is simply unable to supply such a premise. From the epistemological standpoint, only a "miracle" could supply the need. It is Descartes's implicit recognition of this that makes him tie his belief in the adequacy of the standards of clarity and distinctness to an assumption about being, in particular, to one about the being of God. God, the being on which all else depends, is assumed to create according to these standards. Thus, on the one hand, the priority of epistemology makes us define even God according its standards; on the other hand, God must guarantee this priority. With this, we return to the circularity discussed in Chapter 1. I need God to guarantee that I reason correctly, which implies that I must prove that he exists and is not a deceiver in order to be certain of my reasoning. Yet I must assume that I reason correctly to have any confidence in this proof. The ontological assumption about the nature of creation thus chases the epistemological one about my reasoning and vice versa.

What motivates this rather nervous process of argumentation is the conception of my nature as possibly deceptive. The emerging sciences of medicine and anatomy suggest that the body (including the brain and the sense organs) is but a "machine." With this, the temptation grows to interpret the knowing relation in material-causal terms. Yet once we do so, we run into the problems discussed above. In material-causal terms, being made "just right," that is, being made capable of grasping nature as it is "in itself," is simply contradictory. If I limit myself to such terms, I have to say that I grasp nature not as it is in itself, but as it is relative to my material makeup. Obviously, any such thought completely undermines the priority of epistemology. It involves the interpretation of the knowing relation in terms of the material-causal one. Yet if such an interpretation is correct, it undercuts the confidence we have in it, since it implies the relativity of knowledge, in particular, our knowledge of the factors of the material-causal relation. Contrariwise, to the point that we do trust our knowledge, we seem to be assuming that it is not materially determined, that is, that its laws and standards are not those of the material causality. Given that such laws and standards are, in the first instance, those of the knowing subject, the assumption seems to demand this subject's immateriality.

With this, we have the third assumption of the Cartesian project. Not only must he assume two "miracles" of creation: that God created him just right and that the standards for knowing that God gave him were also imposed upon being. Descartes must also assume that creating him just right means creating him as a completely nonextended and hence immaterial subject. Behind, then, the infamous mind-body duality is the attempt to maintain the priority of epistemology. The unexpressed, but controlling thought in the positing of the immaterial subject is simply the desire to extricate it from the web of material causality. It is to give the knowing subject a sphere that will allow it to follow its own laws. This, we may note, requires yet another miracle. As immaterial, such a subject is "windowless" in the physical sense. There seems to be no conceivable connection between it and the physical world. Thus, not only must God create Descartes as a nonextended, perceiving substance or Leibnizian monad, but God must also constantly correlate Descartes's nonmaterial actions and passions with corresponding events in the material realm. From this, of course, it is a small step to the miracle required by the Leibnizian universe. We require the intervention of God as the creator and harmonizer of what we each privately perceive. God becomes the agent who has correlated "from the start of things" all the perceptions of all the perceiving monads so as to produce the best possible world.

§2. *Miracles of Empiricism.* Once we admit the lack of connection between the world of perception and the material world, we can, as Hume and Berkeley show, dispense with the latter. Yet having eliminated the notion of a material substrate for our perceptions (or "ideas"), Berkeley still feels that something must support them. This is mind or spirit, "it being perfectly unintelligible, and involving all the absurdity of abstraction, to attribute to any single part of them an existence independent of a spirit" (*Principles,* §6; p. 32). Just as we cannot abstract primary from secondary qualities, so, for Berkeley, we cannot abstract the notion of a perception from that of a perceiver. The former must depend upon the latter. Spirit qua perceiver, thus, takes the place of matter and becomes the new substrate—this on what Berkeley takes as strict empirical grounds.

Yet even if we accept this, a gap in the explanation remains. Eliminating matter does not eliminate the fact that our perceptions of what we took to be material realities are still very different from those of our thoughts. In Berkeley's words: "I find I can excite ideas in my mind at pleasure, and vary and shift the scene as oft as I think fit. . . . But, whatever power I may have over my own thoughts, I find the ideas actually perceived by sense have not a like dependence on my will" (§§28–29; p. 45). How are we to account for this? Berkeley, like the Cartesians, appeals to God. They appeal to him to match the actions of spirit to those of matter. Eliminating matter does not dispense with this appeal. It only shifts it. God now directly takes the place of the material substrate and cause of our perceptions. Berkeley's argument has a breathtaking simplicity. He reasons: Some ideas (or "thoughts") I produce, but since I cannot produce those of sense and since they must inhere in spirit, "there is therefore some *other* Will or Spirit that produces them" (ibid.). This is God. As for the laws of nature, they are now taken as applying not to material things, but rather to the "ideas of sense" which replace them. More precisely, Berkeley calls them "the set rules or established methods wherein the Mind we depend on excites in us the ideas of sense" (§30; p. 46). They are, then, the rules of the divine Mind governing its continuous creation of what for us is the reality of the world.

The notion of a God who immediately provides us with our world is hardly an empirical hypothesis. Yet it seems to be demanded once we accept the priority of epistemology, giving its standards an ontological force, and then go on, as Berkeley does, to interpret knowing in an empirical manner. Empirically, the idea of a thing as *that of which* we are having perceptions, that is, as something which manifests itself through them and yet is *distinct* from them, makes no sense. As distinct, it cannot by definition be experienced. Thus if knowing is experiencing and if it also sets the standards of what can count as being, we have to deny the existence of the material substrate. The denial, however, leaves a gap in our account of the world, a gap that can only be filled by appealing to God to take up the functions attributed to matter. These include providing a support for a thing's independence of the manipulations of our imagination. The same material basis was assumed as a support for the thing's being subject to distinct causal laws, which were assumed to govern its material (as opposed to its intentional or mental) being. The appeal to God makes them laws of the divine Mind, but the latter is not an empirical hypothesis. Thus, having eliminated matter by rigorously applying the empirical version of the epistemological paradigm, we again confront the inability of this paradigm to support itself. The reinterpretation of knowing that empiricism advances leaves it unable, without an appeal to the miraculous, to account for reality.

Hume's much more radical empiricism may be considered an embarrassed reaction to this. Its essential elements, particularly, its denial of the substantial unity of the perceiver, are already present in Berkeley. Thus, within Berkeley's own system, the appeal to God can be eliminated once we realize that the perceiver (as opposed to the perception) is not an empirical concept. In other words, the arguments that work to disprove the existence of matter as that which supports and yet is distinct from an object's perceptible qualities also undercut the corresponding notion of the perceiver. The perceiver, for Berkeley, *has* rather than *is* its perceptions. As such, it is not an empirical concept. Such concepts are generalizations drawn from our perceptual experience. Based as they are on what we experience, they are ill-equipped to uncover the origin or support of experience per se. To attempt to use them for such is to involve oneself in an unavoidable regress. To escape this regress we have to say that whatever we posit as explaining experience, cannot itself be an experience. If it were, it would require the same explanation as the things it was supposed to explain. Qua experience, it would require a ground, and if this were also an experience, it too would require a further ground—this on the premise that experience per se requires a ground or explanation.[2] Berkeley puts the difficulty in terms of signs and causes. He writes: "Those men who frame general rules from the phenomena and afterwards derive the phenomena from those rules, seem to consider signs rather than causes" (*Principles,* §108; p. 94). Here, the regress takes the form of a circle. To derive the phenomena from the rules that are themselves derived from the very same phenomena is to engage in circular reasoning if we take this derivation in a causal sense. Given this, no empirical argument for the origin of experience can be advanced. A *fortiori,* we cannot make one that mind or spirit is such an origin.

Beyond this general position, Berkeley also advances another, more specific reason why mind (or perceiving spirit) must escape empirical observation. The knowledge we draw from our perceptions (or "ideas") does not apply to spirit since, as he writes, spirit and idea are "entirely distinct and heterogeneous" categories of being (*Principles,* §89; p. 82). Berkeley's defense of this is instructive. He writes: "A spirit is one simple, undivided, active being. . . . Hence there can be no *idea* formed of a soul or spirit; for all ideas whatever being passive and inert . . . , they cannot represent unto us, by way of image or likeness, that which acts" (§27; p. 44). To translate this into modern, phenomenological terms, we can say that the idea or perception is passive by virtue of being temporally fixed. Occurring at a specific moment, it sinks into pastness with that moment. As it does so, its content remains unchanged. This is its being "inert." To call it such is to say that, having occurred, it is incapable of newness. For Berkeley, this is the very opposite of soul or spirit considered as an active principle. We cannot capture its activity in an image or idea, since to do to so would be to fix it and hence to lose it.

How, then, do we grasp ourselves? The first sentence of the first part of *On the Principles,* asserts that all "the objects of human knowledge" are ideas. If the self is not an idea, the obvious conclusion is that we cannot know it. Perhaps embarrassed by this inference, Berkeley in the second edition adds, we do "comprehend our own existence by inward feeling or reflection," this even though "in a strict sense we have not ideas [of ourselves]" (§89; p. 82). Hume, as we cited him, simply makes the inference.

---

2. The operative concept here is Fichte's: "By virtue of its mere notion the ground falls outside of what it grounds" ("First Introduction," §2, in *The Science of Knowledge,* p. 8).

There is no impression (and hence no idea) of the self as distinct from its
perceptions; therefore, there is no such self. In drawing this conclusion,
Hume is unmoved by Berkeley's argument that, since the being of a perception is its being perceived, it is "unintelligible" to think of it apart from
a perceiver. The reason for this is not just Hume's position that "all the
perceptions of the human mind resolve themselves into . . . impressions
and ideas," the latter being the memory traces of the former. Hume is
unmoved by Berkeley's reasoning precisely because he has reinterpreted
reason so as to reduce it to impressions and ideas. His sentiments on this
point are worth quoting:

> All probable reasoning is nothing but a species of sensation. 'Tis not
> solely in poetry and music, we must follow our taste and sentiment,
> but likewise in philosophy. When I am convinc'd of any principle,
> 'tis only an idea, which strikes more strongly upon me. When I give
> the preference to one set of arguments above another, I do nothing
> but decide from my feeling concerning the superiority of their in-
> fluence. Objects have no discoverable connection together; nor is it
> from any other principle but custom operating upon the imagina-
> tion, that we can draw any inference from the appearance of one to
> the existence of another. (*Treatise,* bk. 1, part 3, sec. viii; p. 103)

The key point is contained in the last sentence. As Hume elsewhere expresses it: "There is nothing in any object, consider'd in itself, which can
afford us a reason for drawing a conclusion beyond it" (sec. xii; p. 139). If
we accept this, we cannot reason as Berkeley did from the perception to
the perceiver. For Hume, no rational inference from any entity to any
other is really possible. This holds, he adds, "even after the observation of
the frequent or constant conjunction of objects" (ibid.). Such conjunction
does not in itself convey any reason why we should infer one from the
other. That we do none the less make the inference is a matter of "sensation." Frequent repetition gives rise to "custom operating upon the imagination," and this occasions a transfer of the vividness of a present object
to the one we "infer." Our belief in the latter is just this vividness, the
inference itself being "a species of sensation."

There is a remarkable tightness in Hume's account of how "fancy" or
imagination "enters into all our reasonings" (ibid., p. 140). Two "particulars" are foundational: "the constant conjunction of any two objects in all
past experience, and the resemblance of a present object to any one of
them. The effect of these two particulars is that the present object invigo-

rates and enlivens the imagination; and the resemblance, along with the constant union, conveys this force and vivacity to the related idea; which we are therefore said to believe or assent to" (ibid., p. 142). What establishes the link is not the actual repetition itself, but rather the habit or custom this produces. It is, as it were, the "force of habit" which moves us from one to the other of the objects, conveying the "vivacity" of one to the other. As we earlier cited Hume, "the propensity, which custom produces, to pass from an object to the idea of its usual attendants" is what produces the impression of necessary connection and hence gives rise to our notions of causality (see page 33). Behind causality lies, not being, but rather repetition. It has its reality simply as a psychological effect of recurrence.

   In spite of this rather drastic reduction of reason to experience, difficulties with the epistemological paradigm still remain. Essentially they are the same as those found in Berkeley. Berkeley must appeal to divine intervention to explain the stability of nature—that is, to account for the fact that material objects, rather than being subject to our fancy, seem to follow distinct laws governing their material relations. The reinterpretation of such laws in terms of the psychological effects of repetition does not explain, but rather continues to presuppose such stability. For Hume, the fact that the present resembles the past can neither be causally nor rationally explained. Having reduced reason to a species of sensation, no inference is possible by which we could reason from one state of affairs to a subsequent state. Thus, we cannot, as is usually done, invoke the principle of sufficient reason: nothing happens without its cause. Although this would allow us to assume that in the absence of an intervening cause, things will remain the same (and hence patterns will repeat), causality here is supposed to be an effect of repetition, not an explanation of it. Thus, within the empiricist framework he provides, the "particulars" upon which reasoning is founded (the constant conjunction of two objects and the resemblance of a present object to one of them) are simply miraculous. Together, they give us the stability of nature and hence the possibility of Humean reasoning. Yet the fact that his version of the epistemological paradigm cannot account for this stability, but rather must presuppose it, points again to the inability of this paradigm to support itself. In relying on such stability, it seems to rely *not on how we know things, but rather on the way things are*. The dependence, then, is on an *ontological* presupposition. From an epistemological perspective, however, this can only seem miraculous, since the possibility of such a presupposition is precisely what it denies. From its perspective, an ontological assertion is supposed to be a result, not a presupposition of the knowing process.

It is interesting to observe the same presupposition at work in Hume's twentieth-century successors: James and Husserl. James, as we noted, begins with Hume's position that our perceptions or experiences are irreducible primitives. Not composed of anything, needing neither self nor world to support them, they are the fundamental elements of all composition. It was James's insight that, as prior to both self and world, the same experiences could be taken as elements composing either. It all depends on the contexts in which we place them. To explain this, James uses the example of the memory of a room. This memory has many possible "couplings." Some "are inconstant, others are stable. In the reader's personal history the room occupies a single date—he saw it only once, perhaps a year ago. Of the house's history, on the other hand, it forms a permanent ingredient. Some couplings have the curious 'stubbornness,' to borrow Royce's term, of fact; others show the fluidity of fancy—we let them come and go." What James is observing is the same distinction that Berkeley noted in his "ideas." Some seem dependent on fancy and hence display its fluidity. Some, however, do not. They have a "stubbornness" in their relations. They refuse to yield to the manipulations of imagination. This distinction of ideas has now become a distinction of "couplings" or contexts. It continues, however, to mark out two separate worlds. Thus, as James writes a few sentences further: "The two collections, first of its cohesive, and, second, of its loose associates, inevitably come to be contrasted. We call the first collection the system of external realities, in the midst of which the room, as 'real,' exists; the other we call the stream of our internal thinking, in which, as 'mental image,' it for a moment floats. The room thus gets counted twice over" ("Does 'Consciousness Exist?'", p. 177). On one counting, it is "*Gedanke*" (a thought), on another, it is "*Gedachtes*" (that which is thought). It all depends upon whether its connections are "stubborn," that is, resistant to fancy, or not. That there are stubborn connections, James simply takes as given. He cannot explain why there are such, since to do so would not be to take the experiences as ultimate, but rather to seek their cause or explanation. Thus one could explain this "stubbornness" by linking it to the independent existence of a set of external realities. But this would be to depart from the epistemological paradigm according to which the foundational elements of knowledge—for James, the world of "pure experiences"—determine those of being.

Husserl is quite explicit in his acceptance of this paradigm. He writes that "epistemology must not just be seen as a discipline which follows metaphysics or even coincides with it. Rather, it precedes it and all other disciplines like psychology" (*Logische Untersuchungen* [Tübingen, 1968],

I, 224; see also II/1, 21). This precedence means that it determines what can count as being for the particular sciences. As for metaphysics, it is supposed to "grow" out of the epistemological critique of such sciences (see *Die Idee der Phänomenologie,* Hua II, 22–23). Thus, for Husserl, "the possibility of metaphysics, of the science of being in an absolute and ultimate sense, obviously depends on the success of this science [of epistemology]" (ibid., p. 32). Stripped to its essentials, the "science" Husserl is proposing under the rubric of a "critique of knowledge" (*Erkenntniskritik*) is a continuation of the project initiated by Hume and carried forward by James. It is the attempt to reduce being to experience by seeing it as composed (Husserl's favorite word is "constituted") of irreducibly primitive experiences. The "critique" of the individual sciences is the phenomenological analysis of the type of objects they study in terms of the types of experiences that constitute these objects. Different types of objects—for example, mathematical, biological, or physical objects—are the result of different types of experience and connections. For example, the experience that gives us a spatial-temporal object as the unity of a perspectivally ordered series of perceptions is quite different from the experience of counting which results in numbers. With this, we have the general point of Husserl's *Erkenntniskritik,* which is to determine what can be considered as an object of a particular science by analyzing the structures of experience (that is, of "knowing") that constitute its domain.

The analyses he puts forward in carrying out this project are extraordinary, both in their detail and length. Fortunately, none of this need concern us. For our present purposes we have only to note Husserl's admission that "the factual (*das Faktische*) is the course of consciousness." This means that, whatever is given within consciousness, all its experiences and their ordering, is taken as simply given. Out of these factually given experiences a world can be constituted, but such constitution presupposes rather than explains this empirical base. As Husserl continues, "Prior, then, to transcendental phenomenology [which studies world constitution], it is, therefore, a fact that the course of consciousness is so structured that within it a nature as a 'rational' unity can constitute itself" ("Beilage XX," in *Erste Philosophie I,* Hua VII, 393). Now, the assertion that this is a "fact" means that it could be otherwise. This implies, as he later writes: "The existence of the world is a correlate of certain multiplicities of experience marked out by certain essential formations. But it is *not* a matter of insight that actual experience could proceed *only* in such forms of connections." In fact, "it is conceivable that experience swarms with inherently irreconcilable conflicts, . . . that there no longer exists a harmoniously positable, hence, existing world" (*Ideen I,* §49; Hua III/1, 103). All we need for this is to imagine different formations of experience. We can do so since the ultimacy of experience, when taken seriously, does not just mean that everything else can be derived from it.[3] It also means that there is no a priori of experience, that is, that nothing can determine experience beforehand.[4] Thus, all possible connections or lack thereof are possible for its factual course.

The world, whose reality is those interconnections which allow its constitution, thus, can cease to be. It can dissolve in a tumult of disordered experiences. The same holds for the self or ego experiencing the same disorder. As Husserl asks: "What could the ego be which has no nature facing it, an ego for whom—if nature is not even given as something sensibly approximate and yet as a self-persisting illusion—there would, instead, be given a mere tumult of sensations?" (Ms. K IV 2, p. 14, October 10, 1925). His answer is that the ego cannot exist without its centering environment. As he writes in the same manuscript, "a complete dissolution of the world in a 'tumult' is equivalent to the dissolution of the ego" (ibid., p. 10). This point follows directly from the ultimacy of experience. As composed (or constituted) out of it, neither self nor world can determine its course. Both, then, are dependent on a facticity that could be otherwise. This leads the Husserlian commentator, Iso Kern, to write that it seems a matter of "grace" that both continue. "There is always the 'danger' that this 'grace' will be withdrawn from [transcendental life], i.e., that the cosmos will dissolve into a chaos of sensations, or that it will collapse as an ego which has a world, an authentic ego" (*Husserl und Kant,* p. 298).

What Kern calls "grace," we would call a miracle. It is the same miracle of the stability of nature that all the empiricists, from Berkeley onward, must presuppose. Husserl, we may note, comes closest to Berkeley in ultimately tracing the stability of nature to God. Having observed that "it is

---

3. Husserl's idealism is based on this point. It is because everything arises through the connections of experience that Husserl can assert that "the entire *spatial-temporal world* . . . is *according to its sense merely intentional being.* . . . It is a being that consciousness posits in its experiences . . . *beyond* this, however, it is nothing at all or more precisely for this being a notion of a *beyond* is a contradictory one" (*Ideen I,* §49; Hua II, 106). This means that "the existence of nature . . . *is* [Husserl's emphasis] only as constituting itself in the ordered connections of consciousness" (§51; Hua II, 109). As Husserl elsewhere expresses this conclusion, "I thus see that the existence of the thing itself, the object of experience, is inseparably implicit in this system of transcendental connections and without such connections, it would thus be unthinkable and obviously a nothing" (*Erste Philosophie II,* Hua VIII, 179).

4. For a closer study of this point, see James Mensch, *Intersubjectivity and Transcendental Idealism,* pp. 115–25.

not necessary that a unitary and tolerably rational ordering of consciousness has to be produced [or] that a nature must be given," he asks, "Or are there appropriate sources for this necessity? *That would be to demonstrate God*" (Ms. B I 4, pp. 2–3, 1908; cited in Kern, *Husserl and Kant,* p. 300).[5] If this is so, then in a way we have come full circle back to Descartes. Once he had embraced the epistemological paradigm, Descartes had to prove God to assure himself of the reality of the external world. Husserl, working within the same paradigm, also needs God. For Husserl, however, the need is more desperate, since the stability of experience, which only God can assure, is required for *both* self and world.

Absences

§1. *The Absent Subject.* The "miracles" we have been discussing are a sign that something has been left out. A gap has occurred that can only be spanned by either direct or indirect appeals to something the epistemological framework cannot provide. Broadly speaking, the framework is one where the subject is supposed to provide the norms for certainty. Such miracles, then, are a sign that subjectivity cannot perform its normative function. In a certain sense we need not be surprised at this, since subjectivity itself has disappeared in the doctrines we have been discussing. In fact, it is precisely the definition of it as normative which has caused its disappearance.

Descartes provides a good example of what we are pointing to. To establish the subject as an entity whose apprehension cannot be doubted, he must strip from it all that can be doubted. Thus, normally, when I think of myself, I include my social position (my family, my friends, my job). I also include my physical appearance and my psychological attributes, my "character" in the usual sense of the word. None of this is present in Des-

---

5. Under the aspect of "reason" or the "logos," God appears as a determining goal of the constitutive process. He assures the stability of nature, not by determining things in advance (this would violate the ultimate facticity of experience) but rather as their goal. Husserl's position, then, is that "because *the rationality* which facticity actualizes is not such as the essence demands, in all this there lies a wonderful *teleology*" (*Ideen I,* §58; Hua II, 125). The teleology points to God. "God, himself, is not the monadic [subjective] totality. He is rather the entelechy lying within it; this, as the infinite telos of the development of 'mankind' from absolute reason, as the telos necessarily regulating monadic being and regulating it from its free decisions" (Ms. A V 22, p. 46, January, 1931). For a more extended account of this point, see Mensch, *Intersubjectivity and Transcendental Idealism,* pp. 368–74.

cartes's reduced subject. According to Descartes, to rid myself of doubtful elements, I must assume "that I have no senses; . . . that body, shape, extension, motion and location are merely inventions of my mind" (*Meditations,* II; p. 25). At first it appears that the self that cannot be doubted is not an object of thought but only the thinking itself. It is a "thinking thing." Yet "thinking" for Descartes covers a multitude of activities and the self which I cannot doubt is not itself divisible. In his words, "It is one and the same mind which, as a complete unit, wills, perceives, and understands and so forth" (VI; p. 74). It cannot, then, be identified with any of these activities. What I really cannot doubt is actually "that indescribable part of myself which cannot be pictured by the imagination" (II; p. 28). Such a self, in other words, is neither an object of thought, nor thought itself considered a general term for mental activity. It is rather an indescribable unity underlying such activity. As such, it seems to disappear under the weight of normativity. The further we go in attempting to make it an *ens certissimum,* the more elusive it becomes.

The same point can be made concerning the other figures we have discussed, for it has been implicit in our accounts of them. Thus Berkeley's move to make the subject the immediate substrate of perceptions implies, on the one hand, its normativity insofar as the laws of nature become those of mind (*Principles,* §30; p. 46). On the other hand, it also implies the complete otherness of minds and perceptions. Regarding them, we confront "two kinds entirely distinct and heterogeneous," kinds "which have nothing in common but the name [being]" (§90; p. 83). This means that mind is no more graspable in terms of the qualities it supports than the material substrate it replaces. As we cited Berkeley, "There can be no idea formed of soul or spirit" (§27; p. 44). Within the empirical tradition, this essential anonymity of the subject leads to a curious reversal of its normativity. Berkeley's successors see the subject as the *result* rather than the cause or support of its perceptions.

Rather than repeat our arguments regarding them, we should mention the position of the greatest of Descartes's successors: Kant, who took up the Cartesian project with his typical thoroughness. In his eyes, its fundamental elements were the unity and the normativity of subjectivity. Concerning the first, he asserts that the subject is a "thoroughgoing identity" (*Kritik der reinen Vernunft,* A 116). When we regard it, "nothing multiple is given" (B 135). As Kant explains, I am always "conscious of the self as identical with respect to the multitude of the representations which are given to me in an intuition" (ibid.). Like Descartes, he finds that whatever he represents himself as experiencing or doing, he is always conscious of himself as the same. This unitary self is also normative. Indeed, for Kant, without it "there would be no nature, i.e., no synthetic unity of the multiplicity of appearances according to rules." Taken as a "unity of apperception," it is, in fact, "the transcendental ground of the necessary lawfulness of the appearances composing an experience" (A 127).

Kant does more than simply reaffirm the normativity and unity of subjectivity. He unites these two Cartesian principles in a radical manner. For Descartes, as we said, the subject was normative in the sense of providing the most certain object we could perceive. Its perception is, thus, supposed to set the standard for clarity and distinctness. Kant goes beyond this to ask what we mean by "clarity and distinctness," and, as a prior question, what is meant by the perceptual process itself. His answer on one level recalls that of Hume and is more or less taken over by Husserl when the latter speaks of "constitution." For Kant, the perceptual process is one of synthesis, of connecting perception with perception so that, through their ordering, we can have an extended intuition of a unitary object. Clarity and distinctness involve following the rules of this ordering. To the point that such rules are violated, the object fails to appear. Such rules, in other words, are viewed as "conditions for the possibility of experience." They determine in advance how the object can appear. Thus, in the Kantian view, subjectivity is normative insofar as it is seen as constituting, through its synthesis of perceptions, the appearing of the world. The norms we draw from it, those of the synthetic a priori judgments, are based on the "universal and necessary connection of the given perceptions," a connection which is required if we are to intuit a unified, self-consistent world ("Prolegomena," §19; IV, 298; see also ibid., §21a; IV, 304). In terms of the ancient concept of normativity, we can say that, instead of Plato's ideas or forms, we have synthetic a priori judgments, and behind these we have the rules for connecting or synthesizing our perceptions that must be followed if objects are to appear.

Where Kant diverges from Hume and his empiricist successors is in his attempt to tie this view of perception as synthesis to the Cartesian notion of the unitary subject. For Kant, the link is simplicity itself. It occurs once we admit that synthesis requires a synthesizer. As he expresses this deduction, there is "an action of the understanding which we may name with the general title of *synthesis* in order, thereby, to draw attention to the fact that we cannot represent to ourselves anything as combined in the *object* without ourselves first having combined it and that combination . . . can only be performed *by the subject itself* since it is an act of its selfhood" (*Kritik der reinen Vernunft,* B 130). The deduction, then, is from the giv-

enness of the *action of synthesis* to the necessity of the subject as an
active synthesizer. Now, admitting that all combination requires a combiner, this subject must be uncombined. Otherwise, it would be the result
rather than the ground of combination. In Kant's words, given that it is
what "first makes possible the concept of combination," this self must be
an absolute unity (B 131). If it were not a unity, it would be combined,
but then there would have to be another self behind it acting as *its* combiner.

Ingenious as this analysis is, it sharpens rather than solves the problem
of the subject's relation to the world. Given that appearing is a *result* of
the synthesis (or combination) of perceptions, the subject taken as a cause
of synthesis (and, hence, of appearing) cannot appear. If it did, it would be
a result rather than a cause of synthesis. In Kant's terms, this means that
the subject, taken as an uncombined combiner, must be a *noumenal*
rather than a *phenomenal* subject. None of the categories we draw from
experience can apply to it. Indeed, given that the action of synthesis is that
of placing its perceptions in time, even the categories of temporality fall
away. As uncombined, the subject is not extended in time. If we say that it
is "now," it is permanently (atemporally) so. Thus, not only is it nonextended, it is out of time. Given this, its relation to the world, in particular,
its relation to the "transcendent affection" by which the world provides it
with the material of its synthesis, cannot be known.

Kant asserts that "so far as inner intuition is concerned, we know our
own subject only as appearance, not as it is in itself" (B 156). This puts us in
a curious position with regard to the attempt to make it the ground of normativity. Husserl's criticism here is quite penetrating. It is that "Kant falls
into a kind of mythic speech. While the literal meaning of his words points
to the subjective, this is a mode of the subjective which we cannot, in
principle, make intuitive either through actual examples or genuine analo-
gies" (*Krisis,* §30; Hua VI, 116). Thus, on one level, Kant's talk about rules
of synthesis and universal and necessary connections of perceptions seems
to provide a way of understanding the a priori structure of the world. The
ancient normativity of the ideas can, we imagine, be reinterpreted in terms
of subjective "faculties, functions, and formations." We can directly examine these "in the psychological sphere of the human person." Yet, on another level, once we attempt to tie this notion of synthesis to the Cartesian
doctrine of the unity of the ego, the whole structure loses its "intuitively
redeemable sense." This is particularly the case once "we call to mind the
Kantian doctrine of inner sense according to which everything exhibitable
in the evidence of inner experience is already formed by a transcendental

function, that of temporalization" (ibid.). At this point, it becomes obvious that we cannot actually intuit the work of the actively synthesizing, that is, the temporalizing ego. We cannot, because as the uncombined combiner, it is out of time and, hence, beyond our experience, which is structured by time.[6] Once again, then, the subject disappears under the weight of normativity. The Kantian subject exercises its normativity precisely as a combiner or synthesizer. Yet to the point it does so, it cannot appear.

§2. *The Circularity of the Modern Project.* With Kant the mind-body dualism splits into two overlapping dualisms. On one level, it is a dualism of self and world. As we said, the world is supposed to provide the self with a "transcendent affection," thereby giving it material for its synthesis. Yet the connection between the two cannot be known. It cannot because, considered as active, both self and world belong to one side of a second dualism, that between appearances and their nonappearing ("noumenal") grounds. Qua appearing, both the self and the world are part of the phenomenal totality. Considered as that which actively results in such appearing, both are part of the noumenal totality. This is the totality that remains once we abstract from the phenomenal totality all the categories (all the rules of synthesis) the noumenal self imposes upon it to make it appear. Now, a dualism in which both self and world are split between the appearing and the nonappearing leaves us in a curious situation. Although we can distinguish self and world on the side of appearance, we cannot really do so on the nonappearing side. To accomplish this would be to pick out some inherently distinguishing feature, and this would imply some knowledge of them as they are "in themselves." Yet empirically, this, by definition, is impossible. Both self and world might be ego or both might actually be the world understood as the non-ego. We cannot really *know* if, as Kant says, "we cannot have knowledge of any object as a thing in itself, but only insofar as it is an object of sensible intuition" (*Kritik der reinen Vernunft,* B xxvi).

6. In spite of his criticism of Kant on this point, Husserl himself seems to end up with the same nonappearing, actively synthesizing self. Like Kant, he sees the self as constituting time. He writes, "I am. It is from me that time is constituted" (Ms. C I, Hua XV, p. 667). Because of this I am not in time. In fact, "the ego of all accomplishing" is "the ego which is always now." It is "this 'transtemporal [*überzeitliche*] now" (Ms. C 10, p. 18b, 1931). As "not a now in an objective sense," it cannot appear. Thus, "the actively functioning 'I do,' 'I discover,' is constantly anonymous" (Ms. A VII, 11, p. 91, October 26, 1932). See Mensch, *Intersubjectivity and Transcendental Idealism,* pp. 215–22 for further citations on this point, and pp. 232–33 for a way in which Husserl might be conceived as avoiding the criticism he levels against Kant in the *Krisis.*

Fichte's response to this is instructive. Ignoring Kant's assertion that at least we can "think" the difference, he realizes that we confront an essentially unstable dualism. Once we think it through, it actually requires us to choose between two incompatible alternatives. Either we embrace a thoroughgoing idealism and assert that the ego or self produces the world, positing itself as finite within it, or else, taking the opposite "dogmatic" stance, we "construe the self merely as a product of things, an accident of the world" ("First Introduction," §5, in *The Science of Knowledge,* p. 13). Fichte asks, "Which of the two [self or world] should we take as primary?" Given that both are inherently unknown, we cannot decide. As Fichte says, "Reason provides no principle of choice." It cannot because what is at issue is not "a link in the chain of reasoning," but rather "the beginning of the whole chain" (p. 14). In other words, what is at issue is the ground of reason itself.

With this we have the special crisis of modernity. The Cartesian attempt to ground reason in subjectivity by making the latter normative seems ultimately to result in a kind of philosophic schizophrenia. Either we embrace an idealism that ends by positioning subjectivity as an unknowable and, hence, a nonrational ground of the rational or else we attempt to place this ground in the world. In what we shall call the "realist" alternative, the subject becomes an accident of the world in the sense of being contingent on such nonsubjective factors as the particulars of its biology, chemistry, and physics. The debate between the alternatives appeals to the pugnacious; for defenders of either position, once they gain the initiative, seem invariably victorious. Neither side has any difficulty refuting the other, apparently on the same premises.

Regarding their arguments, we face the same sort of situation Kant detailed in his antinomies. The antimonies present us with pairs of arguments proving and refuting such fundamental theses as the world has a beginning in time, is limited in space, has ultimate uncompounded parts, admits of the causality of freedom, and has a first cause. As Kant observed, the difficulty here is not with the argumentation or with reason itself (for example, with the law of excluded middle) but rather with the hidden premise of the arguments. Thus, we cannot assert that *either* the thesis *or* its denial is true if both presuppose a notion that is inherently contradictory. In Kant's words, "If two opposed judgments presuppose an inadmissible condition, then in spite of their contradiction (which is not actually a genuine one), both fall to the ground, inasmuch as the condition, under which alone each of these propositions is supposed to hold, itself falls" (*Kritik der reinen Vernunft,* B 531). As Kant shows, this condition can be discovered by examining the arguments of the antinomies. The examination is actually a kind of deconstruction, a dismantling to find the hidden premise. This, for Kant, is the assumption that the appearing world is the world in itself. Whether or not this is the case in the antinomies he considers need not concern us. We can, however, apply the same process of discovery to the crisis of modernity. The fact that we are presented with a seemingly arbitrary choice, one where each side can defeat the other, suggests that both sides presuppose an inadmissible premise. Both, in other words, involve a contradictory concept, one that splits, with each resulting half allowing us to prove the opposite thesis.

The line of thought we have traced from Berkeley to Husserl fleshes out the alternative that makes the world an accident of the subject. As for the opposing, realist alternative, its position is so familiar that it hardly needs rehearsal. It is daily presented to us in the print and visual media. Each new discovery about the brain is pursued with an avid interest. Much of the language of the realist alternative, particularly that which compares the brain to a computer, has entered into the way people talk about themselves. People now speak of erasing and storing their memories, of processing and computing what they see. The premise of all such talk, which they hardly ever reflect upon, is, for the realist, clear. If it is to have a real, nonmetaphorical sense, then the subject must be an accident of the world. Its categories must be reducible to the nonsubjective ones of the particulars of its organic and inorganic structure. For this to be possible, there cannot be two sets of laws, one for physical, the other for mental processes. The second must be reducible to the first. This means that the laws we observe in nature also apply to mental functioning. What we learn of the world also applies to the organs by which we grasp it. As Freud puts this premise, "Our mental apparatus . . . is itself a constituent part of the world which we set out to [scientifically] investigate, and it readily admits of such investigation" (*The Future of an Illusion,* p. 91). This investigation does not just show the details of its anatomical structure, it also examines the structure's functioning. Since the result of such functioning is our grasp of the world, the investigation also shows how the structure affects the appearing of the world. To cite Freud again: "The task of science is fully covered if we limit it to showing how the world must appear to us in consequence of the particular character of our organization" (ibid., pp. 91–92). Once it has accomplished this, it has reached its goal. It has shown how the subjective categories involved in such appearing can be reduced to the physical ones that specify the "particular character" of our "mental apparatus."

All this seems rather straightforward, yet it involves an inadmissible assumption. To see this, we need only note that this "task of science" can be accomplished only if we assume an implicit identification. We must identify the mental apparatus that is "a constituent part of the world which we set out to investigate" with the mental apparatus whose "particular character" determines "how the world must appear to us." In other words, we must assume that the appearing mental apparatus is the same as the mental apparatus that helps determine appearance. Without this, we cannot base on appearance a study of what helps determine appearance. We can put this assumption in terms of causality. So expressed, it is that the physiology of the brain whose functioning we observe and causally explain is the same as the physiology *by virtue of whose causally determinative functioning* we make these observations and explanations. As is readily apparent, this assumption may be restated as the assertion that we are causally determined (by virtue of our apparatus) to get these causal processes correctly. Thus, we are also asserting that we can get the world in itself, that is, get the relevant causal laws and processes as they actually function.

The difficulty with this assumption has already been noted. Within the context of causality, the appearance of the world must be relative to "the particular character of our organization." But if this is so, then the notion of a world as it is in itself, that is, as it is independent of the influence of this organization, is an empty abstraction. This point also carries over to the laws we infer from our observations of the world. To try to reason from these laws to what the world is "in itself," that is, to what it is in a unique objective sense, is to ignore what the context of causality tells us about these laws—namely, that they themselves, as empirically based, are relative to the special character of our physical organization.

Ignoring this fact gets us into the type of self-referential inconsistency we noted earlier (see page 20). As we said, given that the structure of the brain is contingent—that is, is something that in the course of evolution could have been different—science, in explaining the mental processes that produce its "knowledge," finds itself in the unpleasant situation of relativizing itself. Since it can never actually get the world as it is in itself, it is, like its idealist alternative, reduced to a level of sheer appearance. For Berkeley, the ground of the world is a mind or spirit concerning which we can form no idea. For Fichte, it is the self-positing ego, which, as a ground, lies outside the grounded, that is, the appearing world. The same holds here, except that the place of the ground is taken by that of the world in itself. It too lies beyond the appearing world as its unknown basis.

Like its idealist alternative, the realist stance also involves itself in a certain circularity of reasoning. Here, the circularity is vicious insofar as it involves the part-whole fallacy. The attempt to get at the determining structures of our brains and sense organs assumes that the real conditions of a part of nature—those of these organs—causally determine our empirical knowledge of the whole of nature; this whole, however, is assumed to include, as a particular determined part within its causal nexus, precisely these same real conditions of these organs. This means that the whole, as we know it in its natural laws, is explained by the determining conditions of a part of nature; and to explain just how the part in its real makeup determines this knowledge of the whole, we appeal to the whole as we know it—that is, to its universal, causal laws. Thus, the whole in its lawfulness is explained by a part, which is itself explained by the whole that was to be explained.

We can, without circularity, say that our knowledge of universal, causal laws is determined by the laws of our thought. The circularity only arises when we interpret these latter laws as natural laws. It is then that we explain them in terms of that which they themselves were supposed to explain. The scientific attempt to eliminate the subject is, then, condemned to circularity by the initial premise noted above. To reduce subjective to nonsubjective categories, it must claim that there are not two sets of laws, but only one, that of physical causality. The laws of such causality, however, fail to provide precisely what the attempt needs to make its case. To assume that I have been causally determined by my physiology to grasp nature as it is in itself is to suppose that there is some standard of epistemological correctness in natural, physical causality. This, however, is precisely what such causality lacks. Thus, the same laws of physics (those of electronics) hold whether or not my pocket calculator misfunctions. There are no standards of arithmetical correctness within them.

As a slight reflection shows, the laws of physical causality are inherently incapable of providing these standards. Standards of correctness work by setting up criteria for what we want to grasp (for example, consistency criteria for mathematical sums). Structured by such criteria, the object of our apprehension appears as a *not yet,* as a *goal to be realized* through the performance of the act through which it is grasped (such as doing and checking the sum). In physical causality, however, the line of determination is from the past to the present to the future. The impulse, for example, which I gave a moment ago to a billiard ball determines its present course and this, in turn, determines its future impact when it collides with another ball. With goals, by contrast, the determination is from the future through the past to the present. Thus the goal as set by the standard of correctness determines how far I have to go, given my past progress, and, hence, determines my present activity in meeting the criteria. Insofar as such standards work through goal directed activity, and insofar as such activity is, strictly speaking, unintelligible on the level of physical causality, the two sets of laws can never be collapsed. To do so would be to collapse two different sorts of temporal determination, that beginning with the past and that which begins with the future, that is, with the goal that some standard sets.

Whether or not such laws can be combined, that is, whether some synthesis of them is ultimately possible, is a question we shall later seek to answer. For the present, however, we need only note the essential contradiction implicit in the scientific attempt to eliminate subjectivity by reducing it to nonsubjective, causal categories: *This attempt does not abandon, but still remains within the epistemological paradigm.* Pursuing it, we find ourselves in the position of using the priority of epistemology and, hence, of subjectivity itself to prove that the subject is an accident of the world. To show this, we need only recall the paradigm. What it does is correlate every possible being to the subjective processes of knowing. The latter determine what can count as being. What cannot fulfill their inherent standards cannot count as being. The scientific method is simply a particularization of this. Its initial standards are set by Descartes in his account of his perception of the wax (see page 30). There, he takes the general standards of clarity and distinctness and interprets them in terms of the reduction of the secondary to the primary qualities of the object. The latter (the size, shape, mass, and motion of its particles) fulfill the standards by being immediately quantifiable. As such they are taken as being. They are the reality of the object. The empirical method put forward by Francis Bacon and his successors adds to this the notions of experimental verifiability, which includes that of being repeatable in a controlled situation. A number of further refinements having to do with statistics and the attempt to limit experimental bias have been added to make up the modern "scientific method." They do not, however, affect our general point about the method's being an example of the epistemological paradigm. Thus, what is at issue in any practical debate on this method is the validity of particular standards, but not standards as such. In fact, what makes the debate "real," that is, of practical importance, is the premise that what fulfills the standards for evidence will count as real.

Granting this, we can see the contradiction in applying the method to itself. If we are to explain the functioning of the method in terms of the method, we have to reduce the actual knowing processes it regulates to their nonsubjective analogues. Thus, instead of knowing and its inherent standards, we are forced to speak of neurons, synapses, neurotransmitters, and the like. The ultimate subject of our discourse is the quantifiable biochemical relations that underlie the brain's functioning. On this level, however, the standards disappear. The physical causality the scientific method equips us to analyze is, after all, quite innocent of any notions of epistemological correctness. The standards, then, cannot be grounded on the level whose investigation they direct. To apply them to themselves is to reductively eliminate the area in which they have their sense, this being the *conscious* activities of perceiving and knowing. Such activities are goal directed, yet material relations are not. They have a different temporality.

When we assert that we will only grant being to that which satisfies the criteria of this method, we have yet another case of the self-referential inconsistency we discussed above. If the scientific method is true, then the standards of correctness guiding it are incapable of being instantiated in reality. Its truth, then, casts doubt on its own validity as an actual process. Yet if it is really true, it wrongly casts doubt on itself. Thus, Fitch's remark, quoted earlier, again holds: "If it is valid, it is self-referentially inconsistent and hence not valid at all" (see page 20). Concretely, the inconsistency is that the method's validity would eliminate the subjectivity whose processes it is supposed to guide.

This, of course, is what we should expect in any attempt to base being on subjective processes. All such attempts face what, for them, is the unresolvable question of the ontological status of the processes themselves. Are such processes being? If they are and if the paradigm of basing being on subjective processes holds, then we must ask: On what further subjective processes does the being of *these* processes depend? The basic difficulty here is simply the insistence of grounding being on subjective processes, which, *since they themselves must count as being,* raises the question of grounding again. We can, of course, short-circuit the regress by refusing to categorize such processes as being, that is, by refusing to give them an ontological status. This is what occurs in the doctrines that end in the elimination of the subject. The price we pay, however, is that of self-referential inconsistency.

In an antinomy there are, of course, two sides: not just the thesis but also the antithesis. Although apparently opposed, the refutation of one side does not entail the affirmation of the other. This, as we said, is because both presuppose an inadmissible premise. For the attempt to see the subject as an accident of the world, we have just shown that this premise is nothing less than the epistemological paradigm. The same premise, however, is equally at work in the idealist alternative: that of seeing the world as accident of the subject. We have already traced it from Berkeley and Hume to James and Husserl. For Berkeley the reduction of the world to a perception follows upon the equation of its being with its being perceived. This, however, follows upon the assumption that we can grant being only to what we know. The same holds for Hume's reduction of substance to a bundle of perceptions. It holds as well for Husserl's assertion that "the entire spatial-temporal world . . . is a being that consciousness posits in its experiences . . . beyond this, however, it is nothing at all." As he also expresses this: "The existence of nature *is* only as constituting itself in the ordered connections of consciousness" (*Ideen I,* §§49, 51 Hua II, 117, 121). As we stressed, in each case a gap remains regarding the stability of nature. Having posited the world out of the ordered connections of our experiences, we are at a loss to explain why or how such ordering occurs. What is missing here is the being whose relations would support such ordering. Appeals to God in this context are nothing less than hidden ontological appeals. They are attempts to save the argument by a kind of *petitio principii,* namely, by introducing as *a premise for knowing* an ontological category that according to the epistemological paradigm, can only be *a conclusion of knowing.* The result is the kind of circularity we observed in Descartes's use of God to secure the epistemological paradigm. Similar sorts of circularity can be uncovered in the attempts to bridge the gaps in the other philosophers we have discussed. In form, they parallel the circularity we have just considered in the "realist" or scientific version of the epistemological paradigm. What they point to is the presence of the same paradigm with the same inherent difficulties. *The paradigm itself, then, is the inadmissible premise that realism and idealism share.*

Fichte says that the choice between the two is perfectly arbitrary. Our age sees the choice as one between the humanities and the sciences, with psychology and the social sciences sometimes ranked with the former and sometimes with the latter side. When one engages in humanistic pursuits, one is thought to interpret the world in anthropomorphic terms, that is, exclusively in subjective categories. In the hard sciences, the opposite is the case. Its interpretive categories are formed by excluding the anthropomorphic ones of secondary qualities. Although mutually unintelligible, society usually considers both equally valid pursuits; the choice being considered a matter of disposition, tastes, or economic circumstances. If such a situation is endemic to modernity, it is because both the humanities and the sciences are founded on the paradigm that characterizes modernity: that of epistemology. The overturning of modernity is, then, the overturning of the split between them, their mutual unintelligibility being one of the most striking features of the modern period. The overturning of modernity is, however, the overturning of the paradigm itself. Accordingly, turning from the analysis of modernity, we must now show how this may be accomplished, how we can actually *reverse* the paradigm. We will begin by outlining the conceptual shift that such a reversal implies.

3

The Reversal

The Open Subject

Modernity, in a broad sense, is not just an appeal to the normativity of the subject. It is also an attempt at what we may call "foundationalism." The latter is a feature of its systematic organization of thought, a process that begins about 1600.[1] Descartes, for example, is one of the first philosophers to use the words "my system" to refer to his thought (*Discourse on the Method,* pp. 123–24). The concept of a system is that of things "standing together" (from σύστημα)—this, by virtue of their having some common foundation. This foundation is referred to as their "origin" or "principle." What it does is to provide an explanation of why they are as they are. Principles, too, can have common explanations. When they do, then they can also be gathered under a common principle. A sufficiently rich system is, then, a layered structure with things gathered under common principles, and these in turn resting on their common principles. The ultimate

---

1. As Jacob Klein notes, before 1600, the term "system" "is never applied to thought." Yet after 1600, "there is a sudden and remarkable shift: book after book appears under titles like 'System of Logic,' 'System of Rhetoric,' 'System of Grammar,' 'System of Theology,' 'System of Ethics and Politics,' 'System of Physics,' 'System of Jurisprudence,' 'System of Astronomy,' of Arithmetic, of Geography, of Medicine and even 'System of Systems'" (*Lectures and Essays,* p. 201).

attempt of every system is to find a final founding principle, a "principle of principles," that gives the system a rationally unified character. Descartes refers to this as its Archimedian point, i.e., the fulcrum point which Archimedes claimed could be used to "move the earth from its orbit," if only it were "fixed and immovable" (*Meditations,* II; p. 23). Descartes's search for a similar foundation for thought ends in the subject. On the certainty of its apprehension rest the notions of clarity and distinctness as well as the other principles of his system.

What does not fit in with these principles is, by definition, excluded. Systematic or foundational thinking does not just organize things into a rationally articulated whole; it also excludes. Whatever does not fall under its principles is considered to be groundless, without foundation or reason. Thus, Descartes, at the very beginning of his attempt to construct his system, rigorously excludes all his received opinions "so that they might later on be replaced, either by others which were better, or by the same, when I had made them conform to the uniformity of a rational scheme" (*Discourse on the Method,* p. 89). The stress is on such conformity. Opinions are to be valued, not by virtue of the authority that propounds them, nor even, in the first place, by the arguments or evidence of their proponents; what counts is how well they fit in with the system's "rational scheme," a scheme that normally includes *its own rules* of evidence. One may compare this with the medieval, "cellular" concept of organization. There, growth, as in a cathedral, is by addition. Unit is added to unit; and the principle of compatibility is that of joining rather than that of grounding. The connection is, in other words, by virtue of the interface, rather than a common support or basis. Thomas Aquinas's use of the opinions of his predecessors is a good example of what we are pointing to. He quotes all sorts of opinions in favor of his positions, but he does not thereby imply that all have the same ground. Descartes, by contrast, maintains in the *Meditations* a total silence concerning his predecessors. He will not bring in their views to support his own since such support, *before* he has constructed his "system," would have no place; afterwards, however, it would be useless.

This attempt to turn thought into a system arises in conjunction with the positioning of subjectivity as normative. The norms we draw from it are taken as founding principles, with the subject itself being the system's principle of principles, its Archimedian point. Nowhere is this clearer than in Kant's proposal for a Copernican revolution. He writes:

Previously it was assumed that all our knowledge must conform to objects. But all attempts to establish something a priori about them through concepts which would increase our knowledge have failed under this assumption. We should try then to see if we would not make more progress in the tasks of metaphysics by assuming that objects must conform to our knowledge. This would better agree with the desired possibility of an a priori knowledge which would determine something about objects before they are given. This is precisely the case of the primary supposition of Copernicus. Failing to explain the movements of the heavens on the assumption that the stars turned about the observer, he made trial whether he would not have more success if he made the observer revolve and the stars be still. (*Kritik der reinen Vernunft,* B xvi)

To see objects as conforming to our knowledge is, Kant says, to see the experience through which they can be known as conforming to our concepts. It is based on the suppositions that "experience itself is a type of knowledge requiring understanding; and understanding has rules which I must presuppose as being in me prior to objects' being given to me. These rules find expression in a priori concepts with which all experiential objects must conform and agree" (ibid.). These rules of the understanding are rules of synthesis, the very synthesis that results in objects' being given. It is because of this that the concepts expressing them must apply to the objects. The concepts, then, are a priori in the sense that they are *prior* to objects, being expressions of that which generates them as objects of experience. In Kant's words, by virtue of this origin, the objects "must conform and agree" with the concepts since the latter simply express the rules of syntheses—of connecting perception to perception—which result in our extended perceptual experience of objects. The subject is what engages in this action of synthesis. It is, in its unity, the uncombined combiner of its perceptions. As such, it is the "transcendental ground of the necessary lawfulness of the appearances composing an [objective] experience" (A 127). In terms of his system, the synthesizing subject is the principle of principles. All further principles, such as those of the concepts that express the rules of its synthesis, presuppose it.

Kant's position is typical. Within the modern period foundationalism takes the form of the epistemological paradigm, what Kant calls the Copernican turn to the subject. Granting this, reversing the paradigm reverses the turn. In a certain sense, it is the attempt to make a genuine Copernican revolution. We say this because the actual turn of Copernicus was *away* from the observer as the center of motion. It was his refusal to take the spectator's view of things as a determining paradigm for their actual motions which led to his revolutionary solution. Thus, the proper analogy for the Copernican shift is not that of letting knowledge or the "concept" determine the object, but rather letting the object determine knowledge.

Kant, of course, would object that without the shift to the subject, there would be no a priori knowledge. We could not make universally necessary assertions. In our terms, we would have to "abandon normativity." Yet the attempt to maintain such normativity is beset with two main difficulties. In the first place, rather than providing a single standard, subjectivity itself has been pluralized. The modern age is marked by competing systems, each of which rigorously excludes the insights of the others, each being based on a different concept of subjectivity. The result is that the intellectual discourse of modernity is marked by a series of non-conversations. A Freudian, a Marxist, and a logical positivist have literally nothing to say to one another. Each, through his principles simply devalues the others' statements. Any attempt at mutual interpretation turns into a *metabasis allo genos* (μετάβασις εἰς ἄλλο γένος), a transformation into a completely other kind, one which does not leave the subject matter intact. For a disinterested observer, what is significant is the evidence that each presents for his case. Here, subjectivity seems to provide a basis for every thesis. This, we may note, is the special curse of psychology. Infinitely adaptable, the subject in its content seems to support every form of analysis from the behaviorist to the cognitive. This pliability is a sign of its elusiveness. Completely adaptable on the level of appearance, the more we attempt to grasp the subject as it is in itself, the more it evades us. The second difficulty, then, is the disappearance of the subject under the weight of normativity.

The problem here is not with the ingenuity of the philosophers in their attempts to make subjectivity normative. The problem is with subjectivity itself. If we wish to escape self-referential inconsistency, we must assume that, on some level, subjectivity does grasp the world, that we can trust the account it provides us. Yet to the point that it does grasp the world, it is not an imposition upon, but rather an openness to the world. This is the openness which gives it its peculiar identity with its objects, one that implies its capability of becoming anything and, hence, of supplying evidence for all kinds of theses about itself. The quality we are pointing to was first observed by Aristotle. As he noted, "before it thinks," that is, before it grasps an object, "mind has no actual existence" (*De Anima* 429a24). It is "potentially identical with the objects of its thought"; indeed, this potentiality is its openness. But as Aristotle adds, it "is actually nothing until it thinks" (429b31). This means that it has no inherent content, all such content being derived from the objects it thinks. If he is right, then any attempt to grasp the subject as an object is bound to fail. It cannot be an object, for to be such demands a definite, distinguishing content. A subject, however, has content only in its temporary identity with what is not itself. This shifting identity is the reason for its pluralization on the level of appearance. It also explains why it becomes so elusive once we attempt to grasp its inherent character. We cannot grasp it as it is "in itself" since *per se* it has no content.

According to this insight, the subject is the last place we should look for normative structures. It is open to such structures. It can take them on in its identity with its objects. This very openness, however, signifies its lack of any *inherent* normative structures or laws. Our point is similar to Sartre's when he writes: "There is no law of consciousness, but rather a consciousness of law" ("Consciousness of Self and Knowledge of Self," p. 136). You cannot, he notes, make consciousness an openness and require from it a set of prescriptive laws. Such laws make it "opaque" rather than open. As our account of Kant indicates, they ultimately conceal rather than reveal what is not consciousness. This, of course, does not mean that we shall ever encounter consciousness without its manifesting laws, no more than we shall ever encounter it without its manifesting *some* content. The laws, however, come not from itself, but rather from its identity with its objects, the very identity that gives it its content.

The best way to express this point is in terms of temporalization. As Kant observed, all "our representations . . . are subject to time, the formal condition of inner sense. Time is that in which they must be ordered, connected, and brought into relation" (*Kritik der reinen Vernunft,* A 99). On the level of "inner sense," the sense by which we grasp subjective processes, we are, formally regarded, simply a series of temporal relations. We say "temporal," as opposed to "spatial," since it makes no sense to say that one representation is so many feet from another or is a certain size. We can, however, talk about one being before or after another and, indeed, about the processes by which we grasp this. This insight allows us to see why the subject cannot have any inherent content. Time per se is capable of exhibiting every sort of content precisely because it lacks any content of its own. Its moments are, as it were, empty containers—or rather, place-holders—of possible contents. Indeed, it is this very lack of any inherent, distinguishing content which undercuts the notion of discrete moments. It is a correlative of the continuity of time. Given this "openness" of time, if subjectivity is a field of temporal relations, any content it has must come from its objects. Its being as such a field *is,* in other words, *its openness* to what is not itself.

The Reversal of Temporalization

For Kant, the notion of the subject as field of temporal relations is that of the *appearing* as opposed to the actual, acting subject. The latter is what imposes its categories on the former as it does on appearance *per se,* i.e., on the whole of the appearing world, which includes the appearing subject. Our position is the reverse of this. For us, the subject is not normative, but rather open to norms. It does not impose categories; categories are rather imposed upon it by the world. To arrive at this notion of the subject, we must reverse the modern view of temporalization. Since the seventeenth century, subjectivity has been normative by virtue of serving as the ultimate focal point for the constitution of experience. For this, it must, as Kant saw, involve itself in temporalization. Its universal and necessary rules for synthesis are normative in the sense that they are what first make experience possible. They perform this function by being rules for temporalization, that is, rules for inserting experiences in the before and after of time. In other words, subjectivity is normative because time is what we bring to the data of experience to make the experience of objects possible. Assuming this, to reverse the normativity of subjectivity is to reverse this temporalization. The object must time the subject. The object must be what inserts the subject in the before and after of time according to the rules of the object's temporalization.

With this, of course, we lose any sense of the a priori character of such rules. What we confront is what we actually experience: the pluralization of the subject considered as a field of temporal relations. The subjectivity we daily experience has as many forms as time does. This means we can speak of subjectivity as sheer nowness, subjectivity as temporal flowing, subjectivity as the form of objective synthesis, subjectivity as our being-there in and through other persons, and even of subjectivity as the Kantian unidirectional flow of objective causality (the flow that allows us to suppose that our own inner relations are subject to causal laws). Each corresponds to a different sort of object. When I grasp a mathematical relation, I experience the first form of subjectivity. This is because at the moment of insight I am no longer conditioned by the before and after of time. I experience a very different form playing with others as a member of an ensemble. When I engage in compulsive behavior, yet another form of subjectivity is experienced. The openness of subjectivity is such that in none of these forms are specific contents required. In fact, as open, subjectivity per se is silent (1) on the nature of the nowness it manifests, (2) on the contents which might occupy its temporal stream, (3) on the nature of its relations with other subjects, and (4) on the type of causal laws it might assume it is subject to. As a field of temporal relations, it has a perfect plasticity. It simply provides a place for different types of objects to appear with different rules of temporalization.

To see how this is possible requires something more than the description of the mechanics of the process by which the object times the subject. To understand the process, we need to reverse the metaphysics that underlies modernity. This metaphysics can be summed up in a single sentence: the whole notion of the constitution of reality by the subjective act of temporalization assumes the dependence of reality on temporalization. In other words, *modernity presupposes the dependence of being on time.* Its metaphysics is, then, a special interpretation (which is also a narrowing) of the ancient view that being equals presence. For the ancients, presence is that quality by which an entity appears so as to show itself as it is. Modernity interprets this as temporal presence. For a thing to be, it assumes that it must share a now with us. The now is that quality by which an entity appears so as to be present.[2] The ontological implication here is readily apparent. If being is temporal presence, then time must be the ground of being. It is what makes the entity temporally present.

We have already given a number of examples of this view. Descartes's grid, as we noted, supposes that what cannot be located within it cannot be. A description according to its coordinates thus becomes an ontological account, one that interprets the sequence of coordinates tracing an event as an explanation of coming into being. In the case of Kantian idealism, the grid becomes, so to speak, internalized. The subject, taken as that which places things in time, becomes the ground of their presence. It is that by virtue of which they appear. As such a ground, however, it cannot appear.

---

2. Heidegger falsely attempts to ascribe this view to "the ancient interpretation of the being of entities." According to this interpretation, "An entity is grasped in its being as presence, i.e., it is understood in terms of a definite temporal mode, the present" (*Sein und Zeit,* §6; p. 25). While true for the modern period, such an interpretation does not hold for the ancients. For Aristotle, for example, being is prior, not posterior, to time. This means that time is the effect being has on us. For a concise account of this position, see James Mensch, "Aristotle and the Overcoming of the Subject-Object Dichotomy."

It has no actual existence in the appearing world. The absence which it is, however, is not an Aristotelian openness. It is, rather, the absence on the level of appearance of what imposes the structures of appearance. It is the absence on the appearing realm of "the transcendental ground of the necessary lawfulness of all appearances."

For Husserl, this becomes an absence on the ontological realm *tout court.* Given, as he says, that "temporalization . . . is the constitution of existents," the ultimate ground of temporalization is not *per se* an existent. It cannot be, since were it such, it would require a ground for its own existence, that is, for its own "original concrete [temporal] presence."[3] As an existent, it would require a ground for its temporalization, which, were this also an existent, would require a further ground, and so on indefinitely. To avoid this, Husserl is forced to speak of this ultimate source, not as being, but rather as "the pre-being [*Vor-Sein*] which bears all being, including even the being of the acts and the being of the ego, indeed, the being of the pre-time and the being of the stream of consciousness [understood] as a being" (Ms. C 17 IV, p. 63 als Beilage, 1930). Here, the epistemological paradigm, which takes the subject as the ground of being, overshoots itself. Basing itself on the equation of being and temporal presence, it has to admit that what ultimately constitutes such presence is not the subject—this, at least, if we wish to consider the subject as *a* being. The difficulty, we should note, is the same as the general one of basing being on subjective processes. Once we do this, the question always arises regarding the being of such processes. Are they themselves, as existent, to be based on further subjective processes? If not, then the question always arises of their ontological status. In what sense does the "pre-being," which bears the "being of the ego," count as an existent? Can it exist as the ground of the ego if existence per se demands egological or subjective processes for its ground?

As we noted in our previous chapter, the difficulty here is with the epistemological paradigm itself, specifically with its demand that knowing, taken as a subjective process, determine being. To overcome it by way of reversal, we have to say that subjective processes are themselves based on

3. Husserl, thus, is a preeminent example of the modern tendency to base being on time. The extended quotation here is: "Temporalization, this is the constitution of existents in their temporal modalities. An existent: a present existent with the past of the same existent, with the future coming to be of the same existent. In an original sense, existent = original, concrete presence. It is persisting presence which 'includes', as non-independent components in the stream of presences, both past and future" (Ms. C 13 III, p. 34b, March 1934). In other words, "Every concrete individual persists in time and is what it is because constantly becoming, it passes from presence to presence" (Ms. E III 2, p. 2, 1934).

being. Since such processes are temporal, the reversal demands that time be based on being. The priority of being implies that there are as many forms of time, and hence of subjectivity as an openness, as there are forms of being. Thus the being of a mathematical relation, say that of the diagonal to the side of a square, *is* and yet has no spatial-temporal position as such. Its timing of the openness which is the subject does not place the subject *in* time in the sense of making it manifest the temporal succession of moment after moment. Timed by the relation, the subject that grasps the relation is simply now. It exists on a level of identity with that which has no temporal referent. The case is quite different, to take another example, when I walk through a forest. As I do so, I experience the trees that surround me unfolding themselves in perspectival patterns. Those that are nearer do so more quickly. Those on a distant hillside hardly seem to move. All this is correlative to my having a finite standpoint, more particularly, to my being an embodied perceiver. Such unfolding requires that I have a finite "here," one I can, through my bodily motion, continuously shift. In a word, my openness to finite beings seems to rest on my own embodied finitude. A "modern" standpoint would take such finitude as constitutive of the presence of the finite things that surround me. My body (and its motion) would be taken as part of the way I "time" the world to apprehend finite beings. The perspective we are advancing would reverse this. It would assert that it is by virtue of finite things timing me that my subjectivity displays the features of embodiment. It is through my registering their motion, including especially the motion of my own limbs, that I become finite, that is, become a subject capable of being definitely described by a here and now. The "laws" applicable to me as such a subject are not a priori in the sense of being universal and necessary. As the laws of my openness to finite being, they are contingent on its givenness, that is, on the givenness of the being that determines them.

In spite of its being constituted, both in its laws and in its content, by the world, the subjectivity we are advancing is not epiphenomenal, not an "accident of the world." It is, rather, an openness that lets the world be. Such "letting be" is not to be conceived as letting the world reveal itself through *our* projects, goals, or criteria for being.[4] "Letting be" here means

---

4. Such projects would still be our norms, our modes of constituting the world's appearance. Heidegger's notion of this "pragmatic" disclosure is largely derived from William James. James writes that in disclosing an entity, "I am always unjust, always partial, always exclusive. My excuse is necessity—the necessity which my finite and practical nature lays upon me. My thinking is first and last and always for the sake of my doing, and I can only do one thing at a time." From this, it follows that "the essence of a thing is that one of its properties which is so

letting the world temporalize itself in and through an apprehending subject. The subject times the world, not (as for Kant) by being the origin of time, but by letting itself be timed by it. In the process, it lets the world be by letting the world set the laws of its appearing. In itself, it is simply an openness to these laws. It is such as a field of temporal relations. The grounding of time by being means that these relations are not set by itself (as some form of Husserlian "pre-being," which is supposed to ground being), but rather by the world. Here, we may remark that the question of the being of such subjective processes is itself reversed. The question achieves its urgency when we say that being is determined by subjective processes. We then position such processes as a cause and give them the ontological status of an agent. When, however, we say that subjective processes are determined by being, this ontological status accrues not to them but to the being that grounds them. Given that this being is the world, we can say that subjectivity *is,* yet its existence is not substantial in the sense that it can be by itself. It "is" rather as a function, or better, as a kind of receptivity to the world. By way of contrast, we can say that this view is the opposite of those who see the openness of subjectivity as an *Abgrund*—that is, something which is, as an absolute origin, both ground-less and an abyss.[5] Rather than being ontologically ground-less, subjectivity, for us, is grounded in the world, the very world in and through which it functions.

Since this functioning is also that of the world, there is here a certain ontological identity between self and world. Self, or subjectivity, is inherently pluralistic. Attentive to mathematical objects, it has one form of being, attentive to another self (for example, another musician playing in a quartet), it has another form of being. For Kant, of course, a similar kind of ontological identity held between the subject and its appearing objects, but only because the subject, through its syntheses, set the laws for the

important for my interest that in comparison with it I may neglect the rest" ("Reasoning," in *Psychology, Briefer Course,* pp. 355, 357). The interest, then, is the subjective norm for disclosure.

5. Heidegger ascribes this view to Kant as the cause of his "recoil from the ground which he himself revealed, namely the transcendental imagination." The recoil is actually from the "abyss [*Abgrund*] of metaphysics" (*Kant and the Problem of Metaphysics,* §38; p. 222). Heidegger himself places this ground-less quality of the subject in its freedom. He writes that "freedom is the abyss [*Ab-grund*] of Dasein" ("Vom Wesen des Grundes," *Wegmarken* p. 69). Speaking of the "absolute," his term for the absolute origin, Husserl writes that it "has its ground in itself and has its absolute necessity as the one 'absolute substance' in its groundless [*grundlosen*] being" (*Zur Phänomenologie der Intersubjektivität, Dritter Teil,* Hua XV, 386). All seem to be driven by the same necessity: that of seeing the ultimately grounding fact as ground-less, as an abyss.

latter. Thus, the concept for Kant automatically applies to the object, since both are manifestations of the same synthetic rules. In fact, so is the appearing subject. All manifest a single standard of being, that of appearance as grounded by the rules of subjective synthesis. It is only on the level of the noumenal—i.e., of the nonappearing, actively synthesizing subject or of the noumenal object that provides it with its transcendent affection, that this identity can, at least in thought, be taken as broken. In the appearing world, it holds throughout. Now, when we reverse this determination and speak of the world constituting the subject, the identity of subject and object continues to hold. As we shall see, the notion of synthesis can be reversed with the object playing the role of agent. Yet since in this constitution there is no longer any single standard of being, its action loses its normative component. There are, as we said, as many forms of subjective being as there are forms of time, such forms being determined by the different ways objects come to presence. If we must speak of normativity, what the reversal implies is its shift to the world itself. That the world supports a plurality of overlapping norms is simply a reflection of its containing a plurality of types of being. From the standpoint of the genuine Copernican turn, the world does not seem to permit any metaphysical monism, any appeal to an exclusive standard of what being must be. Needless to say, this move is equally hostile to any form of reductionism. Given that from its perspective the subject is always on a level of identity with its object, being in fact determined by it, the reversal is in the curious position of offering us epistemological certainty without ontological normativity—the normativity of one form of being to the exclusion of others. Here, of course, we have to add that such certainty is never absolute, but only that *appropriate to its object*.[6] It is the object rather than the subject which sets its limits.

The legitimatization of different types of certainty undercuts the distinction between the real and the apparent world. Descartes, we saw, takes our frequent lack of certainty and interprets it according to the scheme of reality and illusory appearance. He cannot ascribe reality to what he cannot be certain of. This, of course, is to base being on knowing. Yet, once we reverse this relationship, our lack of certainty does not inherently imply a distinction between reality and illusion. It may simply mean that the being we are attempting to grasp is not certain and that we, in our openness, are receptive to its dubitablity. Examples of what I am pointing to form the commonest elements of our experience. Whenever we ask, "Does

6. Cf. Aristotle's *Nicomachean Ethics* 1094b25.

this person love me?" "Is this the right course of action?"—in broad terms, whenever we inquire about a political, social, or personal good—we are posing questions that cannot be answered with mathematical precision. Poetry, with its sensitivity to the ambiguity of the world, is a good example of such receptivity. So are certain forms of moral and political discourse.

Implicit in the above is the fact that all distinction between the real and the illusory depends on norms. What fulfills the norm is counted as real. What does not is relegated to the realm of illusion. The distinction between the real and the illusory is, we should add, not necessarily the same as that between the real and the apparent. We can take the apparent as the appearance of being, as its self-manifestation, be this precise or poetically ambiguous. It is the introduction of norms that makes us regard one appearance as genuine and another as illusory. The same holds when a thing shows itself in a number of different ways. Only when we take one set of them as our standard—for example, the set that appears in controlled laboratory experiments—will the rest be counted as illusion.

The best example of what we are referring to is provided by the epistemological paradigm. It introduces the norm of knowability and defines knowledge according to some single standard. By virtue of this, it creates an ontological monism: one standard of being holding for all that is. Everything that fails to meet it is an illusion or "fiction," to use Hume's term. The difficulty with this is, not just that all sorts of things get dismissed as fictions, but that such monism ultimately becomes schizophrenic. We face the competing monisms of realism and idealism. As we saw, each gives us a division between the real and the illusory; yet what each counts as real, the other takes as illusion. Supposedly, we must choose between them: either the subject is an accident of the world; or the world is an accident of the subject. Neither choice is acceptable, since either, if we embrace it, involves us in the self-referential inconsistency discussed above. Paradoxes and circularities appear: particularly that of explaining laws in terms of that which they themselves were supposed to explain—for example, explaining the laws of knowing in terms of the natural laws that were supposed to be explained by the laws of knowing (see page 61). Given that there are two sets of laws (one for knowing, one for natural causality), the epistemological paradigm gives birth to the problem of their incompatibility precisely because it demands an ontological monism, a monism that robs one or the other set of its validity.

If the above is correct, the way out of this impasse is to break such monism by reversing the epistemological paradigm. The reversal, however, cannot be a reaction. It cannot, for example, be a return to a Platonic standard of being taken from ideas. As Plato's analogy of the cave suggests, he too, puts forward an ontological monism, one where being equals intelligibility (see *Republic* 514a–519e). The fact that the ultimate standard for both being and intelligibility is self-sameness indicates that this norm has been drawn from the realm of being rather than knowing. Yet, concealed in this, as his talk of turning from natural science to dialectic shows, seems to be a form of the epistemological paradigm (see *Phaedo* 96a–101e). In Plato's version, it apparently runs, whatever "is" is speakable and, hence, must follow the rules of speech (of dialectic) and be capable of being investigated by these. Whether or not we accept this interpretation, the difficulty of any monism is clear. It is, for Plato as for the moderns, the failure of any single category of being to account for itself and for what it takes to be illusion.

The true reversal, then, is not the shift from one form of monism to another. It is one that overcomes it all together. Its success would be our ability to speak of being without falling into some form of self-referential inconsistency. This, of course, implies that it would not simply reverse the traditional, ontologically based distinctions of reality and illusion. It would rather be to twist out of them, escaping them altogether. How exactly this will be possible will be considered by us later. Our first task is to secure the basic move of the reversal. The next chapter will begin this by giving a concrete example of how we can regard the subject, not as timing, but as timed by the world.

4

An Aristotelian Paradigm

The Aristotelian Reversal

We are fortunate to have in ancient philosophy a concrete example of what we wish to work out in this chapter. This is a view of the subject, not as timing, but as timed by the world. The advantage of this example is that it is not conditioned by the Cartesian outlook. Cartesianism has so penetrated our world that its assumptions have become our prejudices. For many, they have become ingrained to the point that they appear as common sense or even as axioms of reason. Only a serious confrontation with an ancient author can wrest from us these prejudices.

There is, of course, a certain school of thought, that of historicism, which sees such prejudices as insurmountable. Its view is that the prejudices of our time, of our historically conditioned epoch, make it impossible to grasp an ancient text on its own terms. Historicism, however, is part of what is at issue. It is yet another version of the epistemological paradigm. In its more obvious forms, it is a type of neo-Kantianism. In it, the Kantian categories for the possibility of experience continue as categories of synthesis, that is, as general forms for making objective sense out of our experience. Yet they are now viewed as historically determined and, hence, as excluding the possibility of anything escaping such determination. A priori, whatever is not conditioned by these historically conditioned categories is not a possible experience; we cannot make sense of it. To turn this around, what we do make sense of through such interpretive categories is the object that is constituted through them, not the object that does not fit them. There are many versions of this sort of neo-Kantianism. One could make the same kind of argument using linguistically, economically, or sociologically determined categories.[1] Whatever the variant, they fall under the epistemological paradigm. They all take being as determined by subjective processes, which, however, they interpret in different ways. Thus, for historicism, being is determined by knowing, which is understood as a historically determinate process that fixes the knower in the present. There is, as in all forms of Kantianism, an identity between subject and object, between concept and thing. Yet, as usual, there is a price to be paid. In this case, it is the inaccessibility—the escape into the noumenal—of anything past. The past, for example, the doctrine of an ancient author, cannot be properly known, since we can only interpret it (constitute its sense) according to our present, historically conditioned categories. Knowing, thus, determines being to the point that the past as past cannot count as real for us.

If we accept the epistemological paradigm, the arguments for this version of it, from Dilthey and Spengler to its more modern variants, are extraordinarily powerful. Their only defect is a certain circularity that arises once we try to confirm that *all* knowledge (not just that which characterizes the present age) is historically determined. If we cannot escape our present conditioning, how can we make assertions about the past? Our concern, however, is not with the particulars—such as the circularity or lack thereof—of their arguments. What is at issue for us is the paradigm by which they stand or fall. Their circularity can be traced back to *its* circularity. Yet if we step outside of these forms of the epistemological paradigm, we can, in fact, hear Aristotle speaking in terms that are meaningful yet foreign to our age.

§1. *The Dependence of Space and Time on Being.*   The modern view of space and time, we said, is based on the the Cartesian grid with its associated time line. With it, we can identify each object with a mathematical set of coordinates giving its position and time. As such, it opens the way to the

---

1. Viewed in this light, some brands of analytic philosophy are forms of neo-Kantianism. The Heideggarian, Vattimo, combines linguistic determinism with Heidegger's notion of the "epochs of being." He writes: "It is primarily in language that the originary familiarity with the world unfolds which constitutes the non-transcendental, always historically finite and 'situated' condition of the possibility of experience. . . . [T]his horizon [of language] is not, however, the always identical transcendental screen of Kantian reason. It is instead historical and finite" (*The End of Modernity,* p. 66).

mathematical description of nature. Crucial to this account is the assertion that nothing can exist without being in space and time, while these can continue even while the things within them come and go. Accepting this, space and time become grounding conditions of the objects within them. The mathematical account of something according to its spatial-temporal relations becomes not just a description but also an explanation of its very being. It claims to explain why it is as it is.

Aristotle's view is exactly the reverse of this. Space is thought of as place; and place and time are attributes of beings, but are not themselves beings in any primary sense. This means that they cannot be on their own and, hence, cannot serve as grounding conditions. They exist as descriptive predicates grounded in individual existents. The difference between the individual and its attributes is, thus, ontological. By changing, the individual can take on different attributes and yet continue to be. Its former attributes, however, lose their existence as its predicates. With this view, taken from his *Categories,* we already have the basis for Aristotle's relativization of space and time. Rather than being primary realities, space and time are dependent attributes of beings. Thus it is not the case that entities exist by virtue of being placed in a spatial-temporal environment. Rather, entities are what first make possible this environment. They themselves spatialize and temporalize it.

Given this, a place without a body, an empty space or "void," is impossible for Aristotle (*Physics* 213b31–33). Considered in itself, it is a kind of "nonbeing or privation." One can no more characterize it positively than one can find "differences in nothing" (215a11).[2] A place with a body does exist, but it does so only as an attribute of a body. Aristotle, in trying to determine what sort of an attribute it is, states that place can in no sense be considered as a cause of an entity. It answers to none of the four causes or reasons he advances for why a thing behaves as it does. It is neither a body's matter, nor its form (or intelligible structure); it is neither the goal of its development, nor any particular agent causing it to move (*Physics* 208a21–25). Not being a cause, it is, in fact, dependent upon the body. Strictly speaking, place without body (empty space) cannot exist because the body itself is what first spatializes. As such, it causes us to apply spatial categories. The body does this through its motion. In Aristotle's words, "we must keep in mind that, but for local motion, there would be no place as a subject matter of investigation" (*Physics* 211a13). This can be illustrated in terms of Aristotle's definition of place as "the first unmoved

2. All translations from the *Physics* have been taken from Richard Hope's translation of Aristotle's *Physics*. All other translations from Aristotle are my own.

boundary of what surrounds [the entity]" (*Physics* 212a20). Place answers
the question, "where?" My answer to the question of where I am depends
upon my motion. If I am seated writing at my desk, I am in my chair. If I
get up and walk about my office, its walls are now my first unmoved
boundary. If I now pace the hallway, perhaps visiting other offices on the
floor, the appropriate answer to the question "where" is "on the second
floor." If I take the elevator and visit other floors, my "where" is the building itself. Similarly, during the day, I am at the university; during the week,
I am in this university town; during the month, I am in this area of the
country, and so on. The point of this is that the entity itself determines
through its motion its first unmoving boundary and, hence, what constitutes the limits of its environment.[3]

The proper Aristotelian context to understand this determination is that
of "nature." Things have a nature which posses an inherent principle or
cause of motion and rest (*Physics* 192b12). In other words, natural entities can move on their own. Given this, the ultimate cause of spatialization
is that of movement, and this is nature itself. In Greek, the word nature
(φύσις) comes from the verb, to grow (φύω). It has the general sense of
growing, developing, and unfolding so as to manifest that which grows or
develops.[4] The acorn, for example, grows and develops to manifest the
goal of this process: the fully formed tree. This last, as determining the
pattern and direction of growth, sets the parameters of the environment.
Both as an origin and as an accomplished goal of this process, the fully
formed tree is the entity itself. The process is its manifestation. As occurring in and through this process, spatialization can be defined as a dimension of the entity's self-revelation, its self-manifestation through time.

Time itself is also part of this self-manifestation. Like place, it cannot be
considered apart from the moving body. In itself, it is nothing at all. In
Aristotle's words, a stretch of it "consists in non-beings" since it "com-
prises the past, which no longer is, and the future, which is not yet"

---

3. Only if we ignore the issue of motion can we define "place" as the interface between
the body and what immediately surrounds it. Once we do consider motion, then as Aristotle
notes, this definition has to be modified. We have to say that "place is a receptacle which
cannot be transported" (*Physics,* 212a15). Thus the place of a motionless boat is given by the
surrounding water, but once we consider the boat as moving down the river, "it is the whole
river which, being motionless as a whole, functions as a place" (212a19). As the example of
the boat suggests, the place of a body need not be continuous with the body itself.

4. Heidegger gives a good sense of the word when he writes: "What does the word *physis*
denote? It denotes self-blossoming emergence (e.g., the blossoming of a rose), opening up,
unfolding, that which manifests itself in such unfolding and perseveres and endures in it" (*An
Introduction to Metaphysics,* p. 14).

(*Physics* 218a2). If we ask why neither the past nor the future are, two possible interpretations are open to us. The modern interpretation is that neither the past nor the future are in the strict sense present. They are elapsed or anticipated temporal presence. To become past is to depart from this presence, whereas to be future is to be *not yet* present. The conclusion of this argument is that being is temporal presence. If we are to affirm an entity's actual existence, it must share a now with us. Time, then, grounds being insofar as it makes being present—this through its flow from now to successive now. The premodern interpretation reverses this. It argues that neither the past nor the future is because *the being whose presence underlies them* has departed or else has not yet arrived. The assertion here is that the presence of time requires the presence of being. In this (Aristotelian) view, it is not the case that temporality grounds being, but rather that being (in its capacity for presence, for manifesting itself) grounds time. The entity itself is at the origin of the timing or temporalization of its environment. The modern view, by contrast, embraces the relation of time and being that we saw underpinning the epistemological paradigm (see pages 73–74). It takes the flow from now to successive now as the movement from presence to presence and equates temporal presence and being. Time, in making something now, makes it present and, by this definition, makes it be.

The two positions can be distinguished by the different senses they give to the word "presence." For the modern, time can ground being only if being is reduced to presence and the sense of the latter is limited to temporal presence, i.e., to nowness. For such a position, the being of an entity is its nowness. For Aristotle, as we shall see, being is understood as the functioning (ἐνέργεια) that results in the entity's presence to its environment. The presence of an entity is the *totality* of its effects, one of which is the present, i.e., temporal presence taken as the nowness the soul experiences. Since such presence is only one effect of being, one that requires the soul to occur, it cannot logically be equated with being. (See *Physics* 223a15–17.) Only when we equate nowness, presence, and being do we have the modern view that time, in making an entity now, makes this entity be.

For Aristotle, however, "the present [or the now] is not a part of time" [τὸ δὲ νῦν οὐ μέρος] for "a part is a measure of the whole, whereas the present is not such a measure." As he also puts this: "Time does not seem to be composed of 'nows'" [συγκεῖσθαι ἐκ τῶν νῦν] (*Physics* 218a7–8). The necessity for this is more than the logical one that no number of atomic (partless) nows can be summed to produce a whole. It follows from the fact that the presence that grounds time cannot be a part of time. If it were a part of time, then it would, itself, require the same ground or reason for its being that time does. Thus, to function as a ground, this presence—which concretely is the presence of the entity to us—must be *prior* to time. In other words, it is because being (in its presence to a soul) grounds time, that "the present is not part of time."[5]

As in the case of place, such grounding occurs through motion. It is not being's presence pure and simple which occasions time but rather the change of presence. The temporal result of an unchanging presence is an unchanging present or constant now. But as Aristotle observes, "there would be no time" if there were "only a single, self-identical present" (*Physics* 218b28). In other words, "when we have no sense of change, . . . we have no sense of the passing of time" (218b24). The entity, then, grounds time through the change of its presence. This does not mean that this presence manifests a sheer otherness. It combines identity and difference. The identity comes from the identity of the entity whose presence it is. The difference stems from the differences created by the entity's movement. As Aristotle writes: "The moving body . . . is the same . . . , but the moving body differs in the account which may be given of it." In particular, it differs by being in different places "and the present [τὸ νῦν] corresponds to it as time corresponds to the movement" (*Physics* 219b20–23). The assertion here is that the present or now, which "is not a part of time," but rather its ground, is the presence of the body. It "corresponds" to the body by virtue of being part of the body's continuous self-manifestation. The continuity of time depends on this continuity, this lack of any gaps in the body's presence.[6] Similarly, time corresponds to the body's movement

---

5. Failure to grasp this point makes Aristotle's derivation of time circular. If the present is part of time, then to use it to derive time from motion by noting the different presents (nows) associated with the different positions of the moving body is to derive time from itself. Here, we may note that it is not the case, as Denis Corish asserts, that "the asymmetry of movement through space is at least partly a function of time, and cannot be determined merely in spatial terms" ("Aristotle's Attempted Derivation of Temporal Order from That of Movement and Space," p. 249). For Aristotle, the asymmetry is determined not by time but by the end or goal of the motion, which, insofar as it does not change, is not in time. As we shall see, to be further along in motion is to be closer to achieving one's full or complete being. By knowing the latter, one knows the direction of motion. For example, looking at a series of snapshots of a growing child, I can easily tell the direction of the motion.

6. The same point can be made, *mutatis mutandis,* about the continuity of motion. As Aristotle writes in *On Generation and Corruption,* motion is not continuous "because that in which the motion occurs is continuous," but rather "because that which is moved is continuous. For how can the quality be continuous except in virtue of the continuity of the thing to which it belongs?" (337a27–29).

insofar as it manifests the body's shifting relation to its environment. Thus, "it is by reference to the moving body that we recognize what comes before and after in the movement" (*Physics* 219b24). We say, "before, the body was here, afterward, it was there." If, on reflection, we distinguish the before from the after, then the present appears as a division between the two: it is the presence of the body after it left one place and before it went to another. With motion comes the shift of the before and the after and, with this, the appearance of the flowing present or now. This shifting center of the temporal environment is simply a dimension (an attribute, an aspect) of the presence of the body as the shifting center of its environment. Subjectively, then, time appears as a kind of stationary streaming. We experience it as a flow, that is, as a constant succession of the "before and after." Yet we also have to say that the present in which we experience this streaming is itself stationary and remaining. It is not part of time in the sense that it departs with its fleeting moments. Rather, it is always now for us. The constancy of this now is the constancy of the presence of being. We experience it as long as we are aware of being or, what is the same, as long as an entity's presence is manifested to us.

Time, as we actually experience it in the physical world is, thus, the result of a duality in the presence of a body. The constant presence of the body times us such that we experience the constant now, while the shifting presence of its environment modifies the result so that we experience this now as shifting, that is, as the now through which time seems to stream.[7] Going beyond Aristotle, we may note that it is by virtue of this stationary streaming that we can speak of the distinction of self and world. For self and world to separate, the self must remain now while the world in its objects must depart into pastness. This departure is what we may call the creation of transcendence. Suppose, for example, I take a pencil and slowly twirl it between my fingers. As I do, one side gives way to the next. Appearance succeeds appearance; and as each gives way to the next, each departs into pastness. This departure is actually a departure from me as I remain in the present, ongoing nowness of my perceptual act. Were I to become fixed in one of the departing moments, I would grasp only the appearance it contains. Similarly, were an appearance not to depart, not to

7. This duality of the presence of the body can also be expressed in terms of the modern concept of synthesis. Here, the constancy of the now registers the constancy of the sense of the body—that is, the fact that it is grasped (through a synthetic act of identification) as one and the same in the flow of perceptual contents. The streaming of the now registers the change of contents, which in its flowing continues to make this sense perceptually present. Both together yield the stationary streaming now which frames the experience of the body.

give way to another, but remain now with me, once again my grasp would be limited to just one appearance. That it is not so limited means that such moments transcend my present in their departure into pastness; or alternately, that my present transcends these moments by *its* remaining now, that is, by its not being "a part of time." In either case, the basic phenomenon is that of transcendence. The departure of content-laden moments (temporally determinate appearances) from my present is the ongoing manifestation of transcendence.[8] What is behind this manifestation is simply the shift of the perceptual object with respect to its surroundings. My grasp of it, however, is its constitution of me as a stationary streaming. The continual presence and departure from this presence involved in such streaming means that its constitution of me is also that of transcendence. Let me put this in terms of the example of the twirling pencil. My grasp of it as a moving object involves the comprehension of a number of its appearances, those of its successively appearing sides. So apprehended, its concept involves more than its present perception and, hence, more than its present perceiver. The object transcends the latter as enduring, that is, as an entity whose sense embraces a series of perceptions that occupy a stretch of departing time. Directed to the object, the momentary perception thus intends not just what temporally transcends itself, but also what transcends its momentary content (the content of its momentary act) as well.

Such a grasp, of course, requires memory. To grasp the object as containing more than the present moment, we must retain the contents of the departing moments of its successive appearances. The question of retention, of how it is possible and what it involves must be answered in detail if we are to fill out this account. Without it, the notion of the object as constituting the intending subject—that is, the subject that has transcendent intentions—remains incomplete.

Aristotle's focus, however, is more general. His interest is not in the mechanics of retention, but rather in the ontological conditions for the receptivity of the "subject" (in Aristotle's terms, the sensing and understanding "soul" or self). For our project of reversing modernity, two questions regarding these conditions are paramount: (1) How are we to under-

---

8. The insight here is Husserl's. He, however, sees such manifestation as a simple egological creation, since for him the process has no further ground. He writes: "In the whole continuity [of time], I am . . . the present, primary-actual primordium which originally constitutes what is originally past and future. . . . I exist in the streaming creation [*schaffen*] of transcendence, in the creation of self-transcendence, of being as self-pastness, self-futurity and self-presence" (Ms. C 7 I, p. 21a, June–July 1932).

stand receptivity once we give up the notion of space and time as grounding conditions—that is, once we no longer see them as receptacles
through which things are sent and received? This notion of space and time
as receptacles is, we stressed, implicit in Descartes's grid. The grid sets the
frame for the modern notion of the subject-object relation. Thus we also
ask: (2) How are we to understand the receptivity of this relation once we
do give up the grid? Following Aristotle, these questions should be taken
as focusing on being, that is, on the ontological categories required to
understand receptivity.

§2. *The Receptivity of Mind.*   Aristotle's answer to the first of these questions is implicit in his assertion that "before it thinks," that is before it
grasps and apprehends an object, "mind has no actual existence" (*De Anima* 429a24). As he also put this, mind is "potentially identical with the
objects of its thought, but is actually nothing until it thinks" (429b31).
This implies that, apart from an entity's presence, mind ceases. Separated
from the presence of being, mind (νοῦς), which is the perceiving (νόειν)
of being, collapses. When it is perceiving, mind (or rather the knowledge
that forms its content) is identical with its object (430a20). The removal
of the object is the removal of its content. It leaves it in a state where it
has "no actual existence." The implication of these statements gives us the
ontological underpinning of receptivity, that is, of the notion of the object
as constituting us. It is that mind's actual existence is just the presence
which is the self-manifestion of the object. Its actual existence, in other
words, is a function of its identity with the being of its object.

The key term in Aristotle's discussion is "at workness"—a literal translation of energeia (ἐνέργεία). When Aristotle says that before it thinks,
mind has no "actual existence," he is literally asserting that it has no existence "in the at workness [ἐνέργεία] of beings [τῶν ὄντων]." The *object* is
actual, is "at work," in its self-manifestation. For a subject this self-manifestation is the object's presence to it. Yet, as we just said, such presence is
the subject's actual being. When the object is a moving body, such subjective being involves temporality. It manifests the character of stationary
streaming, that is, of an ongoing nowness within a shifting environment of
the before and after. Insofar as this involves transcendence, what is constituted here is the subject as grasping what is more than itself, more than
what is contained in its momentary perception. Insofar as such a grasp
constitutes the subject's functioning, or at workness, a striking conclusion
arises from this view. This is that the subject's and object's actual being are
intertwined.

Aristotle's way of expressing this joining of being or functioning is in terms of the "actual" and the "potential," terms he uses to define "motion." There is, he notes, a certain ambiguity in being: "Being . . . may be only actual or potential or both actual and potential" (*Physics* 200b26–27). The process from the potential to the actual is "motion" understood in the most general sense of the term, a sense that for Aristotle is far wider than simple change of place. Because it embraces both the actual and the potential, motion *is* and yet, as Aristotle says, "is hard to grasp" (201b33). As he explains it, "since any kind of being may be distinguished as either potential or completely realized, the perfecting [ἐντελέχεια] of what is potential as potential is 'being in movement'" (201a11). Motion, then, is the perfecting of the entity through the functioning of its potential. Such functioning is the actual operation of the powers that lie dormant in an entity. Thus dormant in an acorn is the power to develop so as to ultimately manifest its being as a full grown tree. The motion that is the operation of this power is growth. It is also, we can say, its ongoing result. It is the tree itself in its ongoing presence (or self-manifestation) as a living, growing entity. To take another example, we can say that dormant in the student is the power to learn. The functioning of this power is the perfecting of the student in the sense that it makes him actually become what he is capable of being. In learning, he becomes an actual student.

The student, of course, requires a teacher to learn. If we ask where this teacher is, the ontological ambiguity implicit in this description of motion becomes apparent. Considered in terms of his functioning, that is, his activity of "perfecting" the student, the teacher *is* in the student. The student's perfecting is also the teacher's perfecting as a teacher. Thus, generally speaking, as Aristotle puts it: the "movement is in the movable"—this, because "the movement is the perfecting [ἐντελέχεια] of the movable by some mover, and the functioning [ἐνέργεια] of this agent is not different [from the perfecting of the movable]" (*Physics* 202a13–15). As identified with the perfecting of the movable, the agent's functioning is in the movable. Since this functioning is, in fact, the agent's own perfecting—that is, its own operation of its powers—its identification with the perfecting of the movable means that there is in this relation of mover and movable just one perfecting. In Aristotle's words, "movement must be the perfecting [ἐντελέχειαν) of both; since a thing is an agent or mover because it has the power of moving, and is actually moving when that power is functioning [or: is 'at work']. Hence, there is a single functioning [ἐνέργεια] of both alike" (*Physics* 202a16–20). This means that the teacher cannot function as a teacher without the student functioning as a student. They must "work" together. Their "being at work," their actuality, is, in this instance, one.

To appreciate the strength of this claim, we must note again that for Aristotle, the being of entities is this functioning or being at work. An entity has an actual existence (and hence a capacity for temporal presence) through the operation (or functioning) of its powers (*Metaphysics* 1045a24, 1045b19–20). In such a context, to ask: "Where actually is the entity?" is to ask "Where is this functioning?" In the case of the teacher, the answer is clear. The functioning is "teaching," and the place of this is where it is presently at work. It is "in the one taught" (*Physics* 202b7–8). Thus the teacher must actually function in the learner if the latter is to actualize his potentiality to learn. The teaching is "there" in the learner since this is where the teacher's being as a teacher is "at work." It is there as the operation or functioning of the power to make the learner learn. Given that the functioning of teaching requires that of learning, what we have are not two different functionings, but rather aspects of a single functioning, one that requires both teacher and learner if the potentiality inherent in their relationship is to be realized in the learner. To attempt to represent this on the Cartesian grid, we would thus have to collapse the two spatial-temporal positions of the teacher and learner to represent the single actuality that is their combined functioning.[9]

With this, we have an answer to the first of our questions concerning the receptivity of the subject. Receptivity in the Aristotelian context is *receptivity to being*. Being, however, is not conceived in terms of spatial-temporal location. It is thought of as functioning. Granting this, *receptivity is to this functioning or "at workness."* In other words, one receives activities. An activity, say that of learning, is one's own and yet is received. To

---

9. Hippocrates Apostle translates the passage in question by rendering energeia as "actuality": "Neither is it absurd for the actuality of one thing to be in another thing (for teaching is the activity of a man who can teach but it is an activity upon another man; it is not cut off but is an activity of A upon B), nor can anything prevent one actuality from being the same for two things—not in the sense that the essence is the same for both, but in the sense in which potential being is related to being in actuality." He comments: "The two actualities [of A and B] (if we are to call them 'two') are like aspects of one actuality. . . . In a statue, its actuality is the shape and its potentiality is the material (e.g., the bronze). Yet the statue is one thing, and the shape and the material cannot exist apart but exist as inseparable principles of the statue. It is likewise with that which acts and that which is acted upon qua such" (*Aristotle's Physics,* pp. 46, 255). In other words, just as the matter and the form are aspects of one actuality, so also are the student and the teacher.

take another example, my activity of timing the world, that is, of seeing it in terms of my stationary streaming, is my own in the sense that it occurs "in" me. Yet it is also true that it grows out of my grasp of physical motion, a grasp that the motion imposes on me. Going beyond Aristotle, we can draw a general conclusion regarding our interpretative activity. It is equally true to say that I interpret the world (for example, interpret it in terms of the categories of place and time) as to say that it interprets itself through me. The conclusion follows from the fact that interpretation is an activity (a functioning) and, hence, can be understood as received.

Actuality and Potentiality: The Ambiguity of Being

According to the above, we are receptive to being. Being is defined as functioning, on the most basic level, as the functioning that results in a being's self-manifestation. To repeat our second question, we may ask, How are we to understand the subject-object relation in terms of such receptivity? Here, a number of paradoxes appear. Does this notion of being mean that in teaching I really am "there" where my students are, actually present in their learning? What happens to me when I cease teaching? Does my being as a teacher vanish entirely? The same questions can be asked about the perceptible object. For Aristotle, "the functioning of the sensible object" *is* "in the sensing subject" (*De Anima* 426a10). It is where the perception of the object is actually operative. In fact, it is "one and the same" with the functioning of such perception (425b27). Does this mean that its being *is* its presence in some subject? What happens when it is not perceived? Does its being as a sensible object cease entirely? Does it cease to be even something that *can* be perceived? If we answer in the affirmative, then we seem to fall back to Berkeley's position that to be is to be perceived. But this is to embrace again the epistemological paradigm. Insofar as Aristotle's position differs from this, our account of it is incomplete. It is not enough to speak in terms of Aristotle's general category of being as functioning. What prevents his position from approaching Berkeley's is the division he makes in this. As his definition of motion indicates, beyond the actuality of functioning, being also includes the potentiality to function. This second category is crucial to the account of the self's receptivity once we give up Descartes's grid.

§1. *The Teleological Frame.* Aristotle uses the division between the actual and the potential to distinguish the "to be" of sensation from that of
the object sensed. He writes: "The functioning of the sensible object and
that of sensation is one and the same, but not their 'to be'" (ibid.). The
same claim is made about the teacher and the student. The identity of
their functioning does not exclude a difference in their "to be" (*Physics*
202b10). Thus, you can "be" a teacher after class ends in the sense that
you *can* teach again. You have the capability to re-engage in the functioning that identifies you with the learner. Similarly, we can say that although
the functioning of the perceived and its perception simultaneously arise
and cease, "it is not necessary to assert this of their potentialities" (*De
Anima* 426a20). The sensible object still "is" apart from its being sensed
insofar as it *can be* sensed.

This distinction between functioning and the capacity to function is,
then, an *ontological* distinction, one that shows itself in the distinction
of an entity's "to be." Given that being is the functioning that manifests
itself in presence, this is also a distinction in the ways in which entities
can be present. Thus behind the question of how an entity can "be"
without being perceived is the question of how it can "be" capable of
being perceived. What, in other words, is the ontological status of
potentiality? Behind this is the still more fundamental question: How
do we understand potentiality as a mode of presence? How, in other
words, are we to understand it as a manifestation of the functioning
of being?

Even when it is not perceived, a sensible object, we say, is there available for perception. Its potentiality signifies its being there, its *being available* for perception. In appealing to it, we generally do not take the
Berkelean stance that being equals perception. We require only its per-
ceivability or capability to be perceived. Being is what *can* be brought into
presence. What is potential can become present. Its potential for presence
is its ability to take part in a process involving its self-manifestation. The
Aristotelian name for this process is "nature." "Nature," we said, designates
that activity whereby something emerges, grows, develops so as to show
itself as it is, that is, so as to be present in its completed reality (ἐντελέχεια). Thus, as involving presence (more specifically, as a type of being towards being-completely-present), potential being exists in a context
structured by nature.

Nature, for Aristotle, brings things to presence in a quite definite way.
Its temporality is *not* that of the past determining the present, which determines the future. In this unidimensional view of temporal determinism,

the state of the world at one moment is the necessary and sufficient cause for its state at the next:

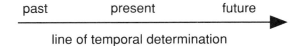

Nature, viewed in an Aristotelian manner, may be symbolically regarded by taking this line of temporal determination and bending it in a circle:

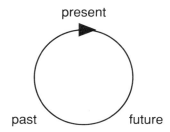

Here, the future determines the past in its determination of the present. As determinative, the future stands as a goal, as a "final cause" of the natural process. The goal makes the past into a resource, into a "material" as it were, for the process of its own realization. The goal thus determines the past in the latter's determination of the present by structuring it as a potential for some particular realization.

The same pattern is present in the temporal determination implied by using standards of correctness to interpret an activity (see pages 61–62). Generally speaking, the same determination is present in every interpretation. It, thus, will form a crucial element of our next chapter's account of the mechanics of the receptivity we are presently describing in Aristotelian terms. Aristotle's conception of goal-directed activity can be illustrated in a number of ways—all of which, from his perspective, are slightly misleading. Suppose, for example, that a woman decides to become a marathon runner. Her being as an actual runner is not a present reality. Neither is it a past one. It "exists" as a *future* whose determining presence is that of a goal. How long she has to train is determined by the resources she brings to the goal—that is, how long she has trained in the immediate *past*. Thus, as the circle indicates, determination by the future is not absolute but occurs through the past. For Aristotle, the determining presence of the past is that of the materials or resources it presents us to accomplish the goal. It is, of course, the goal that allows us to see such materials as materials for some purpose. The goal is what turns the past into a potential to be actualized by our ongoing, *present* activity. To take another example, it is the goal of building that first makes timber into building material. Similarly, the potential of stone to be a statue as opposed to a shelter demands the entertaining of a corresponding goal. What makes these examples somewhat misleading is that they are all from "art" (τέχνη). They are taken from that type of activity where, according to Aristotle, man "imitates" nature. This imitation is an imposition of goals whereby he makes nature participate in his future. Quite apart from man, natural entities have their own goals. Different plants, for example, turn earth, sunlight, water, as well as a host of other factors, into materials for their own particular ends.

What is common to all such processes is the notion of the completed reality, which stands at their end as being *not just the goal but also a cause of its own realization.* As causally determinative, the goal gives us the movement of nature according to which the line of temporal determination can be said to move from the future through the past to the present. This "natural" movement is what situates potentiality as a category of reality.

To speak of determination by the goal is to reverse the modern position that time flows from past to present to future and that, in such flowing, it makes being "be." Were this true, the goal could not be active, since it would not yet be. For Aristotle, however, it is not time that makes being "be," but rather the reverse. Being is the ground of time, this through the presence that is the result of its functioning. The presence that directs the teleological flow of time—the flow from the future through the past to the present—is the presence of a functioning goal. This point can be put in terms of Aristotle's doctrine that actuality is prior to potentiality. This priority of actuality is, ontologically, the priority of the completed reality (ἐντελέχεια) or the *being at the end* of the process that the process itself is directed to realize. It is also the priority of functioning (ἐνεργέια) over the capacity to function (δύναμις). What can fully function is the completed reality. Taken as a goal or end of a process, its functioning is that of the process's final cause. As Aristotle expresses this relationship: "Everything that comes to be moves towards its source [ἐπ'ἀρχὴν], that is, towards its goal [τέλος]; for its wherefore [final cause] is its source. Its coming into being is directed by the end which is the actuality [ἐνέργεια], and it is thanks to the end that potentiality [δύναμις] is possessed" (*Metaphysics* 1050a8–10).

A number of points are made in this passage. Together they give us the answer to the question: What is potentiality as a mode of presence? The first point is that it is the end, the completed reality, which directs coming into being. It is, thus, responsible for the motion of nature, the temporal reflection of which is time grasped as a teleological flow. Without this end or, more precisely, without its functioning (ἐνέργεια) as a final cause, there would be no natural coming into being and, hence, there would be no potentiality as a category of reality. Thus, what is potential can "be" without being presently actualized, but not without that which directs its coming into being. The same point can be expressed slightly differently by noting that causality for Aristotle is exercised by being. It is, in fact, an effect of its functioning. Given that being is what appears at the end of a natural process, we cannot talk of causality in the sense of the past being a necessary and sufficient condition for the present, which serves, in turn, as a similar condition for the future. The presence that could function as such a condition must be that which has achieved completed being (ἐντελέχεια); but in natural, developmental processes, such being is at the end. It is thus "thanks to the end that potentiality is possessed." In other words, the end acts as a final cause determining coming into being, and as such, it makes potentiality possible.

Let us relate this to our point that entities, rather than being a result of their spatial-temporal determinations, are what first determine space and time. Both space and time, we said, result from motion. Their ultimate basis is found in those "natural" entities which have within them a beginning or source of the motion whereby they manifest themselves. This source is the completed reality that stands at the end of this process and determines it as a final cause. Understood as an aspect of the entity's self-manifestation, space can be be seen as a system (or "place") of those places that an entity occupies as it unfolds itself under the direction of this cause. Similarly, time can be taken as the temporal dimension of this unfolding as it manifests itself to us. It is our registering the changes in the entity's presence. The determination of this motion by the completed reality at the end of this process is, then, the determination of the space and time through which such manifestation occurs. Rather than being independent realities, space and time exist "for the sake of" such manifestation. They are, as it were, its *material or medium.* We essentially say the same thing when we say that they exist "thanks to the end." They are *aspects of the potentiality that the end,* in determining coming into being, *makes possible. They are, then, potentiality taken as a mode of presence.*

There are two complementary ways of expressing the above. We can note that insofar as space and time depend on motion, they are determined by the end that acts as the final cause of such motion. To reverse this, we can say that the final cause makes possible both potentiality and the motion that is the actualization of this potentiality. As a consequence, it also grounds the space and time that are the measures of this motion. This implies that space and time are grounded by entities only insofar as they are capable of motion, that is, possess a potentiality that is not completely actualized. The complete actualization of a potentiality exhausts the capability for motion and, hence, for being determined by space or time. This implies that the grasp of what is completely actual, what Aristotle calls the "forms" and formal relations ("ratios") of things, involves neither space nor time. Thus, the relation between the side and the diagonal of a square is not in one place rather than another, nor is it at one time rather than another. Receptive to this ratio, mind is equally timeless. This follows because potentiality taken as a mode of presence no longer applies.

With this, we have the answer to our second question. The self's receptivity, once we give up the grid, is not grounded by space and time, but rather grounds them. It does this insofar as the being it receives implies potentiality as a feature of its presence. Such a view, as is obvious, undermines the idea of perception as the grasp of a replica whose original is somehow "out there."

§2. *Original and Replica.* By contrast, the modern view of the subject-object relation involves, as we noted, the problem of transcendence (see pages 16–17). Given the grid, in knowing, we must transcend our "here" to reach the object, which appears "there" at a physical remove. Regarding the latter, we assume in Descartes's words, "that this alien entity sends to me and imposes upon me its likeness" (*Meditations,* III; p. 37). The overriding question is how I can ever know whether "the ideas [sense perceptions] which are in myself are similar to, or conformable to, things outside myself"? (p. 36). How do I ever know that the replica in myself is "like" the original out there? Following the Aristotelian paradigm, we have to say that this view is the result of a couple of category mistakes. The first mistake takes space and time as essential rather than accidental determinants of being. The second compounds this error by confusing potential with actual being. If Aristotle is right in asserting that the sensible object is actually one with its sensation, there is no original out there with which we could compare our sensation. In Gertrude Stein's phrase, there is no "there there," since the *actuality* (the functioning) of the perceived *is its*

manifestation through our perception. Qua sensible object, this manifestation is its competed reality. It is, in other words, the final cause of the
process resulting in its perception. As such, it is what directed the process
from the start.

What about the sensible object when it is not being perceived? As we
cited Aristotle, even though the sensible object and its perception have a
single actualization, "we need not assert this of them according to their
potentialities." We can, in other words, speak of the potentially sensible.
Does this make the latter a standard we can apply to judge the validity of
our perceiving? Can the potentially sensible object with its different "to
be" count as an original against which we can judge the "replica" in our
heads? Such an interpretation reverses what for Aristotle is their true relation. We can only speak of potentiality in terms of actuality. The "to be" of
the former is that of serving as material for the latter. Thus the potentially
sensible object is such only as offering the material basis for an actual
perception. The latter, rather than being a dependent replica in our head,
stands as a final cause directing the process. It is what, in the first instance,
makes possible the sensible object's potentiality. Given this, there is no
replica and original to compare. To attempt to do so would be rather like
attempting to evaluate a finished statue by comparing it with the material
it came from. In fact, admitting that the original is the perceptual presence,
we have to say that "the perception of [the senses'] proper objects is always true" (*De Anima* 428b19).[10] We can err when we attribute something to objects we do not perceive, but we cannot err (in the sense of
failing some correspondence test) when we do perceive them. We cannot
because, as we said, there is no "there there"—that is, no object actually
possessing the sensible qualities we perceive other than the one which
manifests itself in us.

The assertion that there is no "there there" puts us in a curious position
in describing the place of the teacher. It points to the fact that such place
cannot in a Cartesian manner be specified beforehand. It is dependent on
the manner of being, that is, on functioning or the potentiality to function.
Thus there are as many answers to the question of "where?" as there are
senses of being or functioning. The teacher is wherever her functioning
has effect. Writing at the blackboard, pushing the chalk along, she is at the
place of this physical functioning. Speaking and setting up the movements
of perception and understanding, she is also present in her students' learn-

---

10. The same holds for "knowledge or intellectual perception" (ἐπιστήμη ἢ νοῦς) according to Aristotle (*De Anima* 428a18).

ing. Here, her place, taken as the first unmoving boundary of her functioning, is the classroom. In general, she is, in her being, wherever her presence (as grounded by her functioning) extends. Other beings may also be
in the same "place." Indeed, her own actual being or functioning may be
an essential part of their functioning. Since the senses of her being include
the "to be" of potentiality, the same assertions can be made about her
serving as the material for another's actualization. Finally, insofar as her
teaching is successful, that is, results in the actuality of the genuine perception (νοῦς) of unchanging contents, the teacher's presence escapes
both time and place. The effect of her functioning becomes simply part of
the cogitational actuality of unchanging contents.

§3. *Questions Posed by the Paradigm.*   As the foregoing answer indicates,
Aristotle leaves us with a somewhat messy situation with multiple senses
of being or functioning, one where beings interpenetrate beings and assist
in establishing one another in such functioning. It is not one inherently
orderable according to the Cartesian grid, nor is it, in general, inherently
mathematizable. Its one overarching principle is that of nature, in particular, that of the teleology implicit in natural motion.

Both factors have been heavily criticized. Modernity, in fact, initially
defined itself in terms of this critical response. Thus, the Aristotelian ambiguity of being, the fact, as Aristotle put it, that "being can be said in many
ways" (*Metaphysics* 1003a33), was decried as standing in the way of the
emerging science of physics. The latter's success involved reducing being
to a single sense, that of a mathematizable physical nature. This understanding eschewed final causes. The mechanics of Galileo and Descartes
contented itself with describing the causality that proceeded from the past
to the present to the future. Its position was, in Descartes's words, "that all
causes of the type we are accustomed to call final are useless in physical or
natural affairs" (*Meditations,* IV; p. 53). Not only was the attempt to bring
teleological insights to bear seen as an inadmissible form of anthropomorphism, it was also considered presumptuous. The defenders of the new
sciences derided it as a vain attempt "to discover the impenetrable purposes of God" (ibid.).

In spite of his attempts to separate himself from modernity and its
"metaphysical" traditions, Heidegger, we may note, renews these criti-
cisms. Asserting that the term "actuality" points back to the act of an agent,
he finds its ultimate referent is "Dasein's productive mode of behavior"
(*The Basic Problems of Phenomenology,* §11a; p. 105). Dasein (or the
human existent) anticipates what it will produce. When it makes some-

thing, it has in mind the shape or form of the product. This "anticipated look" is both form (*eidos*) and final cause. In Heidegger's words: "All forming of shaped products is effected by using an image, in the sense of a model, as guide and standard. The thing is produced by looking to the anticipated look of what is to be produced by shaping, forming. It is this anticipated look of the thing, sighted beforehand, that the Greeks mean ontologically by *eidos,* idea" (§11b; p. 106). The anticipated look is the formal-final cause of the productive process. It "shows the thing as what it is before the production and how it is supposed to look as a product" (p. 107). Granting this, Aristotle's attempt to universalize this paradigm in his account of nature seems to turn every being into a product. This, Heidegger asserts, evinces an "intolerable one-sidedness" (§12a; p. 115). He asks: "Can every being be taken as a product and can the concepts of being be attained and fixed by having regard to productive comportment?" (ibid.). The cosmos, he adds, "is surely not produced by the Dasein [the human existent] as a producer" (ibid.).

On one level, the criticism here is the same as that of Descartes and Galileo. It is that of an intolerable anthropomorphism, an illegitimate attempt to interpret things in human categories. Aristotle does, as we indicated, interpret nature in terms of "art" or *techne,* conceiving the latter in terms of the processes of making or producing. Admitting, as we must, that such processes are teleological (as, indeed, those of mind generally), Heidegger is asking: With what justification can we impose them on the world? On another level, his criticism goes beyond that of his predecessors. Once we do attempt to define being in terms of "productive comportment," we not only anthropomorphize nature, we do so in such a way that we leave the human person, the *anthropos,* out. In other words, once we define being in terms of products, then the fact that Dasein itself is not a product makes it ontologically groundless. The question, then, is "whether anything like *Sachheit,* thingness, whatness, reality, essentia, ousia"—all of which, for Heidegger, are originally categories of production—"can belong to the ontological constitution of the Dasein" (§12c; p. 119). To be a product is to be conceived in terms of the anticipated look. It is to be thought of as a "what," that is, as what is to be produced. Yet Dasein (the human existant) is not a "what," but a "who" (120). It is not a product, but a producer and so escapes these ontological categories.

If Heidegger is correct, then Aristotle's position involves the same circularity of reasoning as we saw in the epistemological paradigm. In Heidegger's account, Aristotle takes the productive comportment or behavior of Dasein as determinative of being; yet the resulting categories of being cannot account for the determiner. Once again, we are faced with a position that cannot account for its own standpoint, one that leaves out of account the being of the subject who propounds it. In such a view, Aristotle almost appears as a founder of modernity or, at least, of modernity's productive, "technological" conception of being. It is little wonder that, espousing such a view, Heidegger feels compelled to go back beyond the age of classical Greek philosophy to the pre-Socratics to find an example of an alternate tradition.

For our part, however, the assertion that Dasein is not a "what" but a "who" is not axiomatic. Its mere assertion is not sufficient to close off the Aristotelian position or, by itself, to advance the argument a single step in another direction. Instead, we may ask what would happen if we actually took seriously the view of Dasein as a product. To do so would be to take the world as a producer, one of whose products is Dasein or the human person. It would be to see the human subject as capable of being constituted by the world. The crucial point here is that Heidegger's critique of this is cogent *only if we fail to make the reversal* detailed in the previous chapter. It is only when we continue to see being as determined by *subjective* processes (including those of productive behavior), that the being of the subject appears groundless. Being a producer, rather than a product, Dasein then escapes the resulting ontological categories. When, however, we view the productive capacity of the human agent, not as determining being, but as determined by it, this objection fails to hold. Such a view immediately anchors it in being. At this point, we no longer impose the subject's teleological categories on the world. We take the world in its being as imposing them on the subject.

To this, of course, it can still be objected that the reversal does nothing to account for the fundamental point underlying Heidegger's criticism. Even if we make the world determine the subject, the subject is still not just another natural product. Human existents are not like the animals who more or less repeat the patterns imposed upon them by nature. Animals seem to be fixed in their behavior, such behavior being a determinable function of their environment, both animate and inanimate. By contrast, the human subject's special quality is its "standing out." It asserts itself as existent precisely by freeing itself from the constraints of its environment. This point is not a modern insight. As Sophocles writes in *Antigone,* "Many are the wonders, none is more wonderful than what is man. . . . He has a way against everything" (*Antigone,* lines 332, 360). A list follows of the ways in which human beings overcome the limits imposed by the seas, the land, and the seasons. He concludes, however, by observing that this very ability to escape constraints can lead to good or evil: "With some sort of cunning, inventive beyond all expectation, he reaches sometimes evil and sometimes good" (lines 367–68). This dual result follows from the human capability to do everything. To exercise it is, literally, to "stop at nothing." In other words, no unnatural act is beyond human ken. This, of course, is part of the insight of the play, *Oedipus the King*.[11] Oedipus, who is called, "first among men," knows that "man" is the answer to the Sphinx's riddle. He is, in his daring, taken as the exemplar of what it is to be human. Yet this very daring leads him to become unnatural, to murder his father, marry his mother, and engender (since they have the same mother) daughters who are his sisters and sons who also are his brothers. For the attentive reader, these plays stress the unnaturalness that follows upon human nature. By virtue of reason, which has a universal compass, humans can do anything, but this is to "stand out" of the bounds definitive of "nature" understood as the set of natural products.

Does the foregoing imply that we are totally separated from what counts as our world? Such a separation would imply that our freedom would be absolute. Contrariwise, this absolute freedom would signify our total lack of any grounding (any determination) by anything outside of ourselves. So defined as a "who," we would have to say with Heidegger, "Freedom is the abyss (*Ab-grund*) of Dasein." It is our character as groundless (*The Essence of Reasons,* p. 129). Refusing to go to this extreme is to recognize that we do, in fact, draw our motives, reasons, and projects from the world. It is to recognize that the essence of reason is *not,* as Heidegger asserts, our freedom (p. 123). Its ground is, rather, the world—this, through a special type of receptivity we have to the world. By virtue of it, we can grasp the projects the world is capable of sustaining. At least in thought, we can do and be anything that the world can sustain. Aristotle, thus, positions the mind as a kind of "place of the forms," seeing it as a place where every possible wordly form (and hence every possible final cause) has a possibility of presence.

We are not yet prepared to discuss this receptivity. For the present, it will have to suffice to remind ourselves that our unnaturalness in Sophocles' sense comes from this capacity to do everything. As the poem makes clear, the root of this capacity is our "cunning" or reason. The latter, as a universal tool, can be used for good or bad purposes. What this universality indicates is, as we said, the special quality of our minds. In Aristotelian terms, it indicates the capacity mind has, as a nonsubstantial "place

11. The actual title is Oedipus the Tyrant (τύραννος), which is significant insofar as the tyrant, rather than being part of the body politic, separates himself from it. He is not bound by its laws.

of forms," to be open to all sorts of forms and, hence, to every sort of final cause or goal. Granting this, such openness does not necessarily require, as Heidegger asserts, a shift from the Aristotelian paradigm, which takes our actions as informed by the world.[12] What it points to is the special quality of this informing insofar as it involves human minds. The description of the receptivity of mind as such will have to wait until we have covered more elementary matters—in particular, until we describe the type of receptivity (and the corresponding "standing out") we share with sentient life in general.

What about the criticism that Aristotle, in introducing final causes in nature has engaged in an illegitimate anthropomorphism, illegitimate because, as we quoted Descartes, "Final [causes] are useless in physical or natural affairs"? Insofar as Descartes's view assumes that animate (as opposed to inanimate) agents do pursue goals, it implies a kind of unstable dualism. On the one side, we have the type of teleological causality and corresponding temporality characteristic of animate nature; on the other, there is the material causality and unidimensional temporality definitive of nature regarded as inanimate. Generally speaking, what is wrong with dualism is not the distinctions it tries to make. It is rather its incoherence, its inability to relate the poles of the duality it uncovers. This incoherence shows itself in its instability, in its inherent tendency to reduce one side to the other. Thus the moderns have resolved this duality of causal paradigms in favor of the inanimate. Descartes, for example, while still admitting final causality in human actions, reduces animals to the status of machines. Later writers include human beings in this reduction.[13] By contrast, Aristotle, at least in the traditional way he was interpreted in Descartes's time, reduces the inanimate to the animate. Even the four elements were, he thought, moved by final causes to seek their "proper places."[14]

12. In particular, it does not call for the palpable misreading of the first chorus from *Antigone* (lines 332–72), which Heidegger uses to define being human. For Heidegger, what makes human beings "strange" or "wonderful" (δεινός) is their creative "violence." This violence springs from their not being bound by the rules of the city or, indeed, by any other rules. It, thus, refers back to the "abyss" of human freedom (*Introduction to Metaphysics*, pp. 149–58). The chorus, however, in pointing to human cunning [δοφός] seems to indicate that the source of this strangeness is the mind. Thus, given that a universal is a one-in-many, the mind's ability to grasp it is its ability to grasp what can be put to a multitude of possible uses, both good and bad. This seems to be what Sophocles is pointing to when he writes: "With some sort of cunning, inventive beyond all expectation [man] reaches sometimes evil and sometimes good" (*Antigone*, lines 367–68).

13. This includes, for Pavlov, the reduction of the activity of the scientist himself. It too is to be explained in terms of the laws of material causality. See his "Natural Science and the Brain," in *Lectures on Conditioned Reflexes*, p. 129.

14. Simplicius's views in Galileo's *Two New Sciences* are a good example of this interpretation.

With our talk of two types of temporality, have *we* introduced a similarly unstable dualism, one whose collapse would lead to an "intolerable one-sidedness" similar to that which Heidegger complains of? Expanding our focus from the human to the animate in general, what is wrong with such one-sidedness is that it does not allow the animate to "stand out." It does not stand out if it is a product of the world, that is, an "accident" of its material causality. The same holds if, embracing an idealist standpoint, we make the world the product of the animate, that is, make it relative to its ways of bringing it to perceptual presence. The "standing out" must contain, then, both the escape and ground, both the standing out and that from which such standing out occurs. This means that it must involve both the temporal determination appropriate to the world, materially viewed, as well as the teleological one appropriate to the capacities of animate agents. In other words, to stand out the animate subject must be both a cause in a teleological sense of being motivated by the goals it attempts to achieve and yet be caused in a material, physical sense. The standing out must be of the first with regard to the second.

How is this possible? What we are asking for is a joining of two different types of temporal determination. The first, that of the world, viewed as an inanimate process, proceeds according to the pattern, past-present-future, the conditions of the earlier time determining those of the later. The second, that of the goal-driven process, proceeds from the future to the past to the present. Now if we regard the circle which we drew to illustrate what we took to be Aristotelian causality, we see that it actually embraces both:

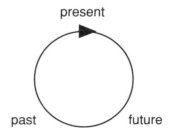

Beginning with the past, the line of determination reads: past-present-future. Beginning with the future, it reads: future-past-present. What the circle symbolizes is that the two types of temporal determination are not opposed. They are actually part of one process. Thus the teleological process, which begins with the future, must include the mechanical one, which begins with the past. It must accomplish the realization of the goal not by bypassing but by using such material-causal means. This, of course, is what the animate subject does in all of its projects. It uses the processes of inanimate nature to accomplish its goals. It is this ability that makes it "stand out," that is, not be simply an accidental product of material-causal factors. That it is not, does not, of course, exclude its being a product of the world in another, teleological sense—the sense in which the world grounds it in its causality by providing it with goals. Given this inclusivity, the "intolerable one-sidedness" that Heidegger complains of is not present in the circle itself. It springs, rather from the attempts to abstract from it opposing lines of temporal determination. It is this which results in the modern dualism of mind and body as well as the type of philosophical schizophrenia of Fichte's arbitrary choice between realism and idealism.

To overcome these, we must move beyond the symbolism of the circle to unpack its actual processes. Our immediate focus will be to see knowing as a teleological function, one that involves the whole of the circle. Before we turn to this task, which will occupy the next chapter, we should mention again the two insights from the Aristotelian paradigm that will be guiding us. The first is the reversal of the roles of original and replica as they function in perception. The original is not to be regarded as some "alien entity" at a spatial-temporal remove. It is rather, as we said, the perceptual presence itself. It is the actuality of the sensible object functioning as a final cause. As such, it guides from the beginning the perceptual process. Insofar as this process involves interpretation, it serves as its principle. Interpretation is, of course, an activity. It is part of the functioning of the subject as a perceiver. Given that receptivity is receptivity to being and that being, in this paradigm, is functioning, the second insight we will be drawing on is the notion that this activity of perception is, itself, received. Interpretation, in other words, is a received functioning. Because it is, we can, as we noted, say both: "I interpret the world" and "the world interprets itself through me." The possibility for both comes from the fact that the principle of my interpretive activity, the principle that acts as its final cause or goal, is itself received. The insight, then, is that the world acts in and through me insofar as it imparts to me its goals.

Our immediate task will be to transform these insights into a concrete, phenomenological description of the perceptual process. This will involve describing not just how goals are received but also the performances by which the goals, once received, control the process.

5

Knowledge as a Teleological Function

Breaking the Circle

The attempt to explain knowing as a material-causal process involves, as we noted, a certain circularity. The world, as we know it in its natural laws, is explained by the determining conditions of one of its parts—the brain and its sense organs, what Freud calls our "mental apparatus." Yet the world as we know it in its universal causal laws is itself used to explain how this part, through its material conditions, determines this knowledge of the world. The circularity is such, then, that we explain the whole in its lawfulness by a part that is itself explained by the whole that was to be explained (see pages 60–61). The only way such a procedure could be justified would be if the part were determined by the whole to get the latter "just right." In other words, if the brain were determined by the laws of nature to apprehend the latter correctly, then such laws could be used to explain its own functioning. Pavlov provides a nice example of this assumption. He argues: "As a part of nature every animal organism represents a very complicated and closed system, the internal forces of which, at every given moment, as long as it exists as such, are in equilibrium with the external forces of its environment. . . . The time will come, be it ever so distant, when mathematical analysis, based on natural science, will include in majestic formulae all these equilibrations and, finally, itself" ("Natural Science and the Brain," in *Lectures on Conditioned Reflexes*, p. 129). Thus, in including itself, science explains its own formulation of these laws of "equilibration." It takes this formulation as an event arising through the operation of the very same laws. Since these are laws of causal determination, the assumption is that the scientist has been causally determined to apprehend such laws correctly. This implies that there is some standard of epistemological correctness in material causality. Yet this, as we saw, is precisely what such causality lacks. For it, the determining factors of an event must include the material makeup of the interacting bodies. Regarded in terms of material causality, the scientist, as we noted, grasps the object, not in itself, but relative to his material makeup.

The difference between a material-causal law and a standard for correctness can be put in terms of the difference between the conditions for applicability and those for validity. The arithmetic laws embody standards of correctness. If they are valid, then, in following them, we will get our sums right. These laws can be instantiated both in men and machines. Both can "do" sums. Very different causal laws, however, are involved in their processes. In machines, the arithmetic laws can be instantiated in mechanical or electronic calculators. In one case, the laws governing the instantiation are those of the gear and lever, in the other those of electronics. Given that the laws governing the instantiation or application are different, but the laws actually instantiated are the same, the two sets of laws cannot be identical. In fact, physical, causal conditions govern the former, but not the latter. As we noted, the laws of such conditions are completely indifferent to standards of correctness. The electronic calculator obeys the same laws of solid state physics whether it adds correctly or not. The designer of the calculator uses these laws to set up the physical structure of the calculator to do sums correctly. She could, however, just as well have made use of the same laws to design a calculator that always did them incorrectly. What ultimately determines the design, then, is not the laws of the physics of the machine, but rather the laws of arithmetic, taken as standards for doing sums correctly. As we said, the difference here is ultimately one of temporality. If the law of material causality describes a line of determination stretching from the past to the present to the future, the law that expresses a standard makes an object, such as sum, appear as a not-yet, as a goal to be realized through the performance of the act through which it is grasped, such as doing and checking the sum. Here, the line of determination is from the future through the past to the present. Thus the goal of arithmetic correctness as specified by the arithmetic laws determined the designer to give the machine the structures that regulate its present activity of doing the sum.

The circularity involved in the project of modern science, the project of explaining things through material causality, arises only when we fail to grasp this. Thus we can without circularity say that our knowledge of the laws of material causality is determined in part through the laws of our thought. The circularity, we said, only arises when we interpret as material-causal laws the laws by which we know such laws. It is then that we explain them in terms of that which they themselves were supposed to explain. Breaking this circle, thus, means conceiving these laws in some other fashion. It means, in fact, recognizing them as teleological, that is, as laws for processes that are future directed. Having said this, the question of course remains. If escaping circularity requires our conceiving knowing as a teleological function, we still must ask: How are we to do this? How, in the first place, are we to conceive the condition of what we called the "standing out" of animate existence, this being its grasp of the world in terms of goals? We must in this chapter answer these questions in some detail.

§1. *Sense and Reference in Knowing.* To begin, we have to first clarify what we mean by knowing. The relation of knowledge involves something more than the mere bodily presence things have to one another. When we know something, we say it appears as an object of knowledge. *Objectum* in Latin signifies that which is placed or thrown before us. The German equivalent, *Gegenstand,* means that which "stands against" us. Both point to the fact that what we know has a specific epistemological, as opposed to bodily, presence. Present, it appears as other, as that which our knowledge is *about,* as that which stands against such knowing as a goal and as a criterion for its success. This success is measured in terms of our grasping the object's meaning.

The two basic phenomena here are sense and reference or, equivalently, meaning and intentionality. Knowing embraces the phenomenon of x meaning y, as when we ask about the meaning of a word, event, or object. It also includes the phenomenon of x, as a mental state, being *about y.* Here it is the ability of thoughts, perceptions, and so on, through their mental contents, to be about objects and events (states of affairs) in the world. As is obvious, the two are intertwined. The knowledge I have *about* some object is capable of being expressed in meaningful symbols, symbols that express the object's *sense.* Although such senses can be abstracted from individual objects, they initially arise through our perceptual contact with them. In fact, when we cannot make sense of our perceptual experiences so as to see them as perceptions of some definite object, their referent is lost to us. Once they do fit together, we say that we are experiencing an object with a definite sense. We also assert that we are not experiencing a hallucination—as well we might if, say, the series of perspectival views displaying a spatial-temporal object suddenly became jumbled in its ordering. As long as one side succeeds another in a regular ordering (an ordering, for example, that obeys the laws of perspectives), we say that we are experiencing an existent object. We continue to regard it as existent as long as we grasp it as one and the same thing showing itself in different perspectives. This very same process of grasping a one in many, however, is a "making sense" of our perceptions. Through it, we grasp the object's sense. In a successful perceptual experience, there is, then, a simultaneity of the assertions of sense and reference—that is, of the "theses" of the meaning and being of the object. We grasp the object as being there at the same time as we grasp it as having a determinable sense. Reference to the object thus seems to be an inherent feature of a perceptually embodied sense.

The notion of sense implicit in the above is that of being a one in many. As we just said, making sense of our perceptions is grasping them as perceptions of individual objects. Contrariwise, a spatial-temporal object appears as such by being apprehended as *one and the same* thing showing itself *in a multitude* of perceptions. Its presence to us then, rather than being a mere bodily presence of contact, such as that of side pressed to side, is a presence of this one-in-many. It is the presence of a perceptually embodied sense; grasping it as a one in many is encountering it as such a sense. We do this whenever we recognize an object as itself. For example, in recognizing a person, we do not have some sort of picture book in our mind which we have to go through to match our current perception with an earlier, stored perception. Such a process would take forever, and it is likely that none of our picture memories would match exactly the content of our present perception. To recognize, say, Mary as Mary, we have to grasp an underlying unity, that is, encounter her as a sense unifying our various perceptions. The essential point here is that not just species or kinds are unities in multiplicity. The same sort of universality is also to be found in the senses ascribed to individuals. For the species, the multiplicity is composed of the individuals falling under its concept. For the individual existent, it is made up of the perceptual experiences through which we grasp its unity.[1]

1. It is likely that a failure to grasp this point is what lies behind the difficulties of the *Parmenides*. What mediates between specific and numerical unity is the fact that both are unities in multiplicity. Phenomenologically speaking, the species can be regarded as the type of perceptual connection that establishes a *type* of object. The actual instance of this type is the actual object as a unity of sense. Thus, the species of spatial-temporal objects is the type

Whenever these experiences reveal an identical content, we grasp both the object and its intuitive sense. This cannot be otherwise, given that, as long as the perceptual process continues, the presence of both is the same. In such a situation, it is almost a tautology to say that the sense bears an inherent reference to the object, that is, has what some call an "intrinsic" intentionality.[2] In terms of their presence, the sense so grasped *is* the object. The sense only refers to the object as something distinct from itself when the perceptual process ceases. When we report what we have seen, the theses of sense and being become separated. The hearer grasps the sense, but cannot grasp the being (in the sense of directly confirming the perceptual object's existence). He can do this only when he experiences the perceptions that can be subsumed under the sense's range. As a one in many, the reported sense embodies the thought of a possible existence that stands as a correlate of a range of possible perceptions. In this way it does have an intentionality, a reference to the object. Yet we should be wary of conceiving this according to the pattern of image and original as if the object were the thing "in itself" independent of and distinct from its sense, the latter being its replica in ourselves. In the view we are presenting, the sense refers to the object, not directly, but through the perceptions making up its range. What underlies this reference is a much more basic form of intentionality: that between the perceptions and the underlying unity that exhibits itself through them. When we speak of intentionality as that basic feature of consciousness according to which it is "of" some object, then the intentionality in question is that between the perceptual experiences making up the field of consciousness and this unity. As we shall see, consciousness becomes such a "field" when, by virtue of its temporal structure, it retains the multiplicity of its past perceptions. In other words, composing its field are just the multiplicities of those perceptual experiences which supply the material for the unities which it grasps. It is their relation to such unities that, properly speaking, is intentional.

The intentional relation is thus inherent in that of sense. This means that when individual experiences are so connected that their succession reveals a single object, each becomes "of" this object. Having this intentional relation means no more (or less) than being part of that relation between

---

of perspectival connections that allows such objects to appear. The individual instance is an object that shows itself through such connections as one thing in a multitude of different perspectives. For an account of this solution, see James Mensch, *The Question of Being in Husserl's Logical Investigations,* pp. 182–85.

2. See, for example, R. McIntyre, "Husserl and the Representational Theory of Mind," p. 109. McIntyre, however, fundamentally misinterprets Husserl by denying the role that interpretation plays in Husserl's account of intentionality. See James Mensch, "Phenomenology and Artificial Intelligence: Husserl learns Chinese," p. 111.

multiplicity and unity which results in sense. Thus the individual experience is considered to be "of" the object insofar as it is taken as an *instance* of what the object in its content can continually exhibit. Suppose, for example, I experience a redness that I take to be "of" Mary's coat. To take it as such is to understand it as part of what the coat makes and can continue to make available to me as I regard it. My sense of the coat's being red inherently implies such availability. What underlies this availability is my grasp of the coat as a sense as well as the fact that sense, per se, specifies its range only as an indefinite multiplicity. It does not specify the exact number of its instances. Similarly, an experience's being "of" an object is its being part of that indefinite multiplicity implied by the object's presence as a sense. This indefiniteness is taken as an indefiniteness of availability, that is, of the object's capability of offering more than what we have already experienced. With this, as we have already noted, the object appears as transcendent, that is, as something which goes beyond (or exceeds) our actual grasp of it (see page 88).

§2. *Perception as Interpretation.*   The foregoing leaves us with the question: How do we grasp this unity in multiplicity? What does it mean for us to make sense of our perceptions? Since the issue concerns our actual functioning, a concrete example should prove helpful. Suppose on a walk, I notice what seems to be something sitting under a bush. Walking closer to get a better look, the pattern of shadows appears to be a cat. As I approach, its various features seem to become discernable. This pattern unfolds itself as its ear, this other as its eye, another as its mouth, the patterns unfolding together to reveal larger unities such as its face, body, and so on. As I continue to draw near, the whole continues to unfold harmoniously in the sense that the patterns continue to reveal particular features and continue to fit together to reveal these features as aspects of the animal as a whole. The nose and eyes appear in the right place, the mouth is where one would expect it to be, as are the body, the tail, and the legs. Suddenly on my approach, the finer-grained features seem to dissolve. While the head, body and legs seem to keep the proper relations, the pattern which I expect to continue to show us the eyes fails to do so. Similarly, the pattern for the mouth fails to keep pace with my expectations. On an even closer approach, the same happens for the larger elements; what I took to be the cat crouching under a bush on a sunlit field dissolves into shadows. Turning away, I say I was deceived or mistaken.

The very assertion that I was mistaken means that during the process I had something to be mistaken about. Nonverbally, I advanced a certain

thesis about what I was seeing, but the thesis, although apparently confirmed for a while, ultimately proved incorrect. The thesis was confirmed
and then disproved through what I saw. This does not mean that I con-
sciously evaluated the thesis through my perceptions. It is not as if I said,
"If this is a cat's ear, then the next perception I will have as I advance will
be the following . . ." Rather, the reverse of this occurred. I used my thesis
that I was perceiving a cat to evaluate what I saw. Thus the assertion that I
am seeing a cat there under the bush translates itself, perceptually, into a
pattern of perceptions, a pattern that I expect to experience as I approach
the animal. This expectation functions as an interpretive frame. I anticipate
that each new perception will fit into the pattern and interpret it accordingly. This moving shadow must be the tail. This other must be the ear as
it flicks back and forth. Similarly, I interpret the whole of what I see according to the pattern I expect will unfold to me the cat as a whole. As
long as the interpretation is successful, I experience the cat, I grasp it as an
object. "Success," here, of course, is a relative term. The criteria for what
constitutes a successful interpretation becomes more demanding the
closer I approach. With each step, more evidence becomes available to
confirm or deny what I expect. When the denial becomes too evident,
then my interpretation fails. With this, both my thesis and the object are
abandoned. The latter is experienced as dissolving into shadows and I admit I was mistaken.

The above illustrates that perception is interpretation in the sense that
what allows us to grasp the object as an object is not just the sensuous
contents we encounter but also the interpretation we place on them.[3] A
good way to express this is in terms of Kant's distinction between a judgment of perception and a judgment of experience (*Prolegomena,* §18).
The former is, broadly speaking, an "I see" judgment. What it affirms is
simply the content of a perceptual experience. Thus in my approach to the

---

3. Husserl advanced this position in the first edition of his *Logische Untersuchungen.*
Asserting, "perception is interpretation," he writes in explanation: "It belongs to perception
that something appears within it, but *interpretation* makes up what we term appearance—be
it correct or not, anticipatory or overdrawn. The *house* appears to me through no other way
but that I interpret in a certain fashion actually experienced contents of sensation. . . . They
are termed 'appearances' or, better, appearing contents precisely for the reason that they are
contents of perceptive interpretation" (*Logische Untersuchungen,* Hua XIX/2, 762). This latter involves taking them according to some given perceptual sense—for example, that of a
cat. As Husserl, in the second edition, writes describing how "we suppose ourselves to perceptually grasp one and the same object through the change of experiential contents," "different perceptual contents are given, but they are interpreted, apperceived 'in the same sense,'
. . . the interpretation [*Auffassung*] according to this 'sense' is a character of experience
which first constitutes 'the being of the object for me'" (ibid., Hua XIX/1, 397).

cat, my successive experiences can each be taken as contents of an "I see" judgment. As such, none of them refers beyond itself. Each simply asserts what I presently experience. When, however, I assert that such experience is an experience of an object, I move to the judgment of experience. In it, I claim that there is an object of which I am presently having experience. The shift from one judgment to the other is from the assertion, "I see," with its merely private, subjective claim, to the assertion "there is" with its objective claim. The latter asserts the existence of something transcendent, namely, an object whose availability exceeds that of the present perceptual experience. What we are asserting is that the move from the first to the second is occasioned by interpretation. To grasp an experience as pertaining to an object is to interpret it as fitting in with the pattern of experiences that would exhibit the object. Each experience is, thus, taken in the same way in the sense of pertaining to the same series or pattern of unfolding whose objective correlate is the particular object. To take it as such is not to make it a member of some picture book, a mythical album named after the object. Membership here is rather to be thought of in terms of a rule of interconnection. What we are pointing to can be illustrated by the mathematical algorithm that allows us to rotate objects on a computer screen. The algorithm does not specify every element but only the rule of transformation connecting each with the next. It is, as it were, the rule for the perspectival unfolding of the object on the screen. In the same way, the interpretation of an experience as an experience of some object occurs through the interpretation of it as falling under the rule for the object's appearing.

Such a rule can often be quite complex. The horizon or pattern of experiences that exhibit an object is, itself, articulated into subpatterns that exhibit its particular elements. Not just the cat appears perspectivally, but also every feature of it. What we have then are clusters of repeatable experiences, that is, patterns which we can run through again and again as we continue to experience and recognize the object as itself. Behind this recognition is the fact that each feature exhibits itself in a repeatable pattern, one that follows a rule and, by virtue of this, attains the status of a one in many. Similarly, the object as a whole may be regarded as a repeatable pattern of such patterns. The interpretation by which we grasp the whole requires the grasp of *its* rule, its order of appearing. Insofar as this interpretation presents it as a sense, namely, as a unity correlated to an *indefinite multiplicity* of appearances, this presence implies transcendence. The object has the sense of something transcending what we presently grasp. It appears, in other words, as an object of a judgment of experience.

§3. *Some Preliminary Points.*   In our next section, we will consider more closely the mechanics (the actual processes) involved in this view of perception as interpretation. For the present, however, a number of points can already be made. The first is that, as defined through interpretation, the intentional relation is not a material-causal one. The presence of the body that it results in is not a mere bodily presence. There is no push or pull, no physical force of contact, not even any physical "action at distance," which could serve to account for it. This is because what the interpretation grasps is not a body, but a sense. The intentional relation is that of consciousness to the latter. In other words, the epistemological as opposed to the mere bodily presence that interpretation results in is that of this one-in-many-perceptions, this perceptually embodied sense. The fact that the relation is to a sense does not mean it cannot be mistaken. As we saw, the interpretation can fail, and both it and its object—for example, the cat under the bush—can be abandoned. Our second point is that this failure should not be accounted for by some sort of replica-original schema. We do not somehow exit our consciousness to compare a replica found within it to an original out there. In the view we are presenting, the original is the perceptually embodied sense. The failure of our interpretation is the failure of it to appear. This is a failure to embody itself through our perceptions. As we saw with our example, this occurs when it no longer has sufficient sustaining material, that is, when the material no longer fits the pattern the interpretation anticipates.

This leads us to our third point, which is that interpretation is a goal-driven process. In perception, our goal is to grasp a one-in-many and, thereby, to "make sense" of what we see. We do this whenever we take a perceptual multiplicity as pointing to one and the same object. To take it as such is to attempt to interpret it according to the pattern that would yield the object. This involves not just a passive evaluation of our already acquired experience. It also implies action on our part. Thus, in seeing what seems to be a cat, I move to get a closer look. In so doing, I attempt to fill up my interpretive schema with appropriate content. Other concrete examples of what we are pointing to can be found in cases of mistaken identity and dissociation. A striking example of the former is provided by the encounter with a lifelike manikin. Regarding him across the store, I take him for a store clerk. Crossing to get some information, nothing at first strikes me about his appearance. When I glance at him, he appears as I expect. His physical person unfolds in the anticipated patterns of perspectival appearing. At a certain point, however, another layer of anticipated evidence, that of him as an animate being, begins to fail. He does not move, he does not react as I would act under similar circum-stances. I would acknowledge another person's approach. Looking up, I would meet his gaze, respond to his voice, answer his questions, and so on. But he remains in his initial posture. As a consequence, my interpreta-tive stance is disrupted. The interpretation of the figure as a physical ob-ject is confirmed, but that which overlays it, the interpretation of it as animate, fails. I experience, then, almost as a physical sensation, the col-lapse of one of my interpretations, an interpretation which guided from the start my action of approaching him. Dissociation, whether from fatigue or stress provides an extreme example of this almost physical sense of interpretative failure. Suffering from dissociation, you perceive and yet your perceptions have no referent. You cannot put them together to get a world of objects, a world somehow "out there" beyond the immediate presence of the sensations that crowd in on you. Only when the inter-pretation does succeed does the world regain its depth. Your perceptions again become *of* something beyond them. Objects then appear which ex-hibit the sense you make of the experiential flow of perceptual multi-plicities. Each object is a sign of a successful interpretation, the result be-ing that once again you *have* a world, that is, a place where you can act and be.

Our fourth point follows the fact that the same teleological relation is involved in a standard of correctness. Meeting the standard, as we said, is being determined by it as a goal. Our point is that, in perception, this standard is given by the sense I am attempting to grasp. If I am successful, it will continue to maintain itself as a perceptually embodied sense. This sense is both the goal of the perceptual process and its directing ("final") cause. It is the latter as being what I "intend" to see, that is, as an interpre-tive intention which seeks to embody itself in the perceptual flow. The contents of the flow, that is, the contents of my ongoing perceptual experi-ence, serve as material for its purpose. Their function, in other words, is the same as that of the wood for the carpenter's project. They are the means of its realization, of its embodiment. Given that such an embodi-ment results in the thing itself (in Aristotle's terms, the actual "sensible object *qua* sensible"), the embodied sense that is the goal cannot be judged against any standard but itself. It is what determines whether em-bodiment is successful, since it is what first determines what can count as material for its embodiment. The relation, then, is precisely that which we saw in the "Aristotelian paradigm" discussed in the last chapter. What de-termines the material is the goal of the process. We can, thus, assert with Aristotle that it is "thanks to the end that potentiality is possessed." We can also say this determination of the potential as potential is through the process the goal directs.

For Aristotle, space and time are part of this determination of the potential as potential. Rather than being given beforehand, they are determined by goals as the material or medium for their manifestation (see page 96). To apply this to our present concerns, we need only note that it is by virtue of a successful interpretation that we have a world. When this fails, as it can in cases of dissociation, the world loses its depth. In severe cases, all sense of space and time can be lost. Given this, the activity of interpretation cannot be thought of as dependent on this sense. It must be thought of as *prior* to any assumption that takes space and time as already given. In particular, it must be thought of as prior to any notion of receptivity that assumes such givenness. Our fifth point is that this new conception is that of embodiment. The process of seeing, understood as the activity of interpretation, is that of embodiment. It is the "enfleshment," as it were, of the successful interpretation with sensuous contents. Such a conception, of course, reverses the usual relation between intentionality and interpretation. Normally, we think of intentionality as prior to interpretation. So conceived, intentionality is taken as a relation between two present things, a subject and an object, both located in an already given space and time. In this view, the subject "interprets" the object that is present to it. The object's inherent qualities determine whether the interpretation is correct. In the view we are advancing, the object continues to serve as a standard. This, indeed, is what distinguishes its "epistemological presence" from mere bodily presence. It does so, however, as a goal that is also a standard for successful perceptual interpretation. To the point that interpretation is successful, the interpretation becomes "embodied" with the appropriate contents. The sense that it intends, i.e., the one in many which is its goal, becomes that of perceptually embodied presence, that of the object that stands against the subject as a given pole of the intentional (or subject-object) relation. We can, thus, speak of the contents of our perceptual experience as being contents *of* this appearing object. When we do, however, we have to say that their intentionality is not a cause, but rather a *result* of a successful interpretation. Here, embodiment and intentionality are thought together. The sense we grasp in perception is both the embodied result of an act of interpretation and an intentional goal or standard for this act's success. It can be both a goal and a result because the relation we are here considering is teleological. It is one where what we intend, the goal, brings itself about through such intending. In other words, interpretation sets up the object it intends.

This leads us to the last of these preliminary points. As we have stressed, when we take the laws by which we know the world as material-causal laws, our explanation of the latter becomes circular. Breaking this circle means conceiving the laws of knowing in another fashion. It means conceiving them not as laws for material-causal processes, but as teleological, as laws for goal-driven processes. The account we are giving does this on the most basic level of knowing, that of perceptual experience. It introduces into the account of perception those standards of correctness which a material-causal explanation can never provide. Here, of course, we must admit that this account's success is not yet decided. It depends upon our actually discovering how, in fact, we grasp a one in many.

Synthesis and Openness

In the previous section we spoke about interpretation as "setting up" the object it intends. Yet interpretation is an activity of consciousness, the very consciousness we have defined as an openness. The question thus naturally arises: How do we combine the concepts of interpretation and openness? Specifically, how do we think of interpretation as an openness? The openness of consciousness is, we recall, the openness of time. It follows from the consideration of time's moments as empty placeholders for possible contents. So regarded, time is open in the sense that it can take on any sort of content in any sort of structure (that is, any type of order or temporal arrangement). As a field of temporal relations, consciousness itself seems to possess this same perfect plasticity. As we quoted Sartre, rather than having laws (in the sense of necessary conditions determining its structure), consciousness is conscious of laws. This means that to explore its openness in terms of its particular interpretive structures is to explore it hypothetically. It is to see what, in each case, is required of consciousness in order for it to grasp a particular type of object. The inquiry is not into what forms it must take on (what conditions it must meet *per se,* what interpretive intentions characterize it as such), but rather into what temporal conditions have to obtain *if* it is to be conscious of some particular kind of object.

This emphasis on time must, of course, be qualified. Even though it is our openness, we should not take it as an ultimate, grounding condition. This would make time an "in itself," a fundamental basis for the real. For us, however, time is nothing of the sort. In the present context, it simply designates our receptivity or openness. Thus the form it takes is determined by what we are receptive to. It is the result of the presence of being. Different types of presence (for example, that of a moving body or that of an immobile mathematical relation) result in different types of temporality, that is, different types of receptivity. Given this, the ultimate grounding principles are not those of time. They are, rather, those of the being whose particular presence structures our openness. As in the Aristotelian paradigm, this will turn out to be a presence that is both a cause and a result of such structuring.

§1. *Conditions for Multiplicity: Kant's and Husserl's View.* The notion of perception as interpretation is based on the notion of an object's presence as a one in many. How exactly does interpretation grasp this presence? What are the conditions for it? The first and most obvious condition is the need to apprehend multiplicity as such, that is, multiplicity in the manyness of the object's distinct appearances. We have already mentioned the first requirement for this apprehension. There has to be a distinction between the constancy of the nowness in which I perceive and the fleeting nowness (the departure into pastness) of that which I perceive. Without this, there is no multiplicity of appearances. Thus, were a particular appearance to remain constantly now with the subject, it could not give way to any others. It would be the only one. Alternately, were the perceiving subject to depart into pastness with this appearance, that is, were it to be fixed in the fleeting moment in which it perceived a particular appearance, once again there would be no multiplicity. Thus, multiplicity requires departure. More precisely, it requires the fixing of appearances in the departing moments of time. Departure, here, is departure from me, that is, from the constant, ongoing nowness of my perceptual act. To translate this to the level of being is to see how the object times me. As we noted, such timing is twofold. The constant presence of the object structures my constant nowness. The fact that the object moves, that is, shifts its relation to its environment, makes my nowness stream, makes it a shifting center of *its* environment. Thus the change of the object doesn't just mean that it shows itself differently; it also means that it differentiates the times for such appearances. The same schema holds for an object that changes while remaining in place—for example, the pencil I twirl between my fingers. What times the shifting (streaming) of my now is a shifting perceptual content. It is my experiencing the changing perceptions through which the pencil continues to show itself as one and the same. That it is grasped as the same, as embodying the same perceptual sense, means that it has a constant presence, one that I register in the constancy of my now. Once again, the result is the streaming of my constant nowness. The now that frames my perception of the pencil remains even as it continually differentiates itself in its changing content.

Behind this differentiation there are actually a number of requirements. The first is that each individual appearance, once obtained, must sink back into pastness. The second is that, in this sinking back, it must itself remain unchanged. If it didn't, we would be confronted with a veritable chaos of sensations as our memories of what we have just seen continually transformed themselves—this, even as they were added to by fresh memories. Now, the fact that this does not occur is what allows us to distinguish individual experiences from the object that appears through them. The latter, as a one in many, continually shows itself in different appearances. Taken as an enduring unity, it persists (is present) through this change of appearances. The individual appearance, however, does not itself appear in different appearances in the sense of first showing us one side and then another of itself. Were it to do so, it would not be an appearance of, say, a spatial-temporal object, a part of the multiplicity correlated to its unity. It would itself be such a one in many. It would be something showing itself in different perspectives, each perspective manifesting different sensuous contents. Were individual experiences not to remain unchanged as they sink back into pastness, a regress would, thus, threaten. Experiences would show themselves through distinct content-filled experiences, each of which would show itself through similarly distinct experiences and so on indefinitely. We avoid it when we say that on some level the experience is *not* a one in many, that is, a unity of different content-filled appearances. It is simply a member of this multiplicity. As such, it does not change in time; it departs with it. In a certain sense, its limitation to a given moment means that it has "no time" to change. Bound to just one moment, it keeps its unchanging content.

To grasp an experience as departing with its content is, of course, to remember or "retain," not just this content, but also the moment to which it is bound. Fixed in time, the moment flows away with it. Thus, to grasp the departing experience *as departing*, its content must be retained unchanged and yet possess a changing temporal tag, a marker showing its increasing distance from the present of our ongoing nowness. Such retention is, of course, another condition for grasping the multiplicity. If I do not retain my perceptual experiences, if the instant after their apprehension, they were to vanish, then once again I would be limited to a single appearance, the one I am momentarily engaged in. The retention must not just include the content of the perception, but also its time. The content must be retained as that which was perceived at such and such a temporal juncture, as that which was perceived before one particular content and after another, the juncture itself being grasped as departing into pastness. If I could not do this, then I could not distinguish the content of a past perception from that of a present perceptual experience. Without a temporal tag, all my impressions would be *now*. All would blend in an immediate chaos. Once again the consequence would be the loss of the multiplicity of the extended temporal series *through which* the object appears as a one in many.

How do we retain what we have experienced? How does this retention include its temporal tagging, that is, allow us to grasp the past as past? Kant, in this context, speaks of "reproduction." He writes: "If I were to lose from my thought the preceding impressions . . . and not reproduce them when I advance to those which follow, a complete presentation [of an enduring object] would never arise" (*Kritik der reinen Vernunft,* A 102). Such a presentation requires my retaining the different impressional moments of its appearing. Thus to grasp the flight of a bird through my garden, I must keep in mind not just the present, but also my previous perceptions of the stages of the flight. For Kant, to retain is to re-produce at each moment one's previous impressions, bringing them up again and again to the present. The reproduction includes what we reproduced previously. The past impression we brought up to the momentary present through reproduction is again reproduced with the departure of this present into pastness. Husserl expresses much the same thought when he advances the notion of an increasing chain of "retentions of retentions." In his view, an impression is retained, and then this retention is itself retained and so on serially, the result being a "constant continuum of retentions such that each later point is a retention of an earlier" (*Zur Phänomenologie des inneren Zeitbewusstseins,* Hua X, 29). Now, for the process to result in a grasp of pastness, the retention must not just retain the previous retention. In Kant's language, we must not just reproduce what we previously reproduced. The retention (or reproduction) must also mark what it retains such that we do not take it as something new, i.e., confuse it with the content of the present impressional moment. The consciousness that something is not new is, of course, the consciousness that it is something past. Each retention must, then, tag as not-new or past what it retains. If the latter is itself a retention, it must do the same, and so on down the chain of retentions. The retention of each is, then, a modification that by tagging it as not new, adds a further degree of pastness to its content. If we say that the sense of pastness is that of not-newness, this sense is a relational one. It is a sense of the stretch of retentions of retentions that intervenes between the present retention and the original impression. Regarding the impression's content *through such retentions,* each of which presents itself as a not new or past moment, is grasping this content *through a stretch of past time.* Similarly, if, in retaining the impression, we also retain the pastness (or "not newness") presented by the retentions of its content, then the appearance of the retained content is also the appearance of the pastness *through which* it is given.

We would seriously misrepresent the above view—which is essentially that of Kant and Husserl—if we left the impression that it takes time as already given. Such a view would see the sole activity of the subject as "keeping up," as it were, with an objectively given, ongoing flow of moments—this by retaining them in order to prevent their vanishing or "passing away." Kant's doctrine, however, is that time is an activity *I* engage in. Time is one of the conditions I bring to experience to make it possible, that is, to make possible the synthesis of grasping the identity in multiplicity that results in the presence of an object of experience. The condition that time satisfies is, as indicated, that of allowing us to "distinguish time in the succession of impressions following one another" (*Kritik der reinen Vernunft,* A 99). It fulfills the condition for their being a multiplicity there for me by allowing the differentiation of impressions according to distinct times. Now, if temporalization is a transcendental function that I engage in, then when I reproduce an impression, I am not just preserving it from vanishing into pastness. Rather, I am producing it as a just-past impression. In other words, my re-production of it is a production (a leading forth) of it as a just-past content-filled moment. Before I engage in this activity, this past moment does not yet exist. Unless I continually engage in it, it does not sink back into pastness—that is, become distinguished from other moments by occupying a definite position in the order of departing time.

The same point holds, mutatis mutandis, for Husserl's retentional chain. The lengthening of this chain is the insertion of an impression in time. It is its constitution as an impression-filled moment in receding time. To retain a content is to "modify" it; it is to mark it as "just past." The retention of this retention continues the process with a "modification," which constitutes the further pastness of this just-past impression, and so on. The result, then, is that the impression "is fixed as the same in the changes of its temporal modalities." In other words, "it is precisely through this process [of retentional modification] that it is constituted as the same, as an identical present in the fixed form of the primal now and the just past, etc." (Ms.

C 2 1, p. 11b, 1930; see also Ms. D15, p. 1, November 1932). This "fixed form" is that of time as a continuum stretching from the present "primal now" to the remote past. Thus, the claim of the above is that the retentional process is not the retaining of an already-given moment understood as a member of this continuum. It is, rather, a process constituting this moment (this "present" in Husserl's terminology). The process, he writes, constitutes it as "an identical, immanent temporal position" in departing time (Ms. C III 3, pp. 41a–41b, March 1931).[4]

All this seems straightforward. Yet there is a certain disingenuous quality to it. This becomes apparent once we ask *why* we must engage in reproduction or retention. The first answer is that we must preserve the reproduced. For Kant, without reproduction, I would "lose from my thought the preceding impressions . . . when I advance to those which follow" (*Kritik der reinen Vernunft,* A 102). Now, if we ask what would cause such impressions to be lost, the only answer we can give is one that presupposes time as something already given, that is, as an objective flow in which something, having become present, then becomes past. Its becoming past is taken as its departure, its passing away—this, without any intervention on our part. What we do is act to preserve it, that is, overcome this passing away or loss through reproducing it. The metaphysical presuppositions of this view have already been noted (see page 73). Being is taken as presence and presence is understood as temporal presence. What does not share a now with us does not exist. Its passing away is its departure from being. It is its annihilation.[5]

The difficulty comes when we combine this view with the position that temporalization is an activity which we engage in—in Husserl's words, the position: "I am. It is from me that time is constituted" (Ms. C I, *Zur Phänomenologie der Intersubjektivität, Dritter Teil,* Hua XV, 667). If this is the case, then it is illogical to say that I must act to preserve something from time, that is, to keep it through retention or reproduction from pass-

4. This means that the welling of moments from my "living present" is, as constitutive of departing time, actually a welling up of retentions. In Husserl's words, "the functioning [of temporalization] . . . is a constant letting loose (*aus sich entlassen*) of retentions" (Ms. AV5, pp. 4–5, January 1933). Although these citations are from the late manuscripts, this doctrine actually appears as early as the lectures on inner time consciousness. Speaking of the "retentional modifications of primary contents in their now character," Husserl claims that by virtue of these modifications, "primary contents are carriers of primary interpretations, interpretations which in their flowing connectedness constitute the temporal unity of the immanent content in its sinking back into pastness" (*Zur Phänomenologie des inneren Zeitbewusstseins,* Hua X, 92, see also ibid., X, 82).

5. The dependence of being on being temporally renewed seems to be behind Descartes's proof that God must constantly act to preserve the world. See Meditations III; p. 47.

ing away. Reproduction, after all, is my action of placing it in time in the first place. Thus, on the one hand, the "loss" of an impression is presented as a result of its becoming past (its passing away). On the other hand, such becoming past does not, in this view, happen on its own. It rather occurs through *my reproducing* the impression. From this perspective, however, its becoming past is *my preserving* it, not my losing it. With this, we have the disingenuousness we mentioned: the motive for positing reproduction cannot be to save the impression from vanishing into pastness. This would involve an assumption about time that neither Kant nor Husserl wish to make. It would imply that time is an objective reality whose processes arise without subjective action. The motive for positing reproduction is, rather, to position the subject as the origin of time. It is to see it as that which produces time's moments by reproducing (or retaining) the impression—this, through repeated acts of reproduction (or the retentional modification) of what has already been reproduced (or retained).

§2. *Conditions for Multiplicity: The Reversal.*   All of this, of course, still leaves us with the question of the origin of pastness. How do we apprehend a past impression as past, thereby distinguishing it from the present impressional moment? How do we get a multiplicity of impressions, each with its distinct time, so that when we do grasp a one-in-many, we have the sense of grasping what endures *through* such moments, the object being apprehended as *persisting through* a temporally extended perceptual experience. The situation we have so far considered can be analyzed into two related possibilities. We can see time as an independent reality in the sense that its advance occurs automatically, requiring nothing but itself for its equitable flow. This, we may note, is Cartesian or Newtonian time. Combined with the notion of being as temporal presence, it gives us the idea of temporal departure as a kind of "nihilation." What is now vanishes with the next now, since with it, it becomes part of the past, which no longer exists. To save it, I must, then, keep it present. This means I must retain or reproduce it. Under the assumption that being is temporal presence, the temptation grows to see such reproduction as production—that is, as the actual creation of the past moment as past. This is because the assumption makes us say that the moment exists nowhere else except as the object of this act. Only as such is it *present;* but then only as such does it *exist.* With this, we have the second possibility, which is to consider time as my product. Temporalization is my activity (through reproduction or retentional modification) of overcoming the nihilation of temporal departure. So defined, this second possibility contains an obvious contradiction. Given that I am the origin of time, it is illogical to assert that I need to *act* to save things from time. Quite the contrary, my inaction, which would stop time, would do this quite well.

The above, however, does not exhaust the possibilities. There is yet a third one, which grows out of the reversal. In this, we assert that being, through me, is the origin of time's flow. We say "through me," since what I contribute is my receptivity—the very receptivity which is time abstractly considered. To remain with Husserl's talk of "impressions," we can say that what I receive is not just an impression, not just some particular content. It is also the *presence* of this (strictly speaking, the presence of the being that is acting to "impress" itself on me). Now if I give up the notion of time as some automatic, independently functioning reality, then I need not say that what I receive automatically vanishes—that is, automatically departs into the nonbeing of pastness. The dependence of time on being implies, rather, that the received remains now. Without some change in being, some change that would be registered as a change in presence, there is no time as yet for it to pass away. Thus in the absence of any change in the entity, it remains "now," that is, it remains a "new" impression. First with the change in the entity do we have a change in its presence—that is, a new impression with a new now. This makes what we have already received not-new. The new now makes it a previous now. It, thus, becomes past, but does not for that reason "pass away." We only need assert this if we assume that being is the same as temporal presence—that is, nowness. If we do, then what is not now is not being. It does not exist. In the alternative we are suggesting, time (qua nowness) does not determine being, but rather the reverse. This means that as long as the being whose presence it registers maintains it, the not-now continues. The shift in the entity's presence, thus, does not obliterate what was the present impressional moment, it only frames it with a new presence. In Husserl's terminology, this framing can be considered to be a retentional modification, one that brackets this impressional moment, marking it as past. A further change in the entity results in a further modification, a further framing, with the result that this moment is experienced as sinking further into pastness. Such sinking, however, is not departure into some realm of nonbeing, but rather signifies the fact that this moment shows itself through these modifications. It is present, but present as that which has been framed by a new present and then, with a further present, framed again. The framing does not change its content, but only its temporal referent. What "tags" it as not now is just the frame given by the presence that is the next now.

By virtue of this framing, we have the special quality that characterizes the momentary experience. Since framing leaves its content unchanged, the experience does not show itself perspectively. Thus, rather than offering us anything new, it departs unchanged into increasing degrees of pastness. Such departure is, as we said, what gives us the original transcendence of the intentional relation. Now, the conditions for this departure may seem quite complex in their verbal expression. Mathematically, however, the algorithm is simplicity itself. It can be expressed in a series of parentheses, each further set representing a framing of a later set. Thus, in the series, i, (i), ((i)) . . . , each successive member can be taken as a framing of its predecessor. What allows us to do this is the operational value we give to the parentheses. This demands that we proceed through the parentheses, going from the outer to the inner, for all operations having to do with "i," the original impression. In this way we take account of the fact that in our actual perceptual syntheses, our access to past impressional moments is through the moments that frame them.[6] We will have

6. In LISP a very simple way of expressing retentional framing would be: (defun retention (x impression) (cond ((= x 0) impression) (T (retention (- x 1) (list impression))))), where "x" stands for the number of retentions, and "impression" stands for the original impression. Letting these equal "3" and "i" respectively, (retention 3 'i) yields (((i))). This signifies that "i"—the impression—has sunk back to a retention of a retention of a retention of "i." The function is recursive, i.e., definable in terms of itself. This implies that all the functions governing the temporality of consciousness, insofar as this is based on retentional framing, are similarly recursive. As such, we can use recursive functions to model them. Suppose, for example, that we hear part of a scale consisting of the notes, A B C D E. The departure into pastness of these notes into x degrees of pastness can be modeled by the following LISP function, which includes the above:

(defun phrase-retention (phrase initial-element x)
(cond ((equal nil (cdr phrase)) (retention (- x 1) initial-element))
      (T (phrase-retention (cdr phrase) (cons (cadr phrase)
      (list initial-element)) (- x 1))))).

Its arguments are: "phrase" (for example, A B C D E), a given "initial element" (A), and "x," which signifies the number of retentions. If we let x = 10, (phrase-retention '(A B C D E) '(A) 10) yields ((((((E (D (C (B (A))))))))))). Of the ten retentions, five are used to retain the phrase and result in (E (D (C (B (A))))). Five more occasion the sinking down of the phrase as a whole five further degrees of pastness. This symbolizes that a temporal remove occasioned by five retentions separates the phrase from the present act of perceiving. A corresponding recursive function for interpreting a phrase to see how far back its initial element has sunk into pastness is:

(defun phrase-time-elapsed (phrase)
  (cond ((null phrase) 1)
    ((atom phrase) 0)
    (t (max (+ (phrase-time-elapsed (car phrase)) 1)
    (phrase-time-elapsed (cdr phrase)))))).

Applied to the retained phrase, ((((((E (D (C (B (A))))))))))), for example, it would yield 10. Similar functions can be written for identifying patterns (repeating sequences) in the retained thus allowing us to distinguish changing objects from their backgrounds.

more to say on this matter when we discuss the application of these processes to machines. Here, we will only note that what triggers the action of this framing should be the entity itself. In the absence of any motion on its part, no action on the computer's side is called for. Only when it changes its presence is its previous presence to be framed or "tagged" as past.

The proper understanding of the foregoing depends on an important distinction. The grasp of the past brought about by such framing is what we may call "short-term memory." It is the kind of holding in the mind by which we grasp a snatch of movement. It is, for example, the way we grasp as a temporal sequence the flight of a bird across the garden. Long-term memory is different from this. It is not an original apprehension but rather an imaging of such. It transforms the result of short-term memory into something that can be accessed (or "reproduced") again and again. What is reproduced represents time, but is not itself temporal. It does not, of itself, declare its position in the temporal order. Thus, we can often remember an event without remembering just when it occurred. To discover this, we usually invoke the idea of causality, saying, "This must have first happened and then, as a consequence, that." Here, the dependence of the remembered is obviously on the mind (biologically, probably on the laying down of the memory as a chemical sequence). Reason, employing the ideas of cause and effect, connects these long-term memories to form some coherent picture of the past. Short-term memory, by contrast, is not a reproduction, but rather an original grasp. What is grasped is time itself. It is that which can be ordered into the "before" and "after." What determines it is not the grasp, not the mind considered as an actor engaged in "acts." It is the being whose presence time exhibits in its various moments.

This is the very being that maintains the past impression by framing it anew in a new present. As long as this being exists, the impression remains framed by its presence. Each shift in this presence changes the frame, changing its temporal referent. What appears in the new frame is either new—the new impression which is the occasion of the new presence—or else it is not new. This not-newness is a being *already given,* which, psychologically, we grasp as *pastness.* The repeated presentation of a content as not new or already given thus yields the sense of it as increasing its "departure" into pastness with each frame. This, sense, however, should not be thought of as something already given and preserved. It has, rather, a precarious existence. The sense of pastness, which is required for the grasp of an extended event, exists in immediate dependence on the being whose presence frames it. If long-term memory does not set to work to transform it into a form that can be iteratively reproduced, it vanishes along with this event. To take our example, the immediate sense of the flight of the bird through the garden exists only as long as the bird's presence maintains it. The bird's absence is its absence. Through long-term memory, I grasp not it itself, but rather an image, a reproduction that I can call up at will again and again. This reproducibility is, we may note, a sign that what is reproduced is not really temporal, not really fixed in the order of before and after.

§3. *Grasping the Unity in Multiplicity.*   Once we do grasp a multitude of temporally disparate contents, we have the material for temporal synthesis, but not the synthesis itself. The latter, as directed to a perceptual sense, is a grasp of a unity in this multiplicity. It is in terms of this grasp that we can first speak of knowing as a teleological process. Teleology appears on two levels: that of interpretation and that of its underlying temporality. Having considered the former, we now must turn our attention to the second, more fundamental level.

As with so many other things involving temporality, Kant was the first to describe the conditions for synthesis. He observes that, enduring through change, the object is apprehended as the same in a number of different appearances. This apprehension is, according to Kant, the result of a "synthesis of recognition in a concept" (*Kritik der reinen Vernunft,* A 103). Given that a concept is a one in many, our representations, to relate to an object, "must necessarily agree with one another, that is, must possess that unity which constitutes the concept of an object" (A 104–5). For Husserl, this means that the recognition of the object requires the grasp of the elements of this agreement. The object is intentionally present as a perceptual sense, as a one in many. The grasp of its content thus depends on the recognition of identical elements within the multitude of our distinct impressions.

Such recognition is based on two different factors. The first springs from the nature of our experiences themselves. As we said, they do not change in time; they depart with it. This means they cannot show themselves perspectivally and, hence, cannot be categorized as real, spatial-temporal objects. Given this, their unification should not be thought of on the model of some biological (real, causal) process involving distinct realities. Here, the elements to be manipulated exist on the level of items of information. Their processing is a matter of an algorithm (as instantiated, for example, in a computer), rather than a material sequence specific to some special type of matter (such as that of the brain).[7] It is because of this that the

---

7. John Searle's argument against the possibility of artificial intelligence is based in part on a denial of this fact. For Searle, consciousness with its mental states is a biological product. In his words, "Mental states are as real as any other biological phenomena. They are both caused by and realized in the brain" ("Minds, Brains, and Programs," p. 455). The same holds

result of the process is not some heap of disparate unities, but rather a new item of information—the sense taken as a "unity of coincidence." The second factor is simply the process of unification itself, something which happens by virtue of the co-presence of the experiences in our minds. Husserl describes its result as "a certain relatedness [*Aufeinander-bezogenheit*] which . . . prior to all 'comparison' and 'thinking' stands as a presupposition for the intuitions of likeness and difference" (*Zur Phä-nomenologie des inneren Zeitbewusstseins,* Hua X, 44). In the C manu-scripts, he speaks of "a continuous merging" (*Verschmelzung*) of like con-tents. By virtue of it, the merged qualities "stand out." They reinforce one another and, hence, distinguish themselves from the heterogeneous quali-ties whose union does not result in their merging.[8] The result of this pro-cess is a kind of overlay of simultaneity on succession. The merged experi-ences retain their successive temporal referents. Each, however, in its content, is merged with others with the same content. The result, then, is the object that presents itself as *simultaneously* possessing all of the fea-tures we *successively* experience. With this, it shows itself as other than the experience, as something transcending the latter's momentary pres-ence. This follows, since according to the above, an experience becomes an experience *of* a particular object by virtue of the merging of its con-tent. It does not, however, become this object inasmuch as it keeps its distinct temporal tag. The tag, then, preserves the "manyness" of the ob-ject's appearing. Distinct temporal tags give us the multiplicity in which the object appears as one and the same thing.

Three points follow from the foregoing. The first is that the intentional

---

for the intentionality of such states. "Intrinsic intentionality," he asserts, "is a biological phe-nomenon, caused by brain processes and realized in the structure of the brain" ("Reply to Jacquette," p. 704). Given that mental processes are causally determined—in Searle's words, that "the brain operates causally both at the level of the neurons and at the level of the mental states"—such processes can only be simulated by a computer ("Minds, Brains, and Programs," p. 455). Thus the computer simulation of the digestive system does not itself digest anything. Similarly, simulating the oxidation of fuels in an automobile engine does not itself power an auto. Since consciousness is also physically caused, Searle concludes: "The computational model of mental processes is no more real than the computational model of any other natural phenomenon" ("Is the Brain's Mind a Computer Program?", p. 29). As we said, all this follows only if the experiences to be processed are material realities subject to causal sequences. Searle's error is, then, an ontological category mistake.

8. Ms. C 15, pp. 2a–4a; Ms. C 13 1, pp. 7aff. Richard Lind seems to come close to Husserl's position with his analysis of "focal attention"—in particular, its two opposing ten-dencies to fasten on what contrasts with the rest of the field and to "discriminate similar elements" ("The Priority of Attention: Intentionality for Automata," p. 610). Unfortunately, he does not see the role that retention plays in the process. He simply confines himself to the mention of a certain "focal inertia."

relation, the relation of an experience being "of" some object involves
something more than its being a member of a pattern of contents. Such
patterns are recognized through their recurring. In this recurring, where
we constantly encounter the same contents, a deeper level of intentionality occurs. It exists as the one in many relation involving time and
specific contents. The continuous merging that grounds it also helps establish the inherent relation between intentionality and meaning. The merging makes our experiences (or "impressions") relate to the object, while
allowing the object to present itself, in each of its features, as a sense. Our
second point follows from the fact that the presentation of the object, in
each of its features, as a sense is through an interpretation that takes it as
simultaneously possessing what we successively experience. As such, the
interpretation implies intentionality. It carries with it the thought of the
distinction between the simultaneous possession of content and successive
appearing. Insofar as this distinction gives us our sense of the object's transcendence—of its being, with its specific features, out there, of its possessing all at once the features it shows us perspectivally—this too is implicit
in the intention. The object, we have stressed, embodies itself through the
intention, the intention seeking out, as it were, appropriate contents. Thus,
our third point is that, paradoxical as it might seem, the notion of perception as embodiment comprehends that of the object's being out there.
Aristotle's intuition thus continues to hold. The subject is a kind of place
of places. In fact, it is a kind of openness that includes its own being placed
in the world. Grasping through its intentions the senses of objects transcending itself, it also contains the possibility of intending (and, hence,
locating) itself in relation to what transcends it. Related to them, it is in
the world they define.

To go beyond this, we have to ask for the conditions of merging. We
must ask, what is required for it actually to occur? Such merging could not
occur if experiences were independent, self-sufficient units. The co-presence of such units would, as we said, result in a heap, a collection rather
than a new unity. The temporal conditions for this may be expressed in
terms of the interdependence of moments. Although each moment has its
time, its temporal referent, it has this in the same way that a point has its
position along a line. Time, like the line, is continuous. Its moments, like
the points on the line, are not independent units which sum up to produce
some whole. It is because of this that we experience time as flowing rather
than as proceeding atomistically. The flow points to time's continuity, and
this, in turn, points to the fact that time cannot be divided into independent segments or elements. Now, if we ask for the conditions for this continuity, the first arises from time's openness. The continuity, in the first

instance, is simply a function of its inherent lack of content, a lack that allows it to have a relation to every possible content. By virtue of this, it is "open" in the sense that it can contain any content without altering it. Here, of course, it is slightly misleading to speak of time's moments as "empty containers" of possible contents. They are, in a sense, containers without walls. The emptiness means that we cannot, in fact, think of them as discrete units. Considered in themselves, their "what they are"—or rather their lack of any inherent "what"—is always the same. This is why they form, not a collection, but rather a continuum. Like points, they lack the boundaries, the "walls" as it were, to be considered distinct units. What distinguishes them as they become now can only be what they "contain," that is, their contents. To the point that such contents are the same, merging occurs.

To inquire into the condition of this openness, itself, is to pass beyond time. It is, in fact, to turn our attention to the being whose presence grounds the experienced temporal flow. On this level, the openness of time, which is a function of its inherent lack of content, results from the fact that presence, as presence, is not some content. If presence were equated to some specific content, then only that content could be present. Rather than being any content, the presence we experience is, to speak tautologically, just this content's presence. It adds nothing specific to it except the relation it signifies. The relation is that of the nowness whose inherent lack of content mirrors this quality of being qua presence (the quality of its not being limited to some specific content).[9] Once we grant this, we can say that the continuity of time in its now-points results from the continuity of the apprehended being's presence. The moment exhibits this continuity in its openness, which is also its dependence on or continuity with the other exhibitions of this presence. The best way to put this is in terms of Aristotle's example of a moving body. As we said, the continuous presence of this body results in the continuous presence of the now, while its shift vis-à-vis its environment results in the shift of this now. What we have, then, is simply a modification of its continual presence. Moving, the body assumes different locations; and our registering of this gives us the differentiation of presence which results in its pluralization into different moments. Such moments, however, are modifications of one and the same thing. As such, they cannot be independent. Were they independent, the body would not be the same. The independence of the distinct moments of its presence would be the dispersal of its being into nonrelated

9. Behind this quality is the medieval distinction between existence and essence. For an account of how this distinction still plays a role in Husserl's phenomenology, see James Mensch, "Existence and Essence in Thomas and Husserl," pp. 62–92.

units. To turn this about, its remaining the same is *what makes such moments dependent and, hence, grounds the phenomenon of merging.*

Once we trace the dependence of the moments to the unity of the being that appears through them, the teleology of the perceptual process becomes apparent. Teleology appears in the temporality of the process. The object that is the temporal result of this process is also its cause. It brings about its presence by determining the process (that of merging), which results in its enduring presence. Thus in its actuality as an enduring object, it is both a goal and a cause of its presence. To see this, we must first note the dual character of the interdependence of the moments that exhibit an entity. Each, being nothing for itself, is immediately dependent on those which surround it. These, in turn, are dependent on their surrounding moments. Thus the dependence passes serially through each member of the stretch with the result that each member exhibits a second dependence. Immediately dependent on those which surround it, it is mediately dependent on the stretch as a whole. Given that each moment is incapable of existing by itself—that is, of exhibiting the independent being that entities (or unities in multiplicities) have—each may be considered as grounded by the whole in which it finds itself. The whole, however, is brought into being by such content-filled moments. The sensible object *qua* sensible exists in and through them since it is progressively realized through their merging. The moments, then, are actually dependent on that which they themselves realize. The latter, as grounding the moments in their dependence grounds the merging that results in its own realization as an actual sensible object. Its presence can thus be thought of as both a goal of their merging and as a cause of the same. As such, its action is that of a final cause of a teleological process.

To complete this picture, two further items should be mentioned. The first is that the presence we are speaking of is that which is realized by short-term memory. As we said, this presence does not preserve itself beyond the actual exhibition of the entity. Thus the interdependence of moments does not as such imply the unending continuance of time. Such an inference is an example of a misplaced concreteness that takes time as a kind of thing in itself. Only as such will its existence as a part imply its existence as an unending whole, one with no first or last moment.[10] For us,

10. For Husserl, for example, one of the "a priori laws of time" is that "an earlier and later time pertains to every time" (*Zur Phänomenologie des inneren Zeitbewusstseins*, Hua X, 10). This follows, since no portion of time, qua dependent, can be without an earlier and a later time. In the lectures on internal time consciousness, he uses this to argue for the unending quality of the retentional consciousness. Referring to his time diagram, he writes: "The

the last moment of the entity's exhibition signifies the end of the stretch. Unable to anchor itself in a further moment, the chain of dependent moments can no longer maintain itself. This means that unless it is transformed into a recoverable unit by long-term memory, the last moment is the chain's irretrievable loss. To assert otherwise is to claim that the sensible object as actually sensed could exist apart from the process of its perception. This leads us to our second item. We said above that the now, in becoming past, does not pass away. As long as the being whose presence it registers maintains it, the not-now, we asserted, continues. On one level, this presence is that of the being whose motion we register as time, specifically the time of an appearing, enduring object. It is this being which provides us, in its shifting presence, with ever new moments for the chain of dependencies. Teleologically considered, however, what maintains the not-now is not the moving entity, but rather its actualization as the appearing object. The moving entity provides the material for the realization of this goal. It is its shifting presence that supplies the content-filled, interdependent moments whose merging results in the appearing object. The latter, however, is the mediate object of the dependence of each moment. As we said, each moment, grounded as dependent, cannot be by itself. That it is, demands that its neighbors be. Thus, the next now—that is, the next presence of the moving entity—does not obliterate the earlier, but rather, as we said "frames" it. This framing is a linking on to it as a support (as an immediate ground) for its own being. The result is that the presence of the moving entity as a now and the framing or retention of the just-past now (the just-past presence of the body) are one and the same. The now that is the momentary presence of the body frames—that is, retains—the just-past now, since in its dependence it demands that the latter also be present. With each shift in the presence of the being there is a new now. Each

---

diagram does not take into account any limitation of the temporal field. It does not suppose an end to the retentions and ideally a consciousness is possible in which everything remains retentionally preserved" (X, 31). In the *Ideen,* the same notion of the interdependence of the moments of time translates it into the assertion that "*no concrete experience* can count *as fully independent.* Each, in its connection, 'stands in need of completion'" (*Ideen I,* §83; Hua III/1,186). Since the dependence is simply that of one content-filled moment on another (and not on the being underlying these), it cannot have an end. Thus we also have the assertion: that every experience, by virtue of its duration, necessarily "takes its position in an unending continuum of durations—a *filled* continuum. It necessarily has an all-sided, infinite, filled horizon of time. This also signifies that it belongs to an infinite '*stream of experience.*'" The individual experience, in having its finite duration, can begin and end, "but the stream of experiences can neither begin nor end" (*Ibid.,* §81; III/1, 182). In our view, however, it ends when the being supporting it is no longer present.

new now requires the presence of the previous now. This happens iteratively with the result that all such presences are held fast in their interdependence, the very interdependence that has as its goal the manifestation
of the moving entity in its own unity. It is only when the process runs out
of material, when the last presence fails to find an anchor in the next, that
the whole which maintained them all vanishes and with it they themselves.
This does not mean that they vanished into some realm of pastness taken
as a place of nonbeing. The vanishing here is of time itself once it loses its
support in the moving body or, teleologically expressed, loses its support
in the enduring, sensibly present object that is the manifestation of this
body—that is, is its reality qua sensible.

§4. *The Mechanical Analogue: Pattern Recognition.* For many readers,
the last few sections may have seemed complex. Some may even regard
them as too concerned with purely speculative matters. The easiest way to
combat this impression is to apply their results to a practical question: that
of pattern recognition in the machine processing of data. This will not just
allow us to show how the teleology we described can be instantiated in a
mechanical process, it will also make our conclusions regarding it easier to
grasp.

There are, to begin with, three major difficulties that confront a machine
when it attempts to grasp a pattern. The first is that of attention focusing.
How do you get the machine to attend and yet be open to something new?
If we divide the visual field into an attended and nonattended part, the
latter is precluded from influencing the attended set of data except at
some mechanically set level. How, then, do we introduce flexibility into
attention?[11] Once we do attend to a part of the visual field, we face the
difficulty of discriminating the object from its background. As Pylyshyn,
the cognitive scientist, writes: if we just use "contrast gradients, light or
dark regions, etc.," then "the lines defined in this manner do not correspond to figure boundaries." Yet if we turn to the figure boundaries of an
actual perception and attempt to capture them through such gradients,
such boundaries "more often than not do not produce lines."[12] Sentient
animals have, of course, already learned to see. They have a large store of
residual knowledge that helps them pick out objects against their backgrounds. We could add such knowledge to a machine in the form of stored
patterns and elements of shapes, but the difficulty of using it effectively

11. See Z. W. Pylyshyn, "Minds, Machines and Phenomenology: Some Reflections on
Dreyfus' 'What Computers Can't Do,'" p. 72.
12. *Ibid.,* p. 73.

would still remain. Blind searches and process by elimination are too cumbersome. What we need, in Pylyshyn's words, are systems "designed to facilitate the use of all available knowledge in working towards their goal—including knowledge gained from the analysis of interim failures."[13] The point is to produce systems that "zero in" on their goals.

Our approach to these problems starts from the premise that pattern recognition cannot be static if it results from synthesis. The synthesis that grasps a one in many is temporal. This means that it grasps the features of the object, not in themselves, but rather *through their recurrence*. We can put this in terms of the position that perception is interpretation. Such interpretation always implies anticipation. When, for example, I interpret the shadows I perceive in the bushes as a cat, I anticipate that further perceptions will confirm this interpretation. This means that, rather than attempting at once to distinguish a figure through contrast gradients in my present perception, I move to get a better look. If it is a cat, then a certain pattern of perceptions will unfold itself over time. The recurrent elements of this perception will, I anticipate, become for me the features of the object. A commonsense interpretation of this is that I always take my perceptions as determined by some object "out there." As we said, I take this object as possessing all at once the features I successively experience. The temporal basis for this is the merging we described above. The teleology inherent in this merging shows itself on the level of my interpretative acts. Here, the whole I am attempting to grasp—that is, the whole that in anticipation, stands as the *telos* or goal of my perceiving—determines the interpretation I place upon my individual perceptions. This shadow is seen as part of the cat's ear. Another is his eye, and so forth. If my interpretations are correct, then the data should form part of an emerging pattern that exhibits these features.

For a machine to imitate this behavior, it must, first of all, process its data according to a series of expanding temporal wholes. When there is something going on, that is, when it registers a change, the brain scans its data for processing every few seconds, but there is no need to repeat the human interval. We could, for example, program the machine to scan its data for processing every second. The first scan for an emerging pattern would then cover the one-second whole of $w1$, the second would cover the whole, $w2(w1)$, for an evaluation of the data of the past two seconds, and the third would examine the three seconds of data accumulated in the whole, $w3(w2(w1))$. The fact, as indicated by the parentheses, that these

13. *Ibid.,* p. 70.

are wholes within wholes points to the temporal tagging (or "framing") of the data of each sweep. This is required if the machine is to grasp a pattern that involves the recurrence of data in the fixed relations of before and after that characterize the perspectival series.

The strategy, then, for distinguishing an object from its background is to turn this into a temporal process, one that imitates our activity of moving to get a better look. We can duplicate this by making the machine attentive, not just to contrast gradients, but to their relative rates of change. The same general strategy can be applied to the problem of attention, that is, of making it flexible. The key here is to note that interpretation is not just anticipation. It is also discrimination. As the machine scans its data, any emergent patterns could be given a reinforcement index number. As the patterns repeat, the numbers would be increased. At any given time, they could be read out as the strength of the machine's objectifying interpretations of what it is seeing. They could also be seen as a discriminatory factor. According to its strength, the machine could be instructed to discriminate against (or set aside) a certain amount of the inharmonious data it is receiving—that is, the data that does not fit into the patterns it has thus far found. This is, in fact, what we do when we perceive. Generally, we only process the information we anticipate we will receive. Within certain limits, the rest is not attended to. To build this flexible focus into the machine, we could have each whole in which an emergent pattern has established itself throw an anticipatory shadow equal to its length. Thus the whole, $w3(w2(w1))$, which repeated the same pattern, would establish a discriminating tendency equal to its length. During this time, the data that did not fit in would, according to the strength of the factor, be stored but not processed.

With our limited capacities, we would suffer breakdown if we had to process everything we received. The same holds for any reasonably finite machine. Giving it the ability to discriminate or focus its attention avoids this. It also, however, makes it capable of mistakes. We are often mistaken in our perceptual interpretations. What we took to be a cat dissolves into a collection of shadows when we get a better look. Our capacity for mistakes is, we can say, a function of the teleology that appears on the level of the interpretative act. The teleology is such that what I anticipate I will perceive determines my present interpretation of what I have already experienced. The latter appears as material for my present interpretation, an interpretation that is itself determined by an anticipated future. To take our example, it is because I anticipate that I will see this pattern of shadows as a cat, that I take what I have experienced and interpret it accordingly. There is, then, the line of determination proceeding from the future to the past, and from thence to the present, which is characteristic of teleology. Now because our anticipations can turn out to be ill founded, the interpretations based on them may turn out to be wrong. We are mistaken, but on the other hand, we are also capable of realizing and rectifying our mistakes. This happens when our discrimination factor starts making us set aside more and more of what we receive as the latter increasingly fails to fit into an anticipated pattern. At a certain point, we snap back and start increasing the amount of data we attend to and process—this, until a new pattern is established.

To give the machine the same flexibility of focus, its discriminatory factor must vary according as the sequence, w1, w2(w1), w3(w2(w1)) . . . , confirms or fails to confirm a pattern. Thus when a pattern stops being reinforced through repetition, the discrimination factor should progressively decrease. Correspondingly, the machine's acceptance of new data for processing should increase until a new pattern (a new interpretation) is established. With this, we have an answer to the difficulty of getting the machine to attend and yet be open to the new. When a changing context disrupts the patterns it has established, it automatically opens up. Similarly, when a pattern begins to emerge, it "zeros in" on it.

To complete this sketch, we must take note of a third possibility. This is when motion stops entirely within the machine's field of vision. It would be a misunderstanding of the foregoing to state that the presence of a static object would result in an increase in the reinforcement index, this because, as the machine scans its data, the same items are received again and again. The scan is not for individual items, but rather for patterns of items that are seen to repeat. It is their presence, rather than single contents, which points to the object as a unity in a *multiplicity*. Here, we have to admit that what may lead to this misunderstanding is our talk of the machine scanning its data. To be true to our fundamental insight— which is that the object, through its motion, times the mind—the object itself should trigger the scan. Only if something changes does the mind register this change as a new present framing the old.[14] For a machine, the analogue would be that the shift from i to (i) would occur only if something new was added. Only if we went from i1 to i2 (two successive impressions distinguished by their content), would we have i2(i1), that is, the second present framing the first.

---

14. Normally, such changes for us include the sense of our own body functions. Such a sense gives us what can be called an "internal clock."

In an actual visual field, there are a number of objects, some of which change while others (in the absence of our own motion) remain static. If one changes, it tends to catch our attention—this, even though it might be on the periphery of our vision. As part of a strategy of introducing a flexible focus in the machine, an analogue to this should be included in our processing scheme. Let us say that a scan of the machine's data is triggered by a change in one object. The scan reveals that the data from the other objects is unchanged. The first object's reinforcement index should have the possibility of being altered, while that of the other static objects should remain the same. This, of course, presupposes the machine's identifying a change in its sensory field as a change pertaining to an object. To do this it must locate this change in a one-in-many, that is, in the object taken as an objectively present sense. For this to be possible, the object would have to define itself in terms of a series of changes in its qualities. Thus, what would be identified as pertaining to an object would be that part of the sensory field which took part in its motion. What would count as such motion would be those changes which would fit into an algorithm for spatial-temporal or perspectival unfolding. These algorithms, as noted, are the same type as those already employed by processors to rotate or otherwise spatially manipulate figures. What we are suggesting is the use of these to process (rather than to manipulate) data. A computer's analogue to the process of something catching our attention would, then, be its triggering the scanning of its data and the processing of it with the goal of identifying the changes it observes in terms of an algorithm of perspectival unfolding.

We seem to have the ability to simultaneously attend to a number of items. We can register their changes and interpret them as changes of different objects. We can also integrate what we thereby grasp in an overarching interpretation, one directed to the state of affairs as a whole. Husserl, we may note, describes such grasp as "polythetic," that is, as built up from a number of syntheses (*Ideen I,* §131; Hua III/1, 303–4). Such syntheses go on in parallel. It is because of this that the brain has been called "a massively parallel processor." Whether or not it actually is, to replicate this ability in a machine, it is probably necessary to treat it as such. This means that when something in the field is experienced as changing, it can be handed on to one of many parallel processors to search for repeatable underlying patterns. Each local area in the field would then be processed in parallel with other areas that exhibit changes. If nothing in the area has changed, then no attending (processing time) is expended on it. Such areas would, of course, themselves be flexibly defined. Rather than being fixed, they would be continually redetermined by the activity experienced. Finally, we may note that given that there are various levels of synthesis, it is probably necessary, as P. M. and P. S. Churchland suggest, to give the machine the architecture of a neural network.[15] In this, different levels of the nodes of the network would correspond to different levels of synthesis, with each node on the lowest level acting recursively to process a particular feature.

§5. *The Dialectic of the Self.* Standing back from the details of the foregoing, we may ask: What is the picture of the soul or self that emerges here? One conclusion is that the perceiving self is not a sheer openness. Rather than remaining a complete "tabula rasa," it manifests an openness to patterns that is also an openness to teleological action. Two phenomena characterize it. On the one hand, we have the search for a pattern understood as a recurring sequence of impressional contents—for example, the perspectival sequence of contents that arise when one twirls a pencil. Depending on the level of discrimination (fine, not so fine, and so on), such patterns may be established on different levels of detail. On the other hand, once we do, on some level, grasp a pattern, there is the attempt to use it as an interpretative filter. Functioning as the "discrimination factor" discussed earlier, the pattern becomes a kind of teleological frame we use to interpret the data.

The result of these two characteristics involves the perceiving self in a kind of hermeneutic circle. The contents it experiences can appear as the contents of an object only by being placed in an interpretative schema. On some level of discrimination (which must itself be flexible), they have to be seen as part of a recurring sequence of contents. This sequence or pattern, however, must be established *through the experienced contents themselves.* The circle, then, is such that the pattern establishes what can count as an objective content, while the latter determines the sequence of the pattern. Thus, the interpretive schema determines the contents, which determine the schema. A good way to express the resulting codetermination is in terms of a dialectic of intention and fulfillment. The dialectic, we can say, is such that not every attempt at pattern recognition is successful. The intentions of the self that seek such patterns (the pattern, for example, of a cat crouching under a bush) are not always fulfilled. The senses they intend are not always embodied by appropriate contents. This means that although every sense of the object (every feature that shows itself in a

15. P. M. Churchland and P. S. Churchland, "Could a Machine Think?" pp. 35–36.

repeating multiplicity of contents) is a sense intended by consciousness, consciousness in its intending the object cannot impose every pattern on what it takes as its contents. In other words, it cannot in its act of interpretation inform the object with every possible sense. The codetermination, then, is such that the self's interpretative intentions inform the object's intuitive presence (making it the presence of some specific object) *only to the point that* the contents which constitute such presence fulfill or embody these intentions.

If an openness to patterns is what characterizes the perceiving self, this dialectic is what first makes such openness possible. Thus it is precisely because not every intention is fulfilled that the perceiving self is not a sheer openness—an openness to some unformed "prime matter" or to some completely undifferentiated "transcendent affection" in the Kantian sense—but is rather an openness to patterns. Concretely, this means that such openness manifests the process of intentions continually arising (on the basis of what seems to be a repetition of a sequence) and continually seeking (in the sense of zeroing in described above) appropriate contents. How much of a repetition is sufficient for the formation of an intention differs according to the circumstance. The level of discrimination is, as we said, flexible. Whatever its character, as long as it exists at some level, this process of arising and seeking (or zeroing in) is that of the *openness to patterns.* As such, it is also an openness to teleological action, that is, *to the "teleological frame" the pattern imposes* on further seeking. As a result, the process exhibits the temporal paradigm of teleological action. Such action is that of the goal (as the not-yet) bringing itself about in and through the material provided to the present by the past. The goal is what makes the material material, that is, gives it its potentiality. In perception, the interpretative intention, taken as the putative pattern, is the presence of the goal. As not yet intuitively present (not yet embodied), it directs the process of realizing itself (of bringing itself to actual intuitive presence) through the contents. Moreover, its presence as a goal is a necessary condition for the contents to be the contents of some object, that is, the material for this object's perceptual presence.

Now, the fact that the intention can fail, that is, that the pattern may not succeed in embodying itself, follows from the teleological circle itself. According to the circle, the present is determined both by the future and the past. The line of determination it symbolizes is that of the future determining the past (qua material) in its determination of the present. Given this, the reduction of experiential content to some kind of prime matter capable of sustaining every kind of interpretation is the elimination of the causality of the past. Only the future determines when the intention, under-stood as the not-yet, invariably succeeds. If, however, what determined the interpretation were simply the contents, in the sense that a shift in con-tents would automatically result in a shift in the interpretative intention, then we would be left with just the causality of the past. The self in this essentially Pavlovian view would act—that is, shift its "equilibrium"—only in response to the material changes of its environment. Once again, the notion of failure would be eliminated. For failure, both the causality of the past and the future is required. The fact that each determines itself through the other is, of course, precisely the point of the dialectic of inten-tion and fulfillment. The dialectic, then, brings with it the possibility of success and failure. Its instantiation is that of the context for their possi-bility. This context is that of teleological action, the action involving a goal that can act as a standard. Given this, we can also say that the dialectic is, itself, our openness to such action. To instantiate it through the routines described in our last section is to instantiate this openness. It is, in fact, to instantiate knowing conceived as a teleological function (see page 109).

The notion of a dialectic of intention and fulfillment has its origins in Husserl's *Logische Untersuchungen*.[16] Husserl advanced it to combat the position that "presentation and what is presented are one and the same," both being reduced to "the mere having of sensations" (*Logische Unter-suchungen* [Tübingen, 1968], II/1, 507). The confusion of the two, which marked the Pavlovian psychologism of his time, resulted, he wrote, from "a refusal to take into account the phenomenological moment of interpreta-tion" (*ibid.*). Interpretation was what distinguished sensations (the physi-cal "presentation") from sense (the object as "presented"). Now, if with Husserl we conceive this dialectic as an attempt to extricate the self from the laws of material causality, that is, to give it its own laws, a difficulty, as the Husserlian scholar, De Boer, points out, still seems to remain. As long as we admit to the reality of consciousness, that is, to its having a material makeup, we still have not overcome "the naturalization of consciousness" (*"Zusammenfassung," De Ontwikkelingsgan in Het Denken van Husserl,* p. 589). Given this makeup, we can see the act of interpretation as a caused fact. But this implies that the dialectic is also caused. It is contin-gent on the material makeup of consciousness, as well as on the sensory influxes we register as impressions. In DeBoer's view, this difficulty ulti-mately caused Husserl to abandon the realistic stance of the *Logische Un-*

16. An account of this is given in Mensch, *The Question of Being in Husserl's Logical Investigations,* pp. 84ff.

tersuchungen and adopt the idealism of his later works. Given that we also assert that consciousness has a material basis and yet have sharply criticized idealism, it may well be asked: How can we avoid this naturalization of interpretation?

Our reply to this essentially takes up the next chapter. Here, we can only say that our position is more radical than Husserl's. It is based on a reversal of the relations of time and being, one that undercuts from the start the basis of this objection. Thus, the naturalization of interpretation presupposes the Cartesian framework with its straight line of temporal determination and its conception of time and space as pregiven receptacles for events. Were we to embrace this framework, we would be driven back to the paradoxes with which we began this book. It has been our working through them that has brought us to this point. Thus, to return to it would be to embrace a kind of neurotic loop, one where we are driven back again to work through the same traumatic theme. To avoid this, we have to say that, as opposed to the view of this objection, interpretation is not a physical shaping or arrangement of some external sensuous matter. Rather than being a physical making, it is, as structured by the dialectic, an openness. Furthermore, once we make the reversal, this openness is not a result, but rather a condition for the object determining our knowledge. This means that what structures this openness are not causal sequences, but rather algorithms. The algorithm for a spatial-temporal object is, we maintain, what first allows it to be determinative as epistemological presence, that is, as an appearing sense.

Beyond these general points, a more complete answer to this objection requires something more than just thinking the self or soul as an openness, as we have done in this chapter. We must use the resulting concept to think through its relation to the body. Fortunately, we need not do this on our own. The notion of the soul as an openness is a pre-Cartesian, primarily Aristotelian concept. Thus, in the first instance, we need to examine this premodern tradition to see if it can provide a framework for avoiding (not solving, but bypassing) the problem of the mind's relation to the body. The result as we shall see will involve a radical shift in the way we normally regard ourselves.

6

Mind and Touch

From the Nonextended to the Immaterial

For Descartes the distinction between mind and body is between the non-extended and the extended. What is nonextended is not divisible, and the mind or soul, for Descartes, is completely indivisible. As he writes, "it is one and the same mind that wills, senses, and understands . . ." (*Meditations*, VI; pp. 97–98). Not that the mind is identifiable with these acts. It cannot be if it remains the same as we pass from one act to the other. Staying the same, it seems to be a nonextended, nonobjective unity of attending underlying all its particular acts. By contrast, as Descartes adds, "no corporeal or extended thing" can be thought by us that we cannot "in thought divide into parts." All bodies are extended and, hence, by definition, physically divisible. Thus, on the one hand, I have "a distinct idea of a body—insofar as it is merely an extended thing, and not a thing that thinks." On the other, I also "have a clear and distinct idea of myself—insofar as I am a thing that thinks and not an extended thing" (p. 93). Given this, the two are "distinct." Yet since between the nonextended and the extended there can be no point of physical contact, Descartes is at a loss to explain how minds and bodies can affect each other. The result of his distinction is, in fact, the absence of mind in the world he wishes to explore with his new science: the world of nature, considered as extended and quantifiable. Concretely, this absence of mind is that of the scientist. Cartesian science cannot account for its own activity, its own concrete presence as the intelligence of the scientist. This, as we noted in Chapter 1, is the paradox of modernity. It is the paradox of the subject that proposes the structures of modernity. Our purpose in this chapter is to explore a model that does not solve, but, rather, avoids its difficulties. To do so, we must begin from a different, pre-Cartesian starting point.

§1. *The Mind as an Openness: The Pre-Cartesian View.*   The notion that the mind is nonextended did not originate with Descartes. Philosophers before him also held this view. There is, however, an important termi-nological shift. Earlier thinkers preferred to speak of the mind as "immaterial." Its lack of extension was a function of its not possessing matter. The nature of this shift can be seen in terms of a different set of epistemological motivations. Descartes is motivated by the search for a being that by virtue of its absolute certainty, can serve as a founding axiom, an Archimedian point, for his system. The requirement of certainty makes him abstract from the mind all that he can doubt. What he cannot doubt is, as just indicated, simply mind's presence as a unity of attending. By contrast, the motivations of the pre-Cartesian tradition focused, not on an indubitable, axiomatic item of knowledge, but rather on the nature of the knowing process. For the process to be possible, the mind, they argued, must be immaterial.

Their argument can be put in terms of the Aristotelian/Scholastic view of reality as informed matter. According to this, a particular thing is what it is because its matter has assumed a particular shape. It is distinguished from its background because it has organized itself as "this" sort of thing, rather than "that." In other words, its formal organization enables it to exist as a "this"—a particular entity. Now, if knowing is to be taken as the process by which the forms of the world "inform" the mind, an obvious limitation to this view must be made. They cannot inform or shape the mind in the way that they shape a material reality. If they did, then as Aquinas says, "The forms of the things known would make the intellect to be actually of the same nature as that which is known" (*Summa Contra Gentiles,* Book II, chap. 50, par. 5; tr. James Anderson, p. 150). In knowing fire, for example, the mind would become fire. It would undergo the same sort of material organization as that which the form of fire imposes on a burning object. If this is not to be the case, then the form must be received immaterially. For this to be possible, the mind itself must be immaterial. Aquinas introduces a host of other arguments to the same effect (see ibid., II, 50, 1–4, 6–9; ed. cit., pp. 149–151). One by one, they point out the difficulties of having a mind involved in the particularities of matter know different objects. In each case, he argues that mind cannot be a particular thing, a "this," and yet be open to other types of objects.

The insight behind these arguments comes from Aristotle. If, in fact, the mind is to be *open* to all objects, "it can," he argues, "have no characteristic except its capacity to receive"—φύσιν μηδεμίαν ἀλλ᾽ ἢ ταύτη ὅτι δυνατόν] (*De Anima* 429a22). If it were "mixed with the body . . . it would become somehow qualitative . . . or even have an organ" (429a25–26). It would, in other words, display the definite qualities that bodies must have as particular organizations of matter. Far from being an openness to all things, it would itself be some particular thing, its qualities standing in the way of its receiving each thing as it is. This point can be put in terms of the consequences of assuming that mind, like the senses of sight and hearing, has a definite organ. According to Aristotle, each of these senses exists as a "ratio," a formula involving its material components. An excess of the sensible object—a blinding light or a deafening sound—disturbs the ratio and, hence, impedes the sense's capacity to function (*De Anima* 424a28–32). Now, if the mind were like this, it would not just be the case that it would be disturbed by an excess of its own object—that is, thinking the more intelligible, it would be unable to grasp the less intelligible. It would also be limited by its ratio to one type of object rather than another. Each sense receives "according to its ratio" [κατὰ τὸν λόγον].[1] To give the mind a material organ would thus be to limit its receptivity to those things conformable to its material makeup. Rather than being a pure receptivity, it would be open only to those things which fit its particular ratio. Changing the ratio, that is, changing its material makeup, would thus change the nature of its understanding. The epistemological situation that Aristotle seems to be trying to avoid can be indicated by citing the nineteenth-century psychologist, G. Ferrero: "Even logic alters with the structure of the brain."[2] An Aristotelian would say that if the brain is the mind's material organ, changing its structure changes its receptivity to particular logical forms.

The alternative to this is to view the mind as an unrestricted openness. Capable of receiving the form of every possible object, it is in itself just

---

1. *De Anima* 424a24. According to Aristotle, the ratio also serves as a mean allowing the sense to judge whether the sensation it receives is excessive or deficient. There is, thus, a certain reflexivity in this judgment. The standard applied by the sense refers not just to object but also to itself. See *De Anima* 424b2.

2. Cited by Husserl in his *Logische Untersuchungen* (Tübingen, 1968), I, 147, 1.

this capability. It is not itself a form, but rather "a place of the forms"—[τόπον εἰδῶν] (*De Anima* 429a27). An analogy Aristotle draws can help us understand this. Explaining why "the soul is like a hand," he writes that "the hand is the tool of tools [ὄργανόν ἐστιν ὀργάνων], and the mind is the form of forms, and the sense is the form of sensible [forms]" (*De Anima* 432a2). The hand is a "tool of tools," not because it is a tool like they are. We do not "use" our hands as we "use" tools. In an important sense, we are our hands. Hand-tools are made to fit hands, not the reverse. This points to the fact that it is only with the hand that the hand-tool can come to presence, that is, actually function as a tool. A pair of pliers, for example, appears as what it is, an instrument for gripping and holding small objects, only in the hand employing it. Similarly, the sensible object qua sensible can only appear within the sense. Without it, there is no place for its presence. Without, for example, the sense of sight there is no place for colors to appear. The same holds for the mind in its relation to intellectual forms. It is the form of forms, not because it is a form, but because it is the only place where intellectual forms as such (as νοητά) can come to presence.

Interpreting Aristotle, we can say that the openness to patterns we described in Chapter 5 gives the mind its openness to the sensible forms—these being the forms of objects conceived as unities of sense. To be a sensible form is to be an intentional one-in-many. It is to be the unity that shows itself through the different experiences. It is to be the one thing to which all the sensible contents making up the pattern of its appearing pertain. Beyond this, a further layer of unity and multiplicity can appear, that of the intellectual forms. Openness here is openness to the similarity of unities of sense, more particularly, to the conceptual unity by virtue of which we call them by the same name—for example, humans by the name "human," pencils by the name "pencil," and so on. Now, at the basis of our openness to the sensible forms, there is, as we noted, a receptivity to time. We can grasp a sensible one-in-many because we can preserve the multiplicity of disparate contents through which it appears. We can do this because we can retain the past as past. The receptivity to the intellectual form, while presupposing this, involves something more. To compare perceptual objects so as to grasp their similarities, we have to recall them. We must, then, preserve the results of temporal synthesis in long-term memory. The objects we do recall, though grasped as temporal unities, are not themselves in time. Thus, we can recall a temporal event, remembering, say, the fall of a lamp in the living room, yet be uncertain when it occurred. If such events were preserved in time—that is, in their temporal order—we would not have to go beyond them to external factors (such as schemes of cause and effect) to place them in their temporal relations. That we must do this indicates, on the one hand, the timelessness of the concepts that form the proper objects of mind. Their status as a one in many different temporal occurrences is, in fact, an abstraction from a position in the temporal order. On the other hand, it indicates a reason why the classic strategies for making machines intelligent (as, for example, in "expert programs") succeed to the point that they do. Basing themselves on conceptual nets linking already given senses, they imitate the mind in its manipulation of what it abstracts from time.[3]

Aristotle makes two further assertions about the mind as an openness. Having asserted that mind "can have no characteristic except its capacity to receive," he adds that "before it thinks," that is, before it grasps its object, "mind is actually none of the existents" [οὐθέν ἐστιν ἐνεργείᾳ τῶν ὄντων πρὶν νοεῖν] (*De Anima* 429a24). This points to its immateriality. Any matter would make it a this—a particular existent, a particular piece of shaped matter. It also indicates that, as a place of forms, mind is not itself a "form" like the forms it receives. As a "form of forms," it is a kind of one-in-many, but only as the *one place in which the multiplicity* of such particular forms *can appear.* Not being a form, it is again disqualified from being any of the existents, since, as shaped matter, they all have form. Does this mean that it is "not," that its essential being is some sort of "absence," some form of Sartrean (or Heideggerian) "nothingness"?[4] This would only be the case if being equaled form, if the actuality (the ἐνεργείᾳ) of the latter were the total sense of "to be." Yet for Aristotle, as we stressed, being includes the sense of potentiality, of capacity. As such, it is relative to that which gives the potential its potentiality. This is the goal for which the latter serves as material. It is, in other words, the form in its actuality (or "at workness") as a final cause. Given this, the declaration that

3. The implication here is that making machines "intelligent" in the sense of giving them problem-solving abilities is different from providing them with intentionality. This is as we should expect, given that large numbers of animals seem to possess intentionality—in the sense of being directed to (and engaging in the perceptual syntheses that result in) objects— and yet do not manifest any of the conceptual abilities associated with mind.

4. Sartre sees this nothingness as the origin of the self-presence that makes consciousness self-conscious: "The being of consciousness qua consciousness is to exist *at a distance from itself* as presence to itself; and this empty distance which being carries in its being is Nothingness. Thus in order for a *self* to exist, it is necessary that the unity of this being include its own nothingness as the nihilation of identity" (*Being and Nothingness*, p. 125). The same nothingness, understood as grounding the possibility of self-detachment, is also at the origin of our freedom (p. 60) and its capability to imagine (p. 62).

mind's only characteristic is its capacity or potentiality (δυνατόν) is not an assertion of its nonbeing, but rather one of its openness to the teleological action that makes this possible. What is asserted is the mind's receptivity to the intellectual forms understood as goals. Immateriality, in this context, does not, then, point to the mind or self's position as an item of knowledge (a particular "most certain thing" in Descartes's phrase). It refers, rather, to an unlimited capacity. Concretely, the reference is to our openness, at least on the level of thought, to every possible motivation.

A similar sort of analysis applies to the assertion that before it thinks, mind has no inherent content. Since it is no actual existent before it thinks, all its content must be drawn from the objects it does think. As before, its lack of content is its openness as a "place." It is its receptivity to content. At the basis of this receptivity is the openness of the sensible part of the soul to sensible content. At the basis of this is its temporal structure. Given that time, in its moments, can contain every possible content, the temptation here arises to distinguish the soul from its content by defining it as a temporal structure. Yet, in saying this, we say too much. From an Aristotelian perspective, the sensible soul is not time, but rather the receptivity that first lets time itself be. As open to time, it is what makes possible the appearance of the sensible form as a temporal pattern.

§2. *One-Way Touch.* How does this immaterial openness interact with the body? Aquinas writes that it cannot be by "contact properly so called. For there is contact only between bodies," which touch by coming "together at their extremities" (*Summa Contra Gentiles,* Book II, chap. 56, par. 6; p. 165). What is immaterial does not have an extremity. It also cannot interact by virtue of the mind's being somehow "mixed" with the body. Things mixed are "altered in [their] relation to one another" (ibid., par. 3; p. 16). But this presupposes some "matter in common," which is just what is lacking here. Having listed the difficulties, Aquinas proposes his solution. He writes: "There is, however, a certain kind of contact whereby an intellectual substance [a soul] can be united to a body. . . . [I]f attention is given to activity and passivity, it will be found that certain things touch others and are not themselves touched" (ibid., par. 8; p. 165). This, he asserts, is the soul's relation to the body. The relation is that of one-way touch. It is distinguished from two-way or mutual contact insofar as "by this contact the indivisible can touch the divisible." The contact is not between the extremities. Rather, "the whole thing" is "touched" by the indivisible agent. It "is touched according as it is acted upon," that is, "inasmuch as the thing is in potentiality" to such action, the potentiality involv-

ing the whole of the thing. With this comes another distinguishing characteristic. The relation of agent to patient is not an extrinsic relation, but
rather intrinsic. In Aquinas's words, "The contact . . . extends to the innermost things, it makes the touching substance to be within the thing
touched and to penetrate it without hindrance" (ibid., par. 9; p. 166). The
two are actually "one with respect to acting and being acted upon" (ibid.,
par. 10; p. 167).

An example he gives makes clear the type of phenomenon he has in
mind. We are often, he notes, affected by things we are not in physical
contact with. It is "in this sense that we say that a person in sorrow touches
us" (ibid., par. 8; p. 167). If we have a sympathetic disposition, we can be
touched to the quick by his plight. The potentiality of our disposition allows it to "penetrate" us "without hindrance." It allows us to be *inwardly*
moved. The motion, we can say, is through the sensitive and intellectual
parts of our soul. But it is through them as our *openness* to the world, in
particular, to the sorrowing person's plight. By virtue of this openness, we
can be moved or touched by someone even if that person remains un-
aware of us. He moves us and yet remains, himself, unmoved.

Once again, the basic insight is Aristotle's. There are, he says, two types
of movers: "One kind of mover can only impart motion by being itself
moved, another kind can do so through remaining itself unmoved" (*On
Generation and Corruption* 323a15). The distinction, he explains, is actually one of touch. Moved movers touch and are touched. Unmoved movers
act through one-way touch. In Aristotle's words: "If anything imparts motion without itself being moved, it may touch the moved and yet itself be
touched by nothing—for we say sometimes that the man who grieves us
'touches' us, but not that we 'touch' him" (323a34–35). When he touches
us, he does not grieve. We are the ones who grieve. The grieving is an
action of our soul; it penetrates our entire bodily being. Yet the basis is our
openness to the man who grieves us. As unmoved, he is the first or prime
mover of this sequence. He moves us, not physically, but as an object of
our thought. As Aristotle states the general position: "The object of desire
[τὸ ὀρεκτὸν] and the object of thought [τὸ νοητὸν] move without being
moved" (*Metaphysics* 1072a26). They do not change or move, rather they
change us. Thus the child on a warm day who turns to walk toward an ice
cream vendor evinces the action of an unmoved mover just as surely as a
person who makes a resolution and attempts to adhere to it. In a certain
sense, we can say that the object of desire or thought—the ice cream or
the resolution—is the agent. Yet it is also equally true to assert that the
person is the mover. He is this because he is the place where the agent can

appear as such. By virtue of possessing sensation and mind, he is where agents can come to presence as objects of desire or thought. As we cited Aristotle, "The functioning of the sensible object" *is* "in the sensing subject" (*De Anima* 426a10). Similarly, the functioning of the intelligible or the desirable object is in the understanding or desiring subject. In each case, "the functioning [ἐνέργεια] of the agent and mover occurs in what is acted upon" (426a5; see also *Physics* 202a13–20). For objects of desire or thought, the motion, thus, occurs within the desiring or thinking person. There is no point in looking beyond or "outside" this person for the reality of their agency. The reality occurs in the only "place" where objects of desire or thought can actually function, this being the perceiving subject.[5]

The teleology implicit in this view should already be familiar to us. If the soul really is a "place" of forms, be these of sensible or intellectual objects, its motive power must be their motive power. Such objects move us as goals. The child, for example, who desires an ice cream desires to eat it. The act of eating it is not a present reality, but rather a "not-yet." It is a *future* condition whose desirability determines his present actions. It moves him to bring about its *present reality.* Of course, we can "change our minds" and, with this, the goals we have "in mind." Considered in their formal character, however, the goals do not change. They are either entertained, that is, function as such in us, or they do not. When they do function, they do not do so in terms of their physical reality, which is something not yet realized. They function simply in terms of their "what" character. They operate *as forms* whose action determines us to accomplish their physical reality. As Aristotle puts this: "There are two principles that cause physical movement." One is obviously physical, as when I am pushed or pulled by something. One, however, is not, "for it has no tendency to change with itself." This is "an unmoved mover." It is also "what anything is or its form," this, insofar as the form functions as "a final cause or goal" (*Physics* 198b1–3). Given that goals do move us without themselves being moved, they are preeminent examples of one-way touch. One-way touch is, in other words, inherently teleological. It is the action of forms functioning as final causes. Insofar as the soul is the place of such functioning, its action must also be regarded as teleological. The relation of one-way touch the soul has to the body is, then, that of the goals it entertains.

5. For an extended account of the epistemological implications of this see James Mensch, "Aristotle and the Overcoming of the Subject-Object Dichotomy."

We can put this in terms of the openness to forms (both sensible and intellectual) that characterizes the human soul. This openness to forms is also an openness to the agency—the energeia (ἐνέργεια)—which *is* such forms (*Metaphysics* 1045a24, 1045b19–20). Forms, for Aristotle, always act as final causes, and one of the places where they can so act is the human soul. When they do, the actuality of their functioning is our own. We are thus both passive and active at the same time. Undergoing their action, we act on our own. I am the one who reaches for the ice cream. I am the person who is touched by the man in sorrow. Their agency is also my own. Thus the openness to teleological action that characterizes the soul permits a double description, one involving both motivation and autonomy. The fact that I do something *for some purpose* in no way stands opposed to my *doing it myself.*

One way to think about such openness is in terms of "disclosive" behavior. My agency or behavior, to the point that it is identified with my openness to the world, discloses it. The desired object, in other words, manifests itself in and through my behavior. Its being—which is its *energeia* (literally, its "at workness") as a form—informs me. It shapes my activity, making me disclose it. This shaping is actually an identity on the level of actuality. For Aristotle, we said, it is senseless to speak of the actuality of a sensible object *qua* sensible apart from the sense organ. Given that such actuality is in the organ, there is no original with which we could compare our sensation (see page 98). The same point holds here. Insofar as our behavior manifests the world, it expresses a relation that *does not involve the notions of original and image.* Our functioning in the world is not to be seen as a copy of it. It is part of an original functioning.[6]

Such functioning does not just occur in us. The whole range of animate existence—from the simple to the complex—manifests it. Far from being monolithic, the world functions differently in different species, each of which exhibits a different openness. A lizard, for example, hears the slightest rustling in the grass. It does not, however, hear a pistol shot fired close by. It does not because it survives by occupying and exploiting its own ecological niche. Its openness is to *its* environment, that is, to *its* advantages and disadvantages, its resources and competitors. It survives by developing an interpretation of its surroundings, a set of rules for the syntheses by which it brings objects to appearance. These are not accidental,

---

6. One of the ways to see our dependence on such functioning is through experiments involving sensory deprivation. Without a surrounding world, the mind's agency itself degrades.

but rather fundamental to its success as an organism; they are integral to the processes of its life. A plurality of such niches thus corresponds to a plurality of types of sensing souls, each of which differentiates itself according to its type of openness. Corresponding to this, there is a plurality of different, disclosive behaviors. A sand swallow, for example, which catches mosquitoes on the wing at the beach, brings to presence a different environment than the piping plover hunting along the sand of the same shoreline.

The fact that each functioning is an original functioning implies something more than the pluralism of the world's functioning. It points to the overcoming of, in the sense of escaping from, the modern distinction between reality and appearance. The world each species brings to presence in its functioning is not a mere appearance, a copy, of some original reality. It is the reality itself. The tradition we are exploring leads, in fact, to a kind of Nietzschean perspectivism. It is one where we can affirm with Nietzsche: "There would be no life at all except on the basis of perspective evaluations and appearancs" (*Beyond Good and Evil,* §34; p. 65). The elimination of these, that is, the abolition of the apparent in favor of a "true" world, would be the elimination of life as a process based on a multitude of perspective evaluations. This implies, as Nietzsche adds, that "if . . . one wanted to abolish the 'apparent world' altogether, assuming you could do that . . . nothing would remain of your 'truth' either!" (ibid.). From an Aristotelian perspective, the same point follows, since the elimination of the apparent world is the elimination of the world as it functions in animate existence. Since the actuality of the mover is in the moved, this is the elimination of the world's actuality as an epistemological presence[7] and, hence, of its "truth." This can also be expressed by saying that the "perspective evaluation," rather than being opposed to the "true" world, is just that aspect of the world revealed in the pursuit of a practical goal. Such a pursuit involves desire, and from desire a set of implications can be made that lead us to the world's presence in a "perspective evaluation." Thus desire implies need in the sense that what is desired is what is not yet actually possessed. This, however, implies finitude insofar as an infinite being would neither lack nor desire anything. This finitude, in turn, implies the desired object's functioning in and through the particular perspectives that define an individual as a member of one species rather than another. Finitude, in other words, implies the finitude (or particularity) of each species's openness.

7. As opposed to its physical presence.

To complete this picture, two further points should be mentioned. The first concerns what can be called the "untidiness" of Aristotle's ontology. As we said, it involves "multiple senses of being or functioning." The situation it leaves us in is one "where beings interpenetrate beings and assist in establishing one another in their functioning" (see page 99). This mutual dependence does not just undermine the modern distinctions of reality and appearance (in Cartesian terms, of original and replica). It undermines the notion of the foundationism inherent in these distinctions. It does not allow us to speak of the world, which functions through us in foundational terms. To see this we must take Aristotle's ontology as actually descriptive of organic life. We must interpret the mutual dependence it proposes in terms of what Darwin called "the web of complex relations" binding different species together. The web, he writes, is such "that the structure of every organic being is related in the most essential and yet often hidden manner to that of all the other organic beings, with which it comes into competition for food or residence, or from which it has to escape, or on which it preys" ("The Origin of Species," Ch. IV; p. 62). For Darwin, the individual features that make up a particular being's structure, from the shape of its legs to the type of eyes it has, are actually a set of indices. Each points to the specific features of the environment in which it functions (see ibid.). Insofar as they shape the animal, the environment can be considered as functioning through it. Since this environment includes other organic beings, each can be considered not just as grounded by the world that shapes it, but also as part of this world insofar as it functions as a determining ground for the beings of *its* environment. Thus, to speak here of the world in its functioning is not to refer to it as some sort of ground or foundation that is distinct from that which it founds. It is not to point to it as the "reality" of which all the various forms of life are the mere appearance.[8] In its functioning through individuals, the world is not a foundation distinct from them. It is, rather, a self-determining plurality of individual actors and actions.[9] To accept this is, in fact, to dissipate the notion of a

8. This view would lead us once again to the type of foundationalism that asserts a single standard of being or functioning, one to which all others could somehow be reduced. It would, thus, return us to metaphysics in Heidegger's sense: "Metaphysical thinking rests on the distinction between what truly is and what, measured against this, constitutes all that is not truly in being" ("Who is Nietzsche's Zarathustra?" in *Nietzsche,* II, 230). Heidegger accuses Nietzsche of such thinking insofar as he equates the will to life an organism manifests with will to power, and asserts the ultimate reality of the latter.

9. Darwin's preferred term for this conception of the world is "nature." Comparing its action with that effected by domestic breeding, he writes: "Man can act only on external and visible characters: Nature, if I may be allowed to personify the natural preservation or sur-

ground. In a situation of individuals determining environments determining individuals, there is no separate first cause, no ultimate determinant. Where each organic being is both ground and grounded, the notion of a ground is robbed of its foundational character. The same holds for the world's functioning in the perceptual syntheses of organic beings. To the point that they do share a common world, it is because these beings function in and through each other. This mutual determination insofar as it precedes through individuals, each working on those beings which form its immediate environment, is not such as to turn this commonality into any single sense or standard of perceptual presence. What we have is a pluralism of environmental niches, one that results in a plurality of different, yet equally valid syntheses.

Our second point concerns what seems to be an obvious exception to the above. This is mind as conceived in the Aristotelian/Scholastic tradition. Nietzsche attempts to place mind on the level of sense. Determined by the needs of its (human) environment, its functioning expresses for him just another perspective, another way of interpreting the world.[10] What prevents us from accepting this view is the immateriality of mind. Such immateriality signifies that, unlike the senses, it has no particular material "ratio" that would limit its receptivity. It, thus, implies the universal, nonperspective character of its functioning. Does this mean that mind puts us in contact with the true, as opposed to the apparent, world? Is what it grasps foundational in the modern sense? Descartes certainly thought so. The primary qualities grasped by mind were in his account the numerical

---

vival of the fittest, cares nothing for appearances, except in so far as they are useful to any being. She can act on every internal organ, on every shade of constitutional difference, on the whole machinery of life. Man selects only for his own good: Nature only for that of the being which she tends" ("The Origin of Species," p. 65). The notion of "the being which she tends" and its benefit becomes highly ambiguous once we bear "in mind how infinitely complex and close-fitting are the mutual relations of all organic beings to each other and to their physical conditions of life" (p. 63). If, in fact, every being is ultimately defined by every other, the "being" tended by nature can only be nature itself understood as the whole web of relations and entities.

10. For Nietzsche, then, the question is not whether the mind's judgment is true or false. "The question is to what extent it is life-advancing, life-preserving, species-preserving, perhaps even species-breeding." This means that "the falsest judgments . . . are the most indispensable to us, that without granting as true the fictions of logic, without measuring reality against the purely invented world of the unconditional and self-identical, without a continual falsification of the world by means of numbers, mankind could not live" (*Beyond Good and Evil*, §4; p. 35). We could not because such notions are *our* survival strategy. Thus, Nietzsche writes in answer to Kant's famous question, "How are synthetic judgments *a priori* necessary," they are necessary "for the purpose of preserving beings such as ourselves" (§11, p. 42). In other words, the use of "the fictions of logic" to interpret the world is simply our way of struggling for existence, our preserving ourselves.

aspects of the world. These, by virtue of their clarity and distinctness, were the reality underlying its various appearances. For Aristotle, however, the immateriality of mind does not signify a focus on some specific aspect of the world—that is, on its numerical as opposed to its other aspects. It implies the universality of its functioning only in the sense that it signifies its openness to all the world's aspects. Its unlimited capability, in other words, is its ability to intellectually grasp all the senses of being which the world is capable of bringing to presence. It is not, in any way, a limitation of such senses. So regarded, Aristotle's conception of the openness of mind allows us to accept the pluralism inherent in Nietzsche's perspectivism without our falling prey to its self-referential inconsistency. This is the inconsistency of asserting the limited quality of mind on the basis of an argument that situates it as just one of many different perspectives that can be discovered and characterized. To make such an argument, the mind must not be limited to its own perspective. But if it is not, the argument is false when it (wrongly) asserts the perspectival character of the mind. Once again, we find the characteristic inconsistency of modernity. At its basis is its inability to account for the subject's ability to put forward the theories it proposes. Nietzsche, insofar as he shares in this, must be accounted as yet another representative of its tradition. To escape from its difficulties is to conceive mind such that it is, by definition, included in any account of the world. This, however, is to consider it as embedded in the world as part of its functioning. It is, in other words, to explore how mind's openness (its "immateriality" in the pre-Cartesian sense) is part of this functioning.

Touch and Consciousness

To pursue this exploration we must first take note of the redefinition of soul implicit in the foregoing. It is one which widens its notion beyond the ability to grasp a one-in-many which characterizes the soul's sensible and intellectual parts. The expansion of its notion results in our seeing soul as involved in the whole of the body's functioning. It thus gives us a context to see mind's place within such functioning.

§1. *Body and Soul.* For Aristotle, in *De Anima,* the soul involves a multiplicity of functions, all of which involve the processes of life. They include our abilities to feed ourselves, to grow and reproduce, as well as our capacities to sense and understand, to desire and to move to attain the things we desire. In general, "the ensouled is distinguished from the non-souled by life" (*De Anima* 413a2). Soul includes whatever functions we ascribe to life. Aristotle puts this in terms of a rather striking example. He writes: "If the eye were a living creature, its soul would be its sight" (412b19). Sight would be the functioning that distinguishes its life. Now, when we say that seeing is the point of being an eye, we are also asserting that seeing is the goal or purpose of its particular material structure. When it sees, it actually is an eye. To use a word Aristotle coined, seeing, the eye is "at-its-goal." Soul itself is defined in terms of this "being at the end or goal" (ἐντελέχεια). In Aristotle's words, soul is "the primary *entelechia*—ἐντελέχεια—of a physical body capable of possessing life" (412a30). Soul, in a broad sense, can thus be defined in terms of the goals or purposes peculiar to bodies capable of possessing life. Such capabilities, Aristotle notes, imply the possession of distinct organs. Being alive is the actual exercise of such capabilities, that is, the actual functioning of the different organs. "Being at its end," that is, actually accomplishing the purposes of its structure, the body is ensouled. The goals of its structure are realized within it.

This definition allows us to specify the soul's relation to the body as essentially teleological. If we ask, *what is a soul*, we have to reply that it is a set of goals a thing must embody if it is to be alive. Insofar as the soul is considered an active (causal) principle, such goals are taken as active. They are understood as final/formal causes. Our reply to the question, *what is an animate body*, follows from this. A living body is such only as material for the purposes that are its soul. In Aristotle's words, "the soul is the cause [of the body] as that for the sake of which [it is]—ὡς καὶ οὗ ἕνεκεν ἡ ψυχὴ αἰτίας (*De Anima* 415b16). As "that for the sake of which it is," it is the body's purpose. The living body lives to provide the material means to accomplish this goal. Since, as Aristotle also writes, it is "because of the goal that potentiality is possessed," we can say that without the soul, that is, without the set of goals definitive of life, there would be no bodies with the potentiality for life" (*Metaphysics* 1050a8–10). The category of living bodies, the category of what we can call "flesh," would disappear.

Once we say that relation of soul to body is that of a *purpose* to the *material required* for its accomplishment, a number of points follow. The first is that their relation does not involve two separate realities. What confronts us are rather two separate ways of considering one and the same process. We can consider the process in terms of its "wherefore," that is, in terms of the end it seems to be achieving. We can also regard the material conditions for this achievement. The process of such achievement is that of life. Concretely, it is the living being taken as a particular type of process. To turn this about, we can also say that the living being is the sort of reality we can examine according to the perspectives of body and soul. Those goals, which are discernable in the processes of its life, determine our account of its soul. Correspondingly, the material requirements for such processes set the parameters for the account of its body. Our second point is that this view allows us to speak of many different types of soul. Soul is as broad a category as that of life. We can, for example, speak of the souls of plants. We can also, of course, speak of human souls. It all depends on the goals the processes manifest. Thus, a plant growing toward the light, a bird hunting on the wing, and a lawyer trying to win his case as he sums up his arguments are all examples of goal-directed activity. Such goals are linked in the sense that some—such as those of nutrition—have to be accomplished for others to be possible. There is, in fact, a certain hierarchy of goals. The nutritive soul—the set of goals embodying basic biological functions—must be present to support the sensitive soul. Sensing is required for the activities of pursuing prey or avoiding predators. It is also required for the activities of mind, since its syntheses furnish the materials for mind's syntheses. Some of the soul's goals are internal to the organism—for example, those of nutrition in the sense of digestion. Some are external such as the prey which is pursued. It would, however, be a false dichotomy to distinguish them by making the soul the set of internal goals. All the goals defining a particular organism involve the world in its functioning through it. Thus the goal involving prey is tied to that involving digestion. The latter, as directed towards assimilating a specific food, is meaningful only within a context that includes the externally directed activity whose object is to provide it with the nourishment it can digest. Thus a further point is that the goals defining an organism are tied together in the sense that, not just the higher, but also the lower, are disclosive. This means that life itself should be regarded as an inherently disclosive process. Not just its organic structure points to the world, but also each of the activities engaged in by this structure. The world that shapes the structure, shapes the activities. The shaping is its disclosure through these activities. Through them, it is revealed as, e.g., digestible material, as prey to be pursued, as an aspect of reality that can be numbered, and so on.

§2. *Subjectivity as Flesh.*   To pursue this further we require a radical redefinition of the Cartesian notion of "subjectivity." Rather than designating a nonextended self, set apart from and doubting its world, subjectivity here indicates a kind of disclosive behavior. Embodied, it behaves "in tune" with the world. What tunes it are its goals. It is, *qua* embodied, material that manifests the purposes of life. As animate matter, we can designate it as the category of "flesh."

Flesh, we can say, has a three-layered structure. The outermost manifests the phenomena of one-way touch. It is behavior animated by goals. As such, it is also an openness to these goals. The particular type of openness it displays depends on its receptivity. In each particular instance, this depends upon its environment. This "tunes," as it were, the organism's senses to particular objects. In general terms, however, receptivity depends upon the type of senses it has. Hearing, for example, is an openness to sound as sound—not to the moving pressure ridges in the air, but to the actual sounding note. Similarly, the sense of sight is an openness, not to a particular range of electromagnetic fluctuations, but to color. Following Aristotle, we can say that each type of sensory openness involves a particular ratio. It is contingent on a particular material organization of the sensory organ. Insofar as this receptivity involves perceptual syntheses, the ultimate receptivity is to time itself. Now, corresponding to each form of receptivity is a type of disclosive behavior. This is directed towards the particular sort of object it receives. Thus, moving to get a closer look at the seen corresponds to seeing; turning the head to better catch the pattern of the sound corresponds to hearing. Considered as a phenomenon of one-way touch, such behavior can be described as the movement of the mover in the moved. At its ultimate basis is the temporal presence of the mover. This is the presence of the time in and through which the perceptual object manifests itself in the syntheses and corresponding behavior of the perceiver.

The same pattern holds for that part of subjectivity we designate as mind. In distinction to the particular senses, it has, of course, an unlimited openness. Thinking, the mind is open to every possible thought. Its disclosive behavior with regard to such thoughts is correspondingly unlimited. This is what makes human beings, in Sophocles' term, "strange" or "wonderful" δεινός (see page 100). Our strangeness is also our being "fearful" or "terrible." Capable, within certain physical limits, of doing everything, we are "strange" insofar as we are not fixed like the animals within the narrow limits of the behavior imposed by a given environment. We are "terrible" because our universal capacity means that we are also capable of stopping at nothing, that is, of breaking all the rules we might, through morality or religion, impose upon ourselves. In a certain sense, both follow from the peculiar capacity of mind to grasp the forms as universals—that is, as conceptual unities in multiplicity. This is an ability to grasp what transcends the particular circumstances of a particular environment. We do this each time we abstract from such circumstances to grasp what is common in them. Apprehending the latter, we have the possibility of practically transcending these particular circumstances. With this, comes the possibility of escaping the constraints of a particular environment. Similarly, the same capability to grasp a one-in-many is behind our ability to apprehend what can be put to a multitude of uses, both good and bad. The same gas, Zyklon B, was used both to delouse the clothes of concentration camp inmates and to kill them.

The above should not be taken as implying that the flesh that is mindful—i.e., human flesh—can literally do or be anything, i.e., escape its physical limitations. A sheer openness on the level of thought does not imply a corresponding openness on the level of those senses which first provide the mind with the materials for its thinking. On the contrary, the mind's dependence on the latter means that it changes as they do. Thus the loss of a sense—for example, sight—profoundly affects it. As the neurologist, Oliver Sacks notes, blindness is not just an absence of seeing, "it is a different condition, a different form of being, with its own sensibilities and coherence and feeling" ("To See and Not See," p. 70).[11] The difference involves our very selfhood. In Sack's words:

> Perceptual cognitive processes . . . lead to, are linked to, a personal self, with a will, an orientation, and a style of its own. This perceptual self may also collapse with the collapse of perceptual systems, and alter the orientation and very identity of the individual. If this occurs, an individual not only becomes blind but ceases to behave as a visual being, yet offers no report of any change in inner state, is completely oblivious of his own visuality or lack of it. (pp. 68–9).

In this occurrence, known as Anton's syndrome, the mind loses all access to the visual material that would allow it to recognize its condition. A complete loss of access to all our sensory systems, not just to their functioning but also to the memories of the already accomplished results of this, would thus seem to close off mind completely. It would seem, in fact, to lead to a complete collapse of our identity, at least, insofar as this identity involved the synthetic processes of the sensitive and intellectual aspects of our souls.

Given the above, the immateriality of mind cannot mean that we must

11. An excellent account of this condition and, in particular, of the transformation of the mind caused by going blind is given by John Hull in his remarkable diary, *Touching the Rock*.

think of it as somehow apart from flesh. The immateriality simply designates a particular type of openness. Dependent on the openness of the
particular senses that provide the mind with its material, it manifests its
own special presence in a particular type of disclosive behavior. In a certain sense, human evil shows this immateriality. It points to our capacity to
stop at nothing. Mind, of course, can also be said to be immaterial in the
sense of being the "place" where the forms appear. As such, it has the
immateriality of a formal/final cause, the cause that can move us without
itself being moved. The same thing, however, can be said about the senses
of animals not possessing mind. They, too, are immaterial in the sense of
being open to their special objects. What moves in each case is the object
that appears through them. This is not the object as a physical presence.
The desired object does not literally pull us toward it by exerting some
physical force. What moves is the object as a "nonphysical . . . unmoved
mover," the object that is functioning as a "final cause or goal" (*Physics*
198b1–3). It moves us through its form. This form can only appear
through our perceptual and intellectual syntheses. As such, it moves us
through the soul taken as the place of forms. What is moved in each case
is, however, material. It is the flesh that, embodying soul, engages in these
syntheses.

§3. *The Temporality of Desire.*   Passing to the second layer of flesh's ontological structure, we may note a point implicit in our last chapter's account of perception. This is that the perceptual process is not a static
gazing at the object. It involves the shifting patterns of contents that arise
and are retained as we move to get a better look at what we intend to see.
Moving to get a better look is movement animated by a particular passion.
So is attempting to find a solution to a philosophical or mathematical problem. So, for that matter, is reaching for a cold beer on a warm Sunday
afternoon. In each case, the unmoved mover moves through desire. Desire,
we can say is the felt presence of the goal. It is the experience we have
when we are touched by it. More concretely, it is our experience of *its*
moving us, its manifesting itself in the motivations of our disclosive behavior. Thus, as long as desire is operative, the person moves closer to get a
better look. What he wants to see works on him, that is, moves him,
through desire.

   Desire has a special quality. It does not just animate my motion towards
some object. It also makes me realize that I am not that object. Confronted
by something I want but do not yet possess, I am, when I compare myself
to it, its absence. Hungry, I am the absence of food; thirsty, I am the ab-

sence of water. The desires that link flesh to the world, thus, also separate it. The behavior they animate discloses flesh as *directed toward* and yet as *other than* the world.[12]

What is disclosed in this dual relationship is, in fact, both the implicit intentionality of flesh and the possibility it has of a pre-reflective self-consciousness. Intentionality is implicit, since being directed to an object (a *Gegen-stand*) is, by definition, being directed to what, in its otherness, can "stand against" one. Insofar as it implies an epistemological, as opposed to a merely bodily presence, intentionality is part of what makes consciousness be consciousness. Another part is the fact that, in a pre-reflective sense, it is aware of itself. Seeing, I know I am seeing, this even in the absence of an explicit reflection on the fact. The root of this implicit self-consciousness is to be found in separation of self and world that occurs with desire; and the root of this is to be found in the teleology of their relationship.

The best way to express this teleology is in terms of the peculiar temporality of flesh. Such temporality is *not* that of the past determining the present, which determines the future. For flesh, the future determines its past in its determination of the present. As desired, the future stands as a goal, as a "final cause" of the process. The goal makes the past into a resource, into a "material" as it were, for its own realization. It thus determines the past in the latter's determination of the present by structuring it as a potential for some particular realization. What we are pointing to can be illustrated by a number of examples. In perception, as we said in our last chaper, what we intend to see—the anticipated object—stands as the goal. The material for its realization is provided by the past in the form of the contents we retain. Together they determine our present, ongoing action of perception. The result is the embodiment of the intended perceptual sense by the changing field of contents occasioned by our moving to get a closer look. The desire to attend to and have a better look at the object is, of course, essential to this process. Manifesting its desirability in the actions of the desiring agent, the desired object embodies or realizes itself as a sensible presence. The same point can be taken from our example of a woman who decides to become a marathon runner. Her being as

12. Alexandre Kojève puts this point rather nicely when he writes: "Desire is always revealed as *my desire,* and to reveal desire, one must use the word 'I.' Man is *absorbed* by his contemplation of the thing in vain; as soon as *desire* for that thing is born, he will see that, in addition to the thing, there is his contemplation, there is *himself,* which is *not* that thing. And the thing appears to him as an *object* (*Gegen-stand*), as an *external* reality, which is not in him, which is not *he* but *non-I*" (*Introduction to the Reading of Hegel,* p. 37).

an actual runner is not a present reality. Neither is it past. It "exists" as a desired *future* whose determining presence is that of a goal. How long she has to train is determined by the resources she brings to the goal—that is, how long she has trained in the immediate *past.* Thus, determination by the future is not absolute but occurs through her past. The determining presence of this past is that of the materials or resources it provides her to accomplish the goal. It is, of course, the goal that allows us to see such materials as materials for some purpose. The goal is what turns the past into a potential to be actualized by an ongoing, *present* activity.

The temporality of such goal-directed activity is the third and innermost layer of the ontological structure of flesh. Within it, the future appears as the goal, as the desired but not yet attained result. The past shows itself as the material for its accomplishment, while the present is their ongoing point of interpenetration. The past meeting the future is, concretely, material embodying a goal. As such, it is flesh or (as an Aristotelian would say) matter that is ensouled. It is matter that distinguishes itself from the inanimate by having a distinct temporality. With regard to self-consciousness, the crucial point here is that such temporality involves reflexivity. Directed towards the future, flesh grasps itself when it grasps the goal. This is because its own history is not some "dead weight" of the past. As the example of the marathon runner indicates, what flesh brings to the present is the very material for the goal's embodiment. Its grasp of the goal is thus through itself, that is, through its history of realizing it.

The temporal reflexivity that makes this possible may be seen by contrasting the teleological with the Cartesian view of temporal determination. In the Cartesian schema, such determination proceeds without self-reference. The future refers to the present as its immediate cause and through it to the past as its more distant cause. No part of it, however, refers to itself. By contrast, the schema of teleological temporality is one where each of the modes of time refers to itself through the others. As we noted, its line of temporal determination is that of the future causing itself to be present and actual *through its determination of the past and the present.* Thus, the past, as we said, is determined as potentiality (as δυν-αμίς) by the future. So determined, it appears a material for the not-yet-existent goal. Similarly, the future determines the present as the place where the actualization of this potentiality occurs. Thus, the reference of the future is to itself *through past and present.* It is through the latter that the future comes to be present and, hence, is now the actual future understood as that which will actually come to be. Similarly the reference of the past is to itself through the other two modes of time. They are what makes it past, that is, determine it as material for a goal. The same holds, mutatis mutandis, for the present. It, too, refers to itself through the other two modes of time. It is not just the intersection point of the past and the future. Through them it determines itself as the point of actualization, that is, of embodiment.

This can be related to the reflexivity of touch. When I touch an object, I perceive both what I touch and that by which I touch, namely, my flesh. In a certain pre-Cartesian sense, my flesh is both perceiver and perceived, both subject and object, in this act. Flesh is the subject insofar as it is (or contains) the organ of touch. It is the object insofar as it is, as Aristotle pointed out, the "medium" of touch, namely, that through which the object appears (*De Anima* 423b14–20). Rémi Brague nicely describes the mystery of this dual function when he writes: "The medium [of touch] is inside. Inside or outside of what? . . . Flesh is so to speak added to itself. Flesh is its own addition: an inner distance that cannot be measured from some external point. Flesh is something like dimensionality without dimension" ("The Mediaeval Model of Subjectivity, Towards a Rediscovery," p. 7). This "inner distance" is between the touching and the touched, the one taken as the subject, the other, as the object of this act. The "distance" separates the two, allowing flesh to grasp itself as *not yet being* (or embodying) its intended object. Its origin, we can say, is the temporal remove that permits the self-reference of each of the modes of time through the "distance," as it were, of the other two. Granting this, what provides this "dimensionality without dimension" is not some hidden spatial remove or relation. It is rather the teleological temporality manifested by flesh. This is what allows flesh to be directed toward its object, understood as the goal of its perceptual process and, in the same process, allows it to grasp itself as other than its object insofar as it does *not yet* embody it. The separation within flesh arises because flesh itself (in the guise of its *presently accumulated* "history") provides the means or "medium" for the goal's *future* realization.

The above will perhaps be clearer if we consider explicitly intentional acts. The teleology inherent in them does not just position the self as embodying the intended object. As we shall see in Chapter 7, there is also a positioning of the self as the performer of the intention. Seeing, the self is positioned as the seer. The performance of the syntheses that present a spatial-temporal world also presents the subject as this world's center—as the "seer" from which it is seen. Similarly, in the attempt to remember, the self is positioned as the being who is attempting to remember. Now, this self is successful or not depending on whether its intention reaches its goal. If it does not reach it, e.g., if it fails to remember, it admits, "I forgot." Here, the result of its performance is compared with what the performance intends, and the comparison carries with it the self-awareness we experience in making this admission. Thus, to say, "I forgot" is to say that I performed an intention (that of remembering) and failed. Because I failed, the intended self (myself as having remembered) and the intending self (the self that is trying to remember but cannot) are incongruent. The basis for this comparison is found in the process that sets up both selves. This is the ongoing interpretative process that measures itself (positioning this as one "I") against its intended result (positioning it as another "I"). Given this, self-awareness is implicit in the interpretative process. It is part of the self-monitoring essential to it. As long as the process is incomplete there is a distance between the goal and the present reality, which translates itself into a duality of the "I." Thus, in trying to remember, the "I" positioned as performing the intention is not yet the "I" positioned as having performed the successful intention. The comparison of the two, which is essential for the self-monitoring of the performance, yields the self-awareness that is inherent in it.

A number of points can be drawn from the foregoing. The first is that self-awareness (at least in its pre-reflective mode) involves duality— namely, that between the self positioned as performer and the self positioned as object of the interpretative process. The second is that this duality is a function of the teleology implicit in performing an intention. It is this which positions one of the selves as a goal. For example, in moving to get a better look to see if there is a cat under the bush, my goal is not just the cat as something perceived, it is myself as perceiving the cat. The process positions me as the one who wants to get a better look. As such, my goal is to make my actual and intended selves coincide. If I am successful, I will embody the latter. I will, in other words, embody my perceptual interpretation (that of seeing the cat) with appropriate sense contents. The third point is that the "distance," so to speak, between the selves is temporal. The self actively attempting to embody the goal is positioned as now; the self that stands as the goal is positioned as not yet. What we have, then, is a teleologically directed interpretative process that generates self-awareness as part of the self-monitoring essential for reaching its goal.

By this, I do not mean to imply that all awareness is self-awareness. This, my final point, can be put in terms of the position that perception, as embodying an intention, is an interpretative process. Interpretation, by definition, involves interpretation and what is *not interpretation,* the latter being what is given (data), namely, *what is there to be interpreted* by the intention. If this is true, we may ask: is there not an awareness of data? If there is not, what is the basis for positing data? In other words, if we do not assume such data, interpretation loses its sense as an interpretation of what is not itself. Yet if we make this assumption, the awareness of data cannot be a result of an interpretation. Given that our self-awareness does arise through the interpretative process, this awareness of data must be prior to this. In other words, we must assume an awareness prior to our pre-reflective self-consciousness. This is a form of awareness that, rather than being a result, is actually generative of the interpretative process with its implicit self-awareness. As Chapter 7 will show, such awareness is a feature of the retentional process itself. Data are there for interpretation because they are retained. Retention is a serial process. It proceeds through an ongoing process of retentions of retentions of retentions, each retention (or framing) resulting in the further departure into pastness of the retained. The original awareness is just this echoing, this placing in time by the repeated retention of what has already been retained. It is, we can say, a kind of clearing (an opening up) caused by the self-distancing of time. As such, it is a feature of temporal distance between the retained and the ongoing nowness of the act of retention. At its basis is, then, the temporal registering of being we described in Chapter 5.

To avoid a possible misunderstanding, we should note that although all the processes we have described are goal directed, not all of them need be considered voluntary. A bird hunting on the wing is engaged in a goal-directed, yet essentially involuntary activity. Its hunting can be taken as a project involving itself. Its goal can be understood as itself catching and eating the insect. Yet it has not engaged in the explicit choice of a self. For the latter something more is required than the separation of the self occasioned by desire. We must move from pre-reflective to reflective self-consciousness. I must reflect on my present conduct and the goal, the goal being what sort of person I want to be. Shall I, for example, tell the cashier that he has given me a fifty instead of a five-dollar bill or should I keep quiet? To simply take the money without any thought is to be attracted by it as a goal (more precisely by the desire that is its felt presence). Yet it is no more voluntary than the simple act of seeing the bill. For it to be voluntary, the above question must be posed. In the answer, a key role is played in the thought of what sort of person I want to be. Shall I be the person who takes what he can get or the person who has determinedly returned the proper change? Choice, thus, involves the grasp of alternate (and, often, multiple) possibilities of the self. For such grasp to be possible, I must escape the narrow confines of the specific behavior imposed by a given environment. For this, however, I must possess mind. Conceptualization, insofar as it involves the grasp of what transcends the particular circumstances of a particular environment, is an escape from the pressure of the desires springing from such circumstances. The "taking thought" involved in choice does not, then, involve the situation of the proverbial ass perishing of hunger and thirst as it remains equidistant between water and hay. It is, rather, a stepping back, one that allows a weighing or measuring of conflicting desires without being immediately subject to them.

So regarded, the openness of mind is the openness of freedom. Both imply the separation of self and environment provided by conceptualization. Thus, negatively, both imply the *lack* of determination of self by the environment. Such separation, however, does not mean that either mind or freedom is absolute. They cannot be, given that mind only works in and through the material (the specific perceptual senses) provided by the environment it experiences. In the absence of any access to such materials, both it and the freedom it implies, collapses. Positively, the identity of the openness of freedom with that of mind, distinguishes freedom from mere whim. The prior fact, here, is mind. Given this, we must reverse Heidegger's assertion that freedom is the ground of reason.[13] Existing only in the context of mind and, hence, of the reason that employs its conceptual units, we have to say that without reason and *its* ability to grasp the "could be otherwise" of a given set of circumstances, there is no freedom. To this, of course, we must add that what makes freedom real is more than the simple conception of alternatives. It is the fact of having to choose. I cannot both take the fifty dollar bill and return it. I cannot because I am finite. I am finite because my subjectivity is embodied. More precisely, as flesh, my subjectivity achieves its goals by embodying them; but as such, it cannot escape the limits of its bodily positionality. Given this, the reality of freedom involves the placing of the openness of mind in the limitations imposed by embodiment. Open to everything on the conceptual level, we must choose if we wish to actually achieve the goals we set for ourselves. This does not mean that the choosing is on the level of embodiment. Embodiment imposes the necessity to choose, but not the choice itself. The choice, to be voluntary, must be worked out on the level of mind. As we

13. In Heidegger's words, "Freedom is the origin of principle of sufficient reason." This is the principle that nothing is without its cause (*Grund*). Since freedom is ultimate, that is, since freedom does not itself have any ground, Heidegger also calls it "the *abyss* of Dasein" (*der Abgrund des Daseins*). It forms its ground-less character. See *The Essence of Reasons*, pp. 123, 129.

said, at issue is what sort of self the chooser wants to be. In considering the alternatives and working out their probable outcomes, the attempt is to arrive at the best "self." In this, there is an analogue to the dialectic of intention and fulfillment discussed in our last chapter. As long as the process continues, different intentions continually arise. Each is directed to a different self, one that arises from a different choice of conduct. These putative selves are tested for their consequences in the light of our experience and the advice of others. The advice of moralists from Plato to Kant and Mill has been directed towards informing this inner debate. Each has given his position, not just on what the best self consists in, but also on the rules for achieving this. That they can hope to be heard points to the fact that the dialectic involved is similar to that by which we grasp a perceptual sense in that it, also, is an openness. It is an openness to the teleological action of the self ultimately taken as the best, that is, taken as the most worthy to be instantiated. We should not look at this "best" self as some sort of original we, through our actions, are creating a replica of. Just as the reality of the sensible object is in the perceiver, so the reality of the self we choose is within us. Its actuality is in the actions that embody it.

§4. *Flesh and Cartesian Dualism.* Returning to the most general level, we may note the interrelation of the elements of our account of flesh. For example, goal and desire are related insofar as the felt presence of a goal is desire. Desire is, we can say, flesh's openness to the teleological presence of being. Thus, to speak of goals and one-way touch is also to speak in terms of desire and the motion it prompts. Given that time is also a function of such openness, we can say that the presence of desire comes with the presence of a distinct, teleological temporality. Flesh, in manifesting it, stands out from the inanimate world. This temporal standing out, this temporal "existence" of flesh, is the way in which desire separates flesh from the world. Animated by desire, flesh discloses itself as other than the world, an otherness that is manifested in a different temporality. The same temporality, as it functions in the perceptual process, allows objects to have what we may call an "epistemological" as opposed to a mere bodily presence. Bodies are present to one another through the causality of inanimate agents. Perceptual objects, by contrast, come to presence as goals. They are the "not-yets" that our interpretative syntheses attempt to make present. By virtue of its intentional relation to such objects, consciousness itself exists, i.e., stands out as something distinct. The fact that the temporality associated with its embodiment involves reflexivity, gives us, as we said, the possibility of self-consciousness. With this, we have the possibility of grasping ourselves in our flesh as other than the world.

This otherness is not that between mind and body, but between flesh and the world. With this, we have our answer to the Cartesian problem posed at this chapter's beginning. The answer is not a direct one; we have not actually related "mind" and "body" as Descartes defined these terms. In drawing on the Aristotelian paradigm, we shifted the ground, our purpose being to transform the categories in which the problem was framed. An example of such Cartesian framing is provided by the problem's contemporary formulation. The mind-body problem, it is asserted, is that of showing how physiological events cause mental events and how mental events, in turn, cause physiological events. My recalling an unhappy event causes my blood pressure to rise. Reciprocally, a rise in my blood pressure causes me to hear a ringing in the ears. Admitting these facts, the question is: How is such causality possible? This formulation is Cartesian because the whole notion of mental events causing physiological ones *presupposes their nonidentity.* We take mental events as conscious and, hence, as spatially nonextended processes. We take their physiological counterparts as spatially extended, nonconscious processes. Thus mental events are examined by questioning a person about his conscious life. In such questioning, we assume, as we must, that it makes no sense to talk of one mental experience as so many centimeters distant from another. Such an assumption is, however, appropriate in the examination of the physiological event. We investigate the latter by examining the chemistry and electrical activity of the patient's brain. As is obvious, to pose the problem in these terms is to become trapped in the Cartesian categories of the extended and the nonextended. Whenever we proceed from the assertion of a reciprocal mind-body causality to an investigation of the distinct agencies of the mental and the physiological, we become engaged in a rhetoric whose terms seem to deny any possibility of an answer.

To escape from this is to realize that the point is not to describe such reciprocal causality. The solution to the Cartesian problem does not come by offering an explanation of how the soul moves the body or the body moves the soul. It arises by understanding their identity in flesh's standing out. This includes the realization that mental life (the conscious element of soul) does not describe a type of being, one that could exercise *its* causality. It describes, rather, a function, namely, that of synthesis. Where matter exhibits it, where it processes information in a way that would allow the presence of an object as a one-in-many, there is intentionality and there is, at least on the perceptual level, a mental life. The result, to use the scholastic term, is a "cogitational existence." It is the kind of being in the mind that a one-in-many exhibits.[14]

Perhaps the best way to put this is in terms of Leibniz's example of the mill. Expanding the mind, taken as "a machine whose structure produced thought, sensation, and perception," to the size of a mill, we "would," Leibniz claims, "only find pieces working upon one another." We would, not, however, "find anything to explain Perception" ("Monadology," §17; p. 254). As we noted, the search in the mill is for "perception" taken as something distinct from the mind's mechanical structure. It is a search for a different type of being, one that could exercise its own type of causal agency. So regarded, the search is doomed from the start by the Cartesian dualism implicit in this example. Now, to actually find perception, we must not attend to the mill as a collection of material elements "working upon one another." Our focus should be, rather, on the algorithm instantiated by such working. The algorithm is not a causal agent. It is rather something instantiated by the causal agency of the material elements "working upon one another." The same point can be made by noting that its laws (the rules it expresses) are not the same as causal laws. Thus the same algorithm (say, that for addition) can be instantiated in a number of machines. With their different material structures, the causal laws applicable to the modern electronic calculator and the old fashioned, crank-operated adding machine are different; yet the algorithm is the same. The same holds for the brain, which, in spite of all the talk about its being like a computer, most resembles, in its material structure, a large secreting gland. It, too, can add. This means that it can, in its own biochemical processes, instantiate the algorithm. Now, if the synthetic function of perception is itself an algorithm, the same set of descriptions apply. The fact that brains instantiate it does not mean that it is tied to brains and their peculiar biochemical processes. It is distinct from them in the same way that the algorithm for addition is distinct. In pointing to it, we point neither to a material process in its material-causal laws nor to some separate substance understood as possessing its own agency. What we point to is a function that when it is instantiated by a material process, makes that process intentional.

We have already given the basic descriptions of (if not the actual algorithms involved in) this synthetic function. On the most basic level, the function involves the receptivity to time that marks the beginning of con-

---

14. Insofar as this being also exists as a goal, mental life also includes the desire that is its felt presence.

scious life. On this level, functioning is registering, retaining, and temporally tagging the appearances of being. Beyond this, of course, it involves
syntheses of the appearances it has so distinguished. It involves, in other
words, the functioning that produces ongoing perceptual sense as a persistent presence within the multiplicities of its temporally distinct appearances. With this, we have the intentional character, the "aboutness," which
stands as the distinguishing feature of the mental as opposed the physiological event. We also have the germ of the subject-object distinction—
this, at least, insofar as the subjective is taken as the sphere of the elements
of synthesis (one which includes the functioning itself), while the objective is taken as the process's result. These distinctions, however, do not
mark off distinct spheres of being. It is not as if, on the subjective side, we
have the mental event with some irreducible quality (one incapable of
further analysis) called "intentionality," a quality absent on the objective
side. The features that mark the intentional relation are, rather, those
which characterize being insofar as it is engaged in a distinct temporal
relation. Through its instantiating the appropriate algorithms in its functioning, being possesses the type of temporality that results in epistemological as opposed to mere bodily presence. The algorithms can thus be regarded
as resulting in a distinct type of openness to epistemological presence.
Given, however, their ontological neutrality, that is, their inherent silence
on the causal conditions that might instantiate them, this is openness that
all sorts of material circumstances are capable of instantiating.

It might be objected to the foregoing that it has only transformed, not
overcome, Cartesian dualism. In place of the old mind-body dualism, we
have introduced a new dualism of two different forms of temporal determination. The temporality of the animate world (of "flesh") is teleological.
By contrast, the temporality of the inanimate world is that of the simple
time line of Cartesian physics. This dualism, it can be objected, plays itself
out in the relations of final to efficient causality. In the position we have
presented, the mind is taken as moving the body as a final cause, while its
muscles (or rather the chemical reactions taking place within them) move
it as an efficient cause. Corresponding to the different forms of temporal
determination, we have assumed two types of causality without giving any
thought to their interrelation. A variant of this objection, we may recall,
was raised against our argument that intentionality could not be characterized as a material-causal relation, since its object was not a material
entity, but rather a perceptual sense. The objection was that the interpretation that resulted in this sense was itself materially caused, since it
took place in a material agent (see page 141). Given this, how can we

assume both the teleological causality of the mind and the material/effi-
cient causality of the circumstances of the mind's instantiation? A sign that
our assuming both amounts to dualism would be our inability to relate the
two. Generally speaking, what is wrong with "dualism" is not the distinctions it attempts to make. It is rather its incoherence, that is, its inability to
relate the duality it uncovers. In the present case, however, *one form of
temporality includes the other.* Thus the circle we used to symbolize teleological temporality contains, as we earlier noted, two different lines of
temporal determination:

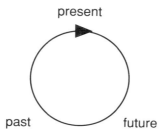

Beginning with the past, the line of determination reads: past-present-future. Beginning with the future, it reads: future-past-present. What the circle symbolizes is that the two types of temporal determination are not
opposed. They are actually part of one process. Thus the teleological process, which begins with the future, must include the material process,
which begins with the past. It must accomplish the realization of the goal,
not by bypassing, but by using efficient causality. This is what happens in
perception with the biological instantiation of the algorithms for interpretation and synthesis. It is also what life does in all of its projects. Life
uses the processes of inanimate nature to accomplish its goals. It is only
when we fail to acknowledge this that we fall into the incoherence of
opposing the animate to the inanimate, or the soul to the body, or the
mind to the brain. Each of these pairs represent opposing, yet complementary aspects of one and the same line of determination. Flesh, as we have
described it in this chapter, actually involves both.

7

Receptivity and Selfhood

Receptivity and the Reduction

All the fundamental positions of this book have involved the assertion of teleological processes. Knowing, for example, has been described as a teleological function. Epistemological, as opposed to bodily presence, has been taken as the presence of a goal. Similarly, it was precisely our attempt to conceive knowing teleologically that allowed us, in Chapter 5, to "break the circle." This was the circle of explaining the knowledge of the laws of material causality through the laws of thought and explaining the latter through the laws of material causality. As we said, "Breaking this circle . . . means conceiving these laws in some other fashion. It means . . . recognizing them as teleological, that is, as laws for processes that are future directed" (see page 109). In our attempt to do this, we introduced the dialectic of intention and fulfillment and took the laws of knowing as the laws of this dialectic. More particularly, we took them as the algorithms whose instantiation would result in this dialectic. This was because such instantiation was, we claimed, actually the instantiation (or embodiment) of an openness to goals. Such openness, taken on the most general level of sentient, animate life, is what makes such life "stand out" or distinguish itself from the inanimate.

Our original motivation for pursuing this path arose from our analysis of

modernity. Specifically, the impulse came from the incoherence of the
Cartesian project—namely, from its inability to account for its foundations, an inability that resulted in its self-referential inconsistency. Given
this, we have to ask: What does the teleology we have advanced imply
about itself? Does it escape such inconsistency? The inconsistency in the
Cartesian project centered around its inability to account for the knowing
subject. The categories of being it permitted made impossible the subject
which could construct the "system" the project called for. Thus they made
impossible that receptivity to being which could result in anything other
than a mere bodily presence. Defined in terms of its receptivity to bodies,
the subject appeared as a mere thing, as an entity capable of having only
bodily relations with other bodies. Turning such thoughts on our own pro-
posals, we have to ask whether they can account for their own foundation.
The questions here are: What are the categories of being underlying our
teleological account of knowing? How do they affect our notions of receptivity and, in particular, our conception of the subject as "the place" of
such receptivity. If we are not to conceive of it as a physical, spatial place
in the Cartesian sense, how are we to conceive it?

§1. *The Question of Receptivity.*   A first answer to such questions comes
from recalling what we said about the reversal of modernity. Without a
conceptual shift involving the basic ontological positions of modernity, the
teleology we have presented is impossible. For modernity, time is a receptacle for events. It is a kind of independent reality that exists prior to
entities as a *condition* for their existing. Given this, the order of the causality of entities depends upon the order of time. What is temporally prior
is taken as the cause of what follows. Assuming, then, that time flows from
the past to the present to the future, the future, by virtue of its temporal
position, can never be a cause of what precedes it. It cannot because, at
the moment of its supposed causal action, it does not yet exist. At a stroke,
we eliminate the ontological foundation of the notion of final causality.
With this, the very concept of teleological action becomes unintelligible.
To assert such action, we must, then, engage in a conceptual shift. We have
to assert that the order of time is dependent on the order of the causality
of entities, not the reverse. Given this shift, if the goal is causally determinative, then it gives us the causal sequence according to which time
moves from the future through the past to the present. This priority of
causality over time is actually a priority of that which exercises causality.
It is, in other words, a priority of being. Thus, our conceptual shift implies
that being, in determining causality, determines time. This is also a reversal

of the modern view, which, in taking space and time as determining the order of causality, understands being as essentially an event resulting from causal processes. Once we do assert that causality is an effect of being, the origin of the causal sequence must occur where the being capable of initiating it first appears. If this being appears at the end of the process, then this is where the source of the causal sequence must lie. In Aristotle's terms, we must treat the end or "telos" of the process as its source. The "coming into being" must be directed by this end. In perception, for example, the positing of the goal is integral to the perceptual process, the goal being what first makes possible the interpretation of the perceptual content. As such, the goal is what directs the "coming into being" of the embodied perceptual sense. Given this, we must assume a corresponding temporal flow. The same holds wherever such goal-directed behavior appears. Our conceptual shift implies that, in each such case, a corresponding causality and temporal flow should be assumed.

The question that remains, once these points have been made, is that of receptivity. How are we to understand it? In the Cartesian framework, its concept is that of one event setting up another. On the one side, we have the original object located at one point in space, on the other, the replica occurring within the perceiver. Its schema is that of the original sending me its likeness across space in time. In Descartes's words, it is "that this alien entity sends to me and imposes upon me its likeness" (*Meditations*, III; p. 37). This imposition is its setting up in the perceiver a set of spatial-temporal processes occurring within the optic nerve and brain. We early on noted the difficulties associated with this account (see page 17). Quite apart from such difficulties, we cannot avail ourselves of it. The account presupposes space and time as already given; we cannot. Our conceptual shift implies, then, that the very factors which, in the Cartesian account, define being, cannot be taken by us as the foundations for its presence. The shift demands that they be taken as the *results* of our receptivity to being. The question is: How are we to think this receptivity without assuming the givenness of space and time?

The same question can be put in terms of the analysis of how we grasp time through the retentional process. One way of analyzing this process would assert that *as time passes,* we register distinct impressional, content-filled moments. Through the retentional process, understood as a process *occurring in time,* we retain not just the impressional content of each moment but also the time (the temporal tag) of its occurring. The synthesis of what we retain, thus, results, not just in the grasp of an objective content, but also of the time through which this content has endured. The important point here is that retention is conceived as a retaining of *already given* moments. It is simply a preserving of what already exists. This, however, is just what we cannot assert once we engage in our conceptual shift. Our position has to be that just as the actuality of the perceptual object is in the perception, so also the actuality of time is in the same perception. In other words, time, like the sensible object, is in the person apprehending it. What is "outside" the perception is material for this, but it is not the actuality. There is no external original against which it can be measured. To be sure, there is change. Various regards to a clock show the hands in different places. This spatial change, however, is not yet a temporal change. Time, as time, finds its reality in the person registering a spatial change. If we grant this, then we cannot talk of a receptivity to time as something occurring in time. To do so, would be to return to the Cartesian conception of time as a receptacle, as a kind of universal placeholder, in which events such as retention have their place. If we wish to avoid this, the actuality of time (like that of the sensible object qua sensible) must come to presence in the subject in some original manner. For this, however, we must conceive of time, not as a condition for our receptivity to being, but as a result of such receptivity. The question, of course, is how we are to do this. How do we conceive receptivity as prior to time? Is this conception to be regarded as the result of a chain of inference— an unobservable yet a necessary condition for experience uncovered through a kind of Kantian deduction—or is there some way of observing such receptivity directly?

The same question can be raised with regard to space. The priority of being over time is also its priority over space. In fact, the latter follows from the former insofar as our sense of space as a three-dimensional continuum requires time. It is dependent on the retention and temporal tagging of our experiences. Temporality, in other words, is implicit in our sense of space, since we achieve this sense through the temporal ordering of experiences into the perspectival series that reveal objects as positioned in space. Objects owe their sense of being "near" or "far" to the relative rates of unfolding of such series. For example, as I walk through a park, trees close by match my progress by receding at the same speed, objects at a middle range glide by at a more stately pace, while objects marking the distant horizon scarcely seem to move. Each, in fact, has its own rate of showing its different aspects, and each rate is coordinated to its changing distance from me. Learning to grasp space is, in large part, learning to gauge these temporally unfolding series. It is, in fact, learning to perform the syntheses that interpret these patterns of perceptions as appearances of objects *in* space. In certain forms of dissociation, the synthetic function breaks down. When this happens, there is a loss of the sense of space. As we noted, the world flattens out; it loses its depth. The same phenomena occur in individuals who have not yet learned how to perform perceptual synthesis. Adults, who have just gained their sight through eye operations, cannot yet put objects together, that is, grasp them as unities of appearance. Because of this, they cannot yet grasp either their own or their objects' positions in space.[1] Given that this sense of space is the result of synthesis, it cannot be taken as a condition for it. It cannot, because to do so would involve us in that circle, so characteristic of modernity, of making something a condition of that which we take as *its* condition. The circle here is that of taking synthesis as a defining condition for space and then taking synthesis as, itself, a space-filling process. The latter positions space as something "in" which synthesis, itself, has to be before it can exist. It makes space a defining condition for synthesis. The same point holds concerning receptivity. As a condition for synthesis, it cannot depend on its result. It must then be thought in terms that are prior to the sense of space arising from synthesis. Similarly, insofar as this sense of space includes the sense of there being objects "out there," that is, spatially distinct from ourselves, receptivity must also be thought of as prior to this sense. In other words, such objects, in their very sense of being "out there," must be thought of as a result rather than a cause of the synthetic processes that begin with our receptivity to being.

This view is demanded by our conceptual shift. The latter, in turn, is required if teleological processes are to be possible. The question, however, remains: How are we to conceive receptivity in this fashion? Are we

1. The neurologist, Oliver Sacks, writes that they all face "great difficulties after surgery in the apprehension of space and distance—for months, even years" ("To See and Not See," p. 63). Reporting on one particular individual, Virgil, he writes: "He would pick up details incessantly—an angle, an edge, a color, a movement—but would not be able to synthesize them, to form a complex perception at a glance. This was one reason the cat, visually, was so puzzling: he would see a paw, the nose, the tail, and ear, but could not see all of them together, see the cat as a whole" (p. 64). "Moving objects," he goes on to observe, "presented a special problem, for their appearance changed constantly. Even his dog, he told me, looked so different at different times that he wondered if it was the same dog" (p. 66). Frequently unable to perform the syntheses that would give him individual objects, his sense of space would also go. In Sacks words, "surfaces or objects would seem to loom, to be on top of him, when they were still quite a distance away" (p. 63). Such observations lead Sacks to conclude that, as generated by visual perception, the idea of space cannot be present before it occurs. In his words: "If one can no longer see in space then the *idea* of space becomes incomprehensible" (ibid., p. 65). This seems to imply that blind people have an idea of motion (as given by their own bodies' movement) quite apart from the idea of space.

left here simply with a deduction, one that, beginning with the teleological conception of knowing, infers the dependence of space and time on synthesis, and from this concludes that synthesis and, hence, receptivity cannot depend on space and time? If we are to escape from having performed a deduction to an essentially unobservable conclusion, there must be a way of intuitively encountering such receptivity. We must be able to observe our registering of being prior to any positing of space and time, that is, before any grasp of space and time in their Cartesian sense as containers of being. Yet, how are we to do this?

The same question of receptivity can be raised in terms of the subject. What do we mean by saying that the sensible object, as actually sensible, is "in" the subject? In a Cartesian sense, for something to be "in" me is for it to be within me spatially. Accordingly, the Cartesian takes the perception as an event occurring in a location—namely, the brain and optic nerve. This sense cannot be assumed here. But if this is so, how are we to think of the subject? What is its sense as the "place" of our receptivity to being? What, in other words, is the nature of its being? What, moreover, is *our access* to this place, given that it is neither placed *within* space nor positioned *within* time in the Cartesian sense?

§2. *The Reduction.*   The key to the question of access is given by Descartes himself, more particularly, by his method of radical doubt. It is radical in the sense that it attempts to get at the root or foundation of things. Its context, in other words, is a situation where what is at issue are not individual particulars, but rather the very categories that set the terms of the debate. Descartes's motive for practicing it is instructive. It is, he says, his realization that many of his initial opinions as a youth were false. This implies the doubtfulness of all he subsequently derived from them. To get a secure beginning, he must, he asserts at the opening of the *Meditations,* raze the whole edifice to its first foundations so as to begin again. The point of this destruction is to avoid thinking of these first foundations in terms of what was later built upon them. It is, in other words, to examine directly the foundations he uncritically accepted and built upon as a youth.

So regarded, the method of doubt is a type of reduction. Rather than engaging in arguments whose categories are at issue, doubt is used to suspend such categories—this, in order to search, unencumbered, for their evidential basis. It is, in other words, a *reducing* of such categories to the evidence which would justify their use. Implicit in Descartes's talk of foundations is, then, the relation of thesis and evidence. Through doubt, we call a thesis into question to examine its evidence. Now, the same relation of thesis and evidence is present in the interpretive syntheses through which we construct our world. The thesis is given by the interpretive intention, that is, by our goal understood as what we intend to see. The evidence consists of the phenomena whose presence is supposed to fulfill this intention. Either the phenomena fit the pattern of appearing required by the intention—the pattern, say, of the appearing of a cat—or they do not. If they do, then their connections allow the ongoing presence of this object. We continue to have the positing belief that the successive appearances are its appearances. To perform the reduction is, here, to suspend this belief in order to regard the evidence for it. I do this when, for example, I begin to doubt that I am seeing a cat and look more closely at what I take to be its appearances.[2] Do they, in fact, fit the expected pattern of appearing? In each case, the point of this suspension is to avoid the logical error of assuming one's thesis as part of the evidence for it. Thus, once I begin to doubt the opinions I acquired in my youth, I cannot use the opinions I have based on them to argue for their correctness. To do so would be to assume their basis, namely, the very opinions I am arguing for. The same holds when I perform the reduction on a perceptually embodied sense. Doubting it, I cannot use this sense as part of the evidence for it. It cannot, itself, be taken as one of the appearances underlying its positing.

The relation of thesis and evidence is often multilayered. In science, for example, a thesis can serve with other theses as evidence for a more complex assertion. This assertion, in turn, can serve as part of the foundation for a further claim. The same holds for perceptual syntheses. This means that the reduction can be exercised again and again to move from synthetic or founded unities to their founding phenomena. In each instance, what we do is attempt to look at the evidence of the phenomena through whose connections the founded appears. When these founding phenomena owe their own appearing to the connections between even lower level phenomena, we can exercise the reduction again. We can employ it on such lower level phenomena. The process can, thus, continue until we reach what cannot be further reduced, namely, an original presence whose appearing is absolutely foundational. This means that were we to go beyond it—this, through suspending our positing belief in its presence—no further presence would be revealed. Attempting to pass beyond it to its foundation, we would be left with nothing at all.

2. This action is a self-conscious, reflective act. As such, it is not part of what we have described as the dialectic of intention and fulfillment. It is, rather, a breaking off from it in order to self-consciously regard its process. The dialectic, in other words, is part of the synthetic process. The reduction is the *reverse* of this.

Given that the point of the reduction is to find what is foundational, we should, then, be able to apply it to the process of synthesis to uncover what is absolutely original, that is, what cannot further be reduced. If, in particular, the appearing of space and time is an original appearing, then the attempt to further exercise the reduction should be fruitless. If, however, we are successful, what we do encounter will be their basis. Having suspended—at least, in thought—all positing of space and time as something already given, we should encounter the coming to presence which is at their origin. This point can be put in terms of a two-stage reduction. Having reduced the phenomena of space to those of time—in particular, to the temporal arrangement of appearances—we should be able to perform the reduction on the latter. If we are successful, we should be able to grasp a coming to be of time that does not presuppose the result of such coming to be, namely, already given time. Thus the presence we encounter should be prior to time.

The success of this reduction would be nothing less than the overturning of the fundamental position of modernity, namely, its assertion of the dependence of being on time. Assuming that being is temporal presence, it understands time as the ground of being. For modernity, as we said, time is what, in its passage, makes the entity temporally present and, hence, be. It is this belief, we may note in passing, that turns its account of the syntheses of consciousness into a constitutive idealism. The basing of being on time makes the temporal synthesis that results in an object's temporal presence actually constitutive of its being. To escape this, we would have to reverse this dependence; we would, in other words, have to successfully perform the reduction on the passage of time. What we would then encounter as founding this passage would not be temporal presence, but rather its ground. The same point can be made with regard to modernity's attempt to base being on knowing. The syntheses of consciousness are, broadly speaking, the performances by which we know objects. Performing the perceptual syntheses that give me, say, a cat, I perceptually know or encounter the latter. The cat is there for me as an epistemological presence. If these syntheses actually constitute being, then the performances by which I know the object also generate its being. Such being is equated with its epistemological presence and, as such, is treated as a result or accomplishment of the knowing process.[3] To reverse this, I need

3. Husserl provides the best example of this. He writes, for example: "Genuine epistemology . . . instead of dealing with contradictory inferences which lead from a supposed immanence to a supposed transcendence . . . has to do with a systematic explanation of the accomplishment of knowing, an explanation in which this becomes thoroughly understand-

not deny that the syntheses in question are those of knowing. But I do have to deny that they are constitutive of being—which I do by reversing the dependence of being on time. The reversal, however, depends on the success of the reduction of temporal becoming to a pre-temporal presence. The being that was such presence could then be seen as foundational for the syntheses that result in knowing. If we take this last view as a kind of realism, opposing it to the "subjective idealism" of its modern alternative, we can say that the outcome of the realism-idealism debate depends on the result of the reduction. Yet nothing we have said indicates that it will be successful. This lack of indication points to its neutrality as a method, that is, to its independence of the issues at stake.

For Descartes, the method of doubt takes us almost, but not quite, to the required level as it leads him from the world to the self. He begins by assuming that there is "no earth, no sky, no extended bodies, no shape, no size, no place"—that is, that all the perceptual evidence he has previously accepted for the existence of the world is actually false (*Meditations*, I; p. 20). If this is so, he cannot assume that he has a physical presence within the world. Doubting this, he writes, "I will consider myself as having no hands, no eyes, no flesh, no blood, nor any senses, yet falsely believing that I have all these things" (p. 22). Turning towards himself, he observes that he cannot assume that he is a "rational animal," since these terms are now highly problematical. Once the world has been doubted, every description of himself whose terms are drawn from the world, becomes doubtful. What cannot be doubted is simply his thinking. As thinking, he exists. He adds, however: "But for how long do I exist? For as long as I think" (*Meditations*, II; p. 26). What remains from his method of doubt is, then, a kind of continuous occurring, called "thinking." Thinking involves the contents of his mental life, the experiences and actions making it up. It does not, however, involve them as part of the world. They are not within the world taken as a spatial-temporal continuum, since they are certain, whereas this world has been dissolved (or suspended) by doubt. Strictly speaking, if we remain faithful to Descartes's method, we cannot, as he does, assert that the self is a thinking thing or substance, since this would imply thought was an attribute of something underlying it, something that could continue even when thought was absent. What we must, rather, do is abstract from

---

able as an intentional accomplishment. Precisely thereby, every being itself, be it real or ideal, becomes understandable as a constituted *product* [*Gebilde*] of transcendental subjectivity, a product that is constituted in just such an accomplishment" (*Cartesianische Meditationen*; §41; Hua I, 118). Reduced to plain terms, this passage asserts that being itself is a product of knowing; it is an "accomplishment" of the "intentional" process of knowing.

the *cogito* or "I think" all content that presupposes the existence of the world. We must think of it as an occurring that is independent of every category drawn from the world.[4]

To proceed any further in this direction is to take up the reduction as it applies to the syntheses of perception. So regarded, its first stage is the suspension of the syntheses that give us a spatial-temporal world. It is, in other words, the holding in abeyance of the positing belief in this world. Descartes does this by supposing "an evil genius, as clever and deceitful as he is powerful," who has tricked him into believing that there is such a world. For us, a simple "thought experiment" can suffice. We can imagine the disordering of the connections by which we experience objects. Husserl's description of this experiment is still the best. He writes: "Let us imagine ourselves performing apperceptions of nature, but such as are continually invalid, apperceptions which are canceled in the process of further experience; let us imagine that they do not allow of the harmonious connections in which experiential unities could constitute themselves for us" (*Ideen I,* §54; Hua III/1, 118). The result is that, in thought at least, "the whole of nature" has been "destroyed"; and this includes human beings taken as part of nature, that is, as "animate bodies [*Leiber*]" (ibid.). This destruction, we may note, is the destruction of space. Once we disorder the perspectival patterns of appearing required for the presence of three-dimensional objects, individual experiences remain; but they are not spatial objects. Were they spatial objects, they could themselves be experienced as *in* space. To be in space is to be capable of being viewed from different sides. This, however, is impossible for them. A perspectival view is not something that can show itself perspectivally.[5] In fact, individually regarded, it has no size at all. We cannot, for example, say that our experience of a meter stick is itself a meter long. The amount of the visual field it takes up is variable. To apportion it, we would have to have some idea of the distance at which it is viewed. Yet, as we have seen, the very notion of distance depends on synthesis, that is, on precisely those connections which we have imagined as disordered. Thus the first result of the reduction is not just the dissolution of space. It is the discovery that it is not irreducible—not something originally given. The pre-spatial elements of experience that found it can be present without its being present. Because of this, we cannot say that space is a founding condition for synthesis.

4. Were Descartes to do this, it would, of course, be far more difficult for him to undo his doubt, that is, to begin the process that leads to the attempt to describe thought as a spatial-temporal process.

5. Were it, a regress would follow: that of perspectives showing themselves through perspectives and so on indefinitely.

The dissolution of the visual, spatial world has a corresponding effect on the self that is correlated to it. As we cited Oliver Sacks: "Perceptual cognitive processes . . . lead to, are linked to, a personal self, with a will, an orientation, and a style of its own" ("To See and Not See," p. 68). Their collapse is its collapse. Thus, with the suspension of the performances giving the self a three-dimensional, spatial world, we have its own suspension as a spatial center of this world. Given that there is no longer any spatial distance in its world, it cannot regard itself as the place from which distances are marked off. Pursuing the reduction, we can imagine the suspension of those processes of syntheses which give us the world we experience through sound and touch. Their collapse would give us a corresponding collapse of the hearing and touching self that is correlated to them. As Husserl notes, the reduction can be pursued to the point that we no longer can regard experiences as "subjective." Disordering the connections that link them to the self (which establish them as "my" experiences), we can imagine their temporal passage without any referent to a person, a psychological subject, who experiences them.[6]

To go beyond this, we have to exercise the reduction on this temporal passage itself. I have a temporal world insofar as I have a past and a future. The past is present to me in the form of the long-term memories by which I preserve the results of my already accomplished syntheses. It also is there by virtue of short-term memories or retentions. These actually give me my immediate sense of expiration or departure into pastness. Both forms of memory provide me with the material for my interpretative intentions which I direct to the future. Expecting that the future will continue the patterns of the past, I experience it as a set of anticipations. Just as the past situates me on one side of its ordered continuum of long- and short-term memories, so the future places me on the other side of its corresponding continuum of anticipations.[7] To exercise the reduction on this structure is, first of all, to disorder the long-term memories. Such memo-

---

6. In Husserl's words, "If there would be something still remaining which could permit the apprehension of the experiences as 'states' of a human ego—experiences in whose changes identical human mental traits manifested themselves—we could also think of these interpretations as robbed of their existential validity [Seinsgültigkeit]. The experiences, then, would remain as pure experiences. . . . *Even mental states [Auch psychische Zustände]* point back to the ordering of the absolute experiences in which they constitute themselves" (*Ideen I*, §54; Hua III/1, 119). The result, then, of this stage of the reduction is the cancellation of any positing of a "mental personality, mental characteristics, mental experiences or real mental states" (ibid.). It is the dissolution of what Husserl calls the "personal ego"—that is, the ego of the ordered connections that form the cogito.

7. Such anticipations are what Husserl calls "protentions." The term designates their status as intentions that "stretch forward" to what is to come.

ries, we noted, do not have, themselves, any sense of temporal position. They achieve this only by our linking them according to schemas such as cause and effect. To scramble them is to put such linking out of effect. With regard to short-term memories, their ordering is the result of two different factors. First of all, we have the continuous process that results in the retention of the retention of one and the same content. This gives us its departure into the past insofar as each retention (or framing) carries with it a sense of the not-newness or pastness of the retained. Synthesized, such elements give the sense of ongoing departure or increasing pastness. Our sense of pastness cannot, of course, depend on a single content. Its departure does not give the continuum of the past, but only one point in this. Such a single point, however, is unthinkable. A moment cannot be *in time* without the others that surround it. For the presence of the past, we need, then, a multitude of contents, all temporally distinguished by the different degrees of their retention. Their synthesis results in the sense of past time as a departing continuum. It is, of course, a synthesis of syntheses, since it includes the syntheses that give the departures of individual contents. To practice the reduction, here, is to suspend these syntheses. It is to imagine, first of all, what would be the case if there were no ordering and putting together of the senses of the different degrees of pastness of *different* contents. It is to imagine, secondly, the result of the failure to order and put together the different degrees of pastness as given by the framing or retention of *any single content.*

A number of conclusions can be drawn as a result of this thought experiment. The first is that all sense of the past would vanish. This follows by definition, given that its sense as a continuum of expiring moments is based on the syntheses we have suspended. With this, our sense of the future would also go. It cannot remain once we lose all access to the materials out of which our anticipations are formed. Given that our sense of self as a temporal center depends upon these two continua—that of past, expiring moments and that of future, approaching moments—it too would go. Perplexed in our inner temporality by a chaos of impressions, retentions, and anticipations, we would no longer have any sense of our nowness as a midpoint between the two flowing continua. It would no longer have the sense of a point of passage, a place toward which time streams from the future and from which it departs into pastness. This does not mean that we would be confronted with total stasis. A suspension of a synthesis is not a suspension of its elements. Indeed, to uncover a synthesis of different elements behind an appearing unity is already to declare that this unity is not originally given, but exists through the elements that can be given apart from it. Thus the occurring of the elements of temporal synthesis can be assumed. What cannot be posited is the temporal extension or positioning of such occurring. Without the past and the future, the occurring is limited to the present; but this is not a present within extended time.[8] What the reduction invites us to do is, then, to regard time's passing through the present simply in the context of this present. When we do, then what appeared to transit through it shows itself as a welling up within it. Passing through, in other words, is exhibited as the successive appearance in this present of what comes, through synthesis, to be regarded as the successive moments of extended time.

The result of this reduction is, in fact, the overturning of the two cardinal positions of modernity. The first is the notion of the irreducibility or original givenness of time. Rather than an ultimate condition for synthesis, time, taken as an extended continuum or receptacle, is shown to be a result of synthesis. It itself rests on a nontemporally extended occurring. Such an occurring, which is nonextended, cannot be in time. To regard this occurring, in a non-Cartesian (Aristotelian) sense, as time itself, is, however, to regard it as dependent. This follows, since, were it independent, it would never stop. With nothing conditioning it, nothing could change or end it. When, however, we sleep, or otherwise end our receptivity, this occurring also ends. Given this, what the reduction uncovers is the welling up of time, which occurs through our receptivity. Its origin, in other words, is our registering being in its changing presence. Given this, we have to abandon the second position of modernity. We cannot take the self as foundational, that is, as some sort of ultimate source point, through its syntheses, of being and validity. This follows because the practice of the reduction is the dismantling of the self. Its last appearance, that of a temporal center, disappears with the suspension of its centering temporal envi-

---

8. Husserl, having performed this reduction, describes its result as a nontemporally extended streaming of the elements of experience. It is a streaming that is limited to the present. In his words: "This streaming, living present is not what we elsewhere, also in a transcendental-phenomenological sense, designated as the stream of consciousness or stream of experiences. It is, *per se*, not a 'stream' according to the pattern of what is properly a temporal (or even a spatial-temporal) whole. . . . The streaming, living present is 'continuously' being *qua* streaming [*Strömendsein*], but it is not such in an apartness of being [*Auseinander-Sein*]. [It is] not [such] in the being that has a spatial-temporal, worldly spatial extension or the being that has an 'immanent' temporal extension. Thus, [it is] not [such] in the apartness which is called succession, succession in the sense of the apartness of positions in what can properly be called time" (Ms. C 3 I, p. 4a, 1930). Unfortunately, Husserl never draws the conclusion that the reduction's uncovering of a nontemporal occurring means that time cannot be an ultimate foundation for being. Because of this, his position remains idealistic.

ronment. More importantly, the reduction shows the condition for this appearing is not the self, but rather the occurring that registers the changing presence of being.

The Situating of Selfhood

To assert that the reduction passes through the self to its founding layers is, of course, to claim that the self is founded. The claim thus carries a corresponding obligation to describe this founding. Yet before we do so, we must make certain what precisely is the "self" that is supposed to be founded. Caution here is justified. Behind the difficulties of the modern attempt to make the self an ultimate foundation is the unavoidable ambiguity of what counts as a self. The ambiguity carries over to the nature of its receptivity.

§1. *What Is a Self?*   If we ask, "What is a self?" a number of answers can be given. I can think of myself in terms of my personal and social relations, that is, as a fully concrete member of the intersubjective community. I can also focus on my physical presence, taking myself as this face, these hands, and so on. Alternately, I can think of myself as the soul or psychological self animating this body. The self is then understood to be my feelings, emotions, experiences, acts, and intentions, in short, everything that goes on in the inner sphere I call my consciousness. Proceeding still further, I can conceive the self as the underlying unity behind all the shifting contents of consciousness. The self is then what remains through their change. The acts are its acts, but it remains even as they shift. Here the self is a kind of unchanging reference point, a point from which all the contents are viewed, all the acts performed.

Each of these answers correspond to a different stage of the reduction. The reduction, as we said, is the dismantling of the self; it is the uncovering of one layer after another by imagining the suspension of the syntheses that present each layer. What it does is undo the process of the self's generation. The self, accordingly, is each of the layers achieved by this generation. It is everything from simple central nowness to the fully concrete person interacting with others. More broadly, it is the continuous process of generation, stretching from one to the other. The process *is* the self in its ongoing achievement of concreteness. As such, it involves both specification and embodiment. With each stage, the self becomes more definite, more individually given. It embodies more and more features as the syntheses making it up become fulfilled or embodied by appropriate contents. Given this, we have a general answer to the question we raised about the notion of something being "in" the subject. To be "in" it is to be present as part of the material for the syntheses that result in the self. In its broad sense, being "in" it is being part of the process that is the "self" in its ongoing constitution.

Having said this, we have not yet said how such syntheses result in a self. Their immediate object is not the self, but rather its surrounding world. Yet their presence is its presence. As we cited Sacks, "Perceptual cognitive processes . . . lead to, are linked to, a personal self, with a will, an orientation, and a style of its own. This perceptual self may also collapse with the collapse of perceptual systems, and alter the orientation and very identity of the individual" ("To See and Not See," p. 68). In fact, this linking is a positioning. The "cognitive processes" or syntheses that yield a partic-ular objective environment *also result in the self as its center*. Their col-lapse is the collapse of the centering environment and, hence, of the self as centered by this.

A good example of the above is provided by the constitution of the lowest level of the self, that is, by the syntheses that result in its presence as central nowness. All its stages should already be familiar to us. It begins with the constitution of pastness through the syntheses associated with retention. Such constitution is also that of the original transcendence, this being the transcendence of pastness vis-à-vis the present. An original dis-tance is, thus, constituted. We have the generation of the temporal remove that allows the past to stand over against the present. The result of this is the positioning of the now of the original, pre-temporal occurring as a now in an extended temporal field. It becomes the point of departure, the "place," as it were, where moments well up to depart into pastness. The ultimate basis for this is, of course, the pre-temporal occurring. More pre-cisely, it is the registering of the shifting presence of being. The continuity of the pre-temporal now springs from the continuity of the being whose presence it is. The shift in this presence is what results in the newness of the same now, that is, in its manifesting a shifting content. The first tran-scendence comes, then, from the retentional positioning of this content as past—that is, as what *was* now. A second transcendence arises through a kind of "protending" or stretching forward from the past to the future. All intending is an anticipating and, with the production of the original tempo-ral remove, the intentions that make use of retained material achieve a temporal sense. They become anticipations of what will come to be. Their synthesis yields the presence of the future as that which stands over against the now in its approach to it. Surrounded by a double temporal remove, the original now thus becomes a central now. It achieves its identity as a now *within* an extended temporal environment. The self, *in its identity with it,* becomes the place through which time appears to flow and in which its content-laden moments appear to well up as present and actual.

The result is not just the positioning of the self as temporal center, as a source point for temporalization. It is also its original appearance as an actor. Remaining at the center, the self remains now—this, even though the content of the now shifts. As now, it becomes the place of action, the place where cognitive performances well up as present and actual. Such performances become "mine," that is, egological, by giving rise to a surrounding world. The surrounding world situates the performance. In doing so, it identifies its action with the nowness of the center. This is the center over against which the surrounding world stands. Pertaining to the immediate presence of the center, the action is not part of the objective presence of this surrounding world. It cannot be, because the action is temporally immediate, whereas the surrounding world exists at a certain temporal remove, the very remove that gives it its objectivity (its over-againstness, its nonidentity) vis-à-vis the acting self. Thus, the surrounding world is there by virtue of a synthesis of retained contents. Such contents have already departed from the immediacy of nowness. Their transcendence translates itself into the transcendence of the world. Distinguished from the immediate, ongoing nowness of the cognitive performance, the objective world, thus, "expels" this performance. It situates it as "mine," that is, as pertaining to the center that it transcends.

The consequence is a further sense of what "in" me signifies. Actions are "in" me insofar as they generate the environment that situates me. My situation is their situation. The actions become part of my increasing concreteness. This allows us to refine our original assertion that for something to be "in" me is for it to be part of the material for the syntheses that result in the self. We can now say that the syntheses accomplish this by positioning their own processes (including their material) as *processes of the self.* The constitution of the self's temporal and spatial environments gives the simplest examples of what we are pointing to. Prior to temporal synthesis, there is the pre-temporal occurring, which appears as the ultimate residuum of the reduction. By virtue of the constitution of the temporal environment, this occurring now appears to take place "in" me. In other words, in my identity with my ongoing central nowness, I become the place of the occurring. Its action, thus, appears as my action. Its pre-temporal occurring appears as a welling up "in" the center of an already constituted temporal environment. As this center, I become the locus of action, the place "in" which the content-laden moments appear to well up as present and actual. The same assertions can be made, mutatis mutandis, with regard to the higher-level cognitive processes (primarily those of visual perception) that result in the presence of the spatial-temporal world. Insofar as they make this world present as an environment, they situate themselves within it. So situated, they become localized in the perceiving "self" that embodies them. Situated within the spatial-temporal world, the self, thus, becomes the place where the perceptions generating this world come to presence.

As these last remarks indicate, the self should not be understood as a simple positionality. It would be a misreading of the above to take it as the abstract, central *now* of the temporal field or as a *here*, understood as the empty zero-point of the spatial field. The self is a performance, one which in each case is situated by the result of the performance. The complexity of the performance depends on the level involved, the lowest level being that of temporal constitution. In terms of our last chapter's account of "flesh," we can say that this performance begins the animation of the material being of the performer. It is, in other words, the beginning of his constitution as flesh. Thus, prior to the performance which results in time, we have a pre-temporal occurring that is simply a material registering of the shifting presence of being. The animation of this matter begins with the performance that generates the temporal distances that first allow objects to stand against it.[9] It is only at this point that it can engage in something other than the behavior (the inanimate motion) occasioned by mere bodily presence. The same holds for the much more complex perceptual-cognitive performances involved in the presentation of a surrounding spatial-temporal world. These performances can be described as the animation of the material being of the perceiver by the intentions that make up perception. They are his engagement in the goal-directed behavior that is perception. Accordingly, they are also the transformation of his material being into perceiving flesh. Flesh, as we said in our last chapter, engages in disclosive behavior—for example, the behavior that reveals the world as its visual, spatially extended environment. Revealing the latter, it reveals itself in it. Its performances, in other words, situate themselves as the *here* of the embodied perceiver. This is the *here* to which all the varying rates

---

9. Such performances, themselves, as we said in our last chapter, arise through the instantiation of the appropriate algorithm.

of the perspectival unfolding of its surrounding objects correspond as it changes its position. It is also, however, the *here* to which correspond the perspectival unfolding of its own bodily being. That one's own visual body can be considered objective, that is, as standing over against one, points to the fact that visual constitution of the self and its *here* is not ultimate. It proceeds on the basis of an ongoing temporal constitution. Such constitution yields a central now; and from its perspective, everything else, including one's body, appears as objective.

This central nowness is the deepest layer of the self. It is, in fact, the self reached by Cartesian doubt. To see this, we must first recall Descartes's description of this residuum. It is not a body—not a self having a "face, hands, arms, and all this mechanism composed of bone and flesh and members" (*Meditations,* II; p. 25). In the exercise of his doubt, Descartes assumes "that I have no senses; . . . that body, shape, extension, motion and location are merely inventions of my mind" (p. 23). In fact, he takes all the correlates of his thought as doubtful. What about the thinking itself? On the one hand, Descartes does affirm his being as a "thinking thing" (p. 26). On the other, however, he admits that "thinking" is a generic term covering a multitude of changing activities. The self, however, remains unchanged. This is essential to its indivisibility. As we quoted him, "It is one and the same mind which as a complete unit wills, perceives, and understands and so forth" (VI; p. 74). It cannot, then, be identified with any of these activities. What it is seems to be an underlying unity of attending, a lasting point of view *from which* all the objects of these acts can be regarded. Considered in itself, it is, thus, anonymous. Being neither an object of thought nor any changing act or content of experience, it cannot be described or named in their terms. Regarding it, I regard only "that indescribable part of myself which cannot be pictured by the imagination" (II; p. 28). The only thing that I can say is that it remains the same, that it keeps its unity in the change of its "thinking."

As our reduction reveals, what actually remains the same on the deepest level of the self is the temporal form of the streaming content, i.e., of the acts and experiences that make up such "thinking." No matter what the content, a central nowness with its centering environment remains. It is from the perspective of such nowness that objects are viewed. This cannot be otherwise, given that the very acts which constitute its environment situate their action within this ongoing nowness. Furthermore, to reduce the self to such nowness is to make it anonymous. What is actually anonymous is the nowness itself. Everything objective, that is, everything grasped through the synthesis of retained contents, stands over against it.

My anonymity as a self is, thus, a function of my remaining now while the experiences that just now characterized me depart into pastness. Grasping myself through their objective synthesis, I apprehend not the self I presently am, but rather the self I was. In this sense, I am no different from any other object. Every object I grasp already transcends me by virtue of the retained contents through which it is grasped. As transcendent, it is other than what I am in my central nowness.

We should not conclude from this that such nowness is empty. It is, as we said, the place where content-laden moments well up as present and actual. As such, it is the place of our receptivity, our openness to being. In a certain sense, its anonymity is one with the fact that this openness is such that it preserves itself as openness. No matter what it receives, it still remains receptive or open. This is because, not having any objective qualities, there is nothing to hinder its receptivity. Its anonymity, then, is its immateriality in the Aristotelian sense. As "immaterial," it has "no characteristic except its capacity to receive" (*De Anima* 429a22). This immateriality expresses itself in the fact that on the deepest level of our selfhood, we never become what we receive.

§2. *The Self's Duality.*   This, of course, does not mean that we exist only on this level. That we do not signifies that there is a certain duality of the self. Limited to my immediate nowness, I am anonymous. Another way to express this is to note that none of the senses I can grasp can apply to me. Sense, as such, is a one in many. It is a unity in a plurality of appearing, a plurality whose grasp requires the extension of time. This, however, is precisely what I lack in my immediate nowness. Limited to it, I lack all determination, including any determination of my actions. Given that I act only in the now, I, thus, appear to possess *a complete, if negative, freedom.*[10] Limiting one's focus on the acting self to the nowness in which it acts is, then, to strip it of all objective content and, hence, to strip it of everything that could count as an objective causal determination. Once, however, we expand our focus, we get a second, different view. The self, grasped objectively, has definite features. No longer anonymous, it has what we can call a character. Its grasp excludes, by definition, the nowness of my action. This is because my focus is now on the self, which is grasped through the synthesis of *retained* contents. Undisturbed by the presence of an actual actor, I am free in this "objective" regard to examine all the relations which link my past actions to causally determining factors. I can,

10. My grasp of myself as such is, of course, pre-reflective.

for example, subject myself to psychological or sociological analysis, focusing on my personal or interpersonal determinants. The results of this examination are, of course, the opposite of those of a corresponding "existential" analysis, which would focus on the self's undetermined freedom.

Viewed abstractly, the two types of analyses seem unalterably opposed.
In fact, their perceived opposition is part of the reason for the long-lasting
split between the social sciences and the humanities. Beginning with a
description of the factors *influencing* a person's behavior, social scientists
often slip over to describing such factors as causally determinative. The
freedom of the actor thus completely vanishes from the account. Such
freedom, however, is just as much a part of the self as the determining
factors. The self is both anonymous and objective, both free and determined. It is, in fact, the synthetic process that continually proceeds from
one to the other. Given this, neither answer can be completely correct. As
a consequence, what we face in trying to fix the self is a certain unavoidable ambiguity, a kind of "uncertainty principle" of the self. In physics, the
uncertainty principle applies to the momentum and position of a body. It
states that regardless of a body's particular mass or velocity, the simultaneous determination of its momentum and position is subject to an uncertainty that is at least as large as Planck's constant.[11] Our analogous formulation would be that the objective determination of our character and
our current decision is subject to an uncertainty as least as large as the so-
called specious present, this last being the area of unsynthesised data—
that is, the area of nowness in which we act. This means that a complete
determination of our character still leaves an unavoidable range of uncertainty concerning what our current decision will be. Similarly, a complete
knowledge of this decision leaves a certain unavoidable uncertainty regarding how much our character contributed to it. In spite of the style of
its formulation, this is not meant to be a quantifiable relation. It is meant
simply to express the concealment involved in the self's duality.

§3. *The Overcoming of Foundationalism.*   Two of our conclusions have a
direct bearing on the question of foundationalism. The first is that every
level of the self, from its being as an anonymous center to its appearance
as a fully concrete social being (a fully integrated member of the intersub-

---

11. Algebraically expressed: $\Delta p \Delta x \geq h$ or, dividing by the mass, $\Delta v \Delta x \geq h/m$ where p is
momentum, x is position, v is velocity, m is mass, and h is Planck's constant. The Δ stands for
the uncertainty, that is, the amount of indeterminacy. Thus, Δx can, for example, be read as
the difference of two values for the position of light, $x1$ being the top of a beam passing
through a hole and $x2$ being the bottom. The area of indeterminacy regarding the position
any particle of the light passing through the hole can, thus, be expressed by $\Delta x = x2 - x1$.

jective world), is a constituted formation. Taken as embracing all of these, the self is simply the synthetic process that proceeds without rest from one to the other. The second conclusion is that there is an essential "complementarity" that results from this. Opposite descriptions can be applied to one and the same subject. Depending on our focus we can speak of the self as determined or free. This does not mean that these two aspects are in direct contradiction. It is rather that the focus on the one excludes the perception of the other.[12] These conclusions undermine the foundationalism characteristic of modernity by subverting its attempts to appeal to the self as a foundation. This includes the ethical foundationalism which attempts to base its system of ethics on the premise of an autonomous subject. It also includes its opposite number, the behavioral or psychological foundationalism which bases its account on what it takes to be the "objective," fully determined subject. More importantly for our purposes, they also subvert the epistemological foundationalism which bases itself on a conception of a normative subject. What our conclusions indicate is that none of the systems based on specific notions of the self can be closed, that is, brought to a satisfactory completion. Eventually, they all show their limits—this, because the subject they appeal to is a constituted formation. They, thus, hold only for the levels where this constituted formation has been accomplished. In other words, they hold only so long as the conditions for its constitution obtain, and only within the limits of such conditions. Given that the self is a continuous process of constitution, it is always escaping from such limits. It is, thus, inherently unsuited to be an unchanging foundation. This fact, however, tends to escape the investigator because of the complementarity just mentioned. The objective view of the subject tends to hide the view that focuses on its autonomy and vice versa.

To fill this out, let us turn for a moment to the types of foundationalism just mentioned. Kant provides a good example of the ethical foundationalism based on the autonomy of the self. Such autonomy is a feature of the "I in itself," the self that lies behind its appearances. This is the noumenal I, considered as an indescribable unity, which exists prior to the syntheses that give us a spatial-temporal, causally determinate nature. Kant writes

12. Our use of the term is directly analogous to its use in physics—in particular to its employment by Niels Bohr to describe such phenomena as the wave/particle duality of light. He writes: "The spatial continuity of light propagation, on the one hand, and the atomicity of the light effects, on the other hand, must, therefore, be considered as complementary aspects of one reality, in the sense that each expresses an important feature of the phenomena of light, which, although irreconcilable from a mechanical point of view, can never be in direct contradiction, since a closer analysis of one or the other feature in mechanical terms would demand mutually exclusive experimental arrangements" ("Light and Life," p. 110).

that we must "admit, as is reasonable, that behind the appearances there must also lie at their root (although hidden) the things in themselves, and that we cannot expect the laws of these to be the same as those that govern their appearances."[13] While the appearances in their order and succession are governed by rules of natural causality, the noumenal I (the I behind appearances) exercises a noumenal causality. Not being bound by the natural causality, it is free. In Kant's words, "the notion of a being that has free will is the notion of a *causa noumenon*."[14] As such, of course, none of the categories we take from the world of appearances can apply to it. As nonappearing, it is, in fact, objectively anonymous. The appeal to it is, thus, an appeal to the self prior to the syntheses that would situate it within the world of appearances. We shall not rehearse any of the well-known difficulties with the Kantian system, difficulties that revolve around the reality of a freedom that can never appear. The essential problem with this type of foundationalism is that the self never remains at this level. Its processes are always situating its action (and, hence, its "causality") on the objective, appearing level addressed by the psychological foundationalism of, say, a Freud, a Pavlov, or a Skinner. The latter, however, are equally unable to complete their systems. If the foundationalism of a Kant is unable to bring freedom to the level of appearances, they find that they can never banish it entirely. They are always discovering what Pavlov, in desperation at making his test subject's behavior fit the stimulus response pattern, called the "reflex of freedom." Observing how a dog failed again and again to respond in the expected way to controlled stimuli, he writes:

> In order to place more emphasis on the inborn, reflex character of our reaction, we proceeded further with its investigation. Although the conditioned reflex which was elaborated on this dog, was the food reflex, i.e., the dog was starved for about 20 hours preceding the experiment, and was fed on the stand during each conditioned stimulus, even this was not sufficient to suppress and overcome the reflex of freedom ("The Reflex of Freedom," in *Lectures on Conditioned Reflexes*, p. 284).

The freedom, here uncovered, is entirely negative. It is, to state the obvious, not a function of the dog's possessing mind.[15] It points, rather, to a

---

13. "Fundamental Principles of the Metaphysics of Morals," p. 80.

14. "Critique of Practical Reason," p. 145.

15. Freud finds himself compelled to assume a positive freedom, which does presuppose mind, as part of his explanation of how patients can be cured. As Freud notes, the traumatic events of our past control our behavior by generating "symptoms." Once we uncover them,

level of his being that is sheer nowness. This, of course, is precisely the level that behavioral foundationalism cannot see. That neither it nor the ethical sort of foundationalism can enjoy a complete success is a consequence of the fact that the self is always more than that which any single view can comprehend. It is, in its synthetic processes, always moving beyond a particular perspective's focus. The result, as we said, is the kind of complementarity where we have to assent to supposedly opposite assertions—those of the freedom and determination of the self. As our uncertainty principle indicates, neither can be affirmed beyond a certain degree of assurance.

An analogous form of complementarity appears in the epistemological foundationalism that assumes the normativity of the subject. We have already considered the Cartesian project as an example of this. Its attempt to base certainty on an appeal to the subject positions the latter as the *ens certissimum*. The subject becomes the being whose certainty is such that our knowledge of it can stand as a norm or standard for all other claims to knowledge. This norm is mediated through the concepts of clarity and distinctness. To the point that our perceptions and thoughts of other objects approach the clarity and distinctness of our grasp of the subject, to that point we can be equally certain of the reality of their objects. The difficulty with this is, of course, that the subject is not an object. To the extent that it cannot be doubted, it distinguishes itself from every object that can be known. Descartes's search for subjective certainty, thus, points in opposing directions: both to the self as a most certain object and to the self as anonymous. We, thus, have another example of the complementarity where we face the necessity of making opposing descriptions. Here, it appears in the paradox that Descartes's "most certain being" turns out to have no content, that is, no objective features to which he can attach certainty.

A similar sort of complementarity appears in Kant's brand of epistemological foundationalism. His attempt to base knowledge on the sub-

---

that is, change them from unconscious to conscious determinants of our actions, they lose their coercive power. In Freud's words: "Symptoms are not produced by conscious processes; as soon as the unconscious processes involved are made conscious the symptoms must vanish. . . . Our therapy does its work by transforming something unconscious into something conscious, and only succeeds in its work insofar as it is able to effect this transformation" ("Eighteenth Lecture, Fixation upon Traumas: The Unconscious," in *A General Introduction to Psychoanalysis,* pp. 290, 291). The implicit premise of this therapy is that consciousness (understood as the realm of intellectual appreciation) is the realm of freedom, that is, of self-determined choice. Its practice consists in making us acknowledge the unacknowledged determinants of our actions. Once we do, they appear as goals we can choose or refuse to realize. I can, for example, choose not to repeat the behavior (the "symptoms") that helped me in childhood to cope with an abusive situation.

ject involves essentially two assertions. The first is that the appearing of the world is the result of synthesis. The second is that synthesis is an action of the subject. The subject, in fact, is what "first makes possible the concept of combination" (*Kritik der reinen Vernunft*, B 131). The difficulties with this center once again around the anonymity of the subject. Taken as a cause of synthesis (and, hence, of appearing), the subject cannot appear. If it did, it would be an effect rather than a ground of synthesis. Thus, for Kant, the subject, taken as an uncombined combiner, must be a *noumenal* rather than a *phenomenal* subject. As we said, none of the categories we draw from experience can apply to it. At a certain level, this subject appears as a nowness; yet, given that the action of synthesis is that of placing its perceptions in time, even the categories of temporality fall away. Not only is it nonextended, it is out of time in the sense that it cannot be considered to be a nowness located within it. Fixed on this level, its relation to the world, in particular, its relation to the "transcendent affection" by which the world provides it with the material of its synthesis, cannot be known. Indeed, insofar as synthesis is an act of this subject's "selfhood" (B 130), it also appears to share in this noumenal character. At this point, the status of such syntheses becomes highly problematical. Are they something that we can analyze and make intuitively clear to ourselves or do they escape our apprehension altogether? On the one hand his famous "regressive method" of searching for the conditions for the possibility of knowledge seems to lead back to the synthetic performances of an observable subject. On the other hand, the method cannot stop here but becomes, instead, a regression to the ground of appearances per se. Such a ground, insofar as it distinguishes itself from the grounded, can never appear. The result is that the descriptions of the syntheses of the ego Kant does provide have to be taken as descriptions of the syntheses of the *appearing* ego. His method exhibits an enforced silence concerning the *actually functioning* ego, which, as noumenal, is positioned beyond all phenomenal experience and description (see pages 56–57). Once again, we face the phenomenon of complementarity. The syntheses supposed to embody knowing in its concrete performance must, themselves, be assumed to be unknowable. Taken as an action of the "selfhood" of the subject, they get drawn into its anonymity.

The failure exhibited by these examples of foundationalism cannot be traced to any lack of skill in their arguments. The systems they proposed are subverted, rather, by the fact that there is no univocal foundation they can appeal to. As we said, the self manifests multiple levels in its ongoing process of becoming concrete. Moreover, rather than being a foundation for its epistemological relation to the world, the self is *founded by* this relation. Thus, cognitive performances, if they are successful, have a dual result. They yield the presence of a corresponding surrounding world. They also result in the presence within this of the subject. The subject or self becomes situated as the actor of their action. Accordingly, the failure of these performances is the collapse of the self embodying their activity. The implication here is that there are as many different selves as there are performances or, indeed, as there are corresponding surrounding worlds. For example, to the point that a surrounding world consists of concepts that abstract from time, that is, to the extent that it is atemporal, so is the self. It becomes an atemporal contemplator.[16] Similarly, if this surrounding world is historical, the self is historical in the sense of being historically determined by this surrounding, situating world. The same holds for economics or, indeed, any "cultural" activity, taking this term in a sufficiently broad sense. One cannot, in this context, seek within the self some specific, objective quality that would make it more receptive to taking on one persona rather than another. To express this somewhat paradoxically, we can say that the receptivity of the self is a function of its not becoming on its deepest level what it is receptive to. Because of this, it can never achieve the latter as an unalterable character. As already indicated, this receptivity is one with its anonymity. Such receptivity, then, points to the absence of any features that could serve as a ground or condition for the adoption of one form of self or persona rather than another. It also explains the complementarity that undercuts the Cartesian/Kantian attempt to position the self as a foundation. The reason why this foundational self cannot be known is because, on its ultimate, supposely foundational level, it is totally transparent to what is not itself. It has no inherent content. Indeed, in its identity with anonymity, the self's receptivity indicates that it is grounded by what it receives just to the point that it receives it. Here, of course, we have to add that memory, too, is part of what it can receive. The self, in a certain sense, can ground itself as long as it has access to the memories of what it has done and undergone.[17]

16. From our perspective, then, there is no reason to doubt the legitimacy of the descriptions of Socrates when he enters this mode of being a self. In Plato's words, "every now and then he just goes off like that and stands motionless, wherever he happens to be" (*Symposium* 175B). At times, this atemporal, unchanging stance can last a whole day: "One day at dawn he started thinking about some problem or other; he just stood outside, trying to figure it out. He couldn't resolve it, but he wouldn't give up. He simply stood there, glued to the same spot. By midday, many soldiers had seen him, and, quite mystified, they told everyone that Socrates had been standing there all day, thinking about something" (220D).

17. The most notable example of such self-grounding is mind. Having once achieved a

§4. *Receptivity and Activity.* To complete this picture, we need to recall that what is grounded is not just the self but the self's activity. As we earlier put this, receptivity is receptivity to being. It is receptivity to it in its functioning or activity (see page 91). Thus, receptivity to being in its shifting presence gives the self its primitive status as the now that streams. Similarly, its receptivity to the economic agency of others makes it an economic agent. Carefully regarded, there is here an overlap between receptivity and activity. On the one hand, we can say that a cognitive performance is also a receptivity—this, in the sense that it is what makes possible something's being "in" the subject. Situating the subject, the performance situates itself along with the material for its syntheses within the subject. It, thus, makes the subject receptive of such material. Moreover, as a result of the same syntheses, the subject can also be said to be receptive of the senses that make up the epistemological (as opposed to the physical) presence of a surrounding world. On the other hand, we also have to say that the activity of these performances can itself be taken as received. Receptivity to the agency of another is a grounding of the self in its activity. A good example of this is Aristotle's description of the relation between the student and the teacher. Without the teacher, the student cannot function as a student. Neither can the teacher function as such without the student (see page 90). It is, then, the student's receptivity to the teaching of the teacher which makes him learn. His actually functioning as a student is his acquisition of this self or persona. The same holds in reverse order for the teacher. The fact that agency (and, hence, selfhood) can be received is, of course, simply an expression of Aristotle's doctrine that the *energeia* of the mover is in the moved. "Energeia," translated literally, is "at workness" or agency. As Aristotle's example of the student and the teacher makes clear, one's receptivity to the agency of another can make one an agent acting on this other. Thus, the student, in his receptivity to the teacher, acts to make the teacher function as such. Similarly, in my receptivity to another person's timing me, I can "time" this other—this, for example, by playing music with him. Receptive to economic motives stemming from others, I can act as such a motive for others, grounding them in their agency. In each case, I help ground others as the active centers of their environments by providing, through my agency, an essential component of the environments that situate such agency.

The result of this overlap between receptivity and agency is a notion of

---

stock of concepts, it can engage in intellectual activity on its own. In Aristotle's words: "When it has thus become each of these objects, . . . it, itself, can then think itself" (*De Anima* 429b10). Mind "thinks itself," since in actual knowledge it is one with its objects, their agency (energeia) being its agency (430a20).

grounding that is essentially nonfoundational. In a situation of individuals determining environments, which, in turn, determine individuals, there is no first cause, no ultimate determinant. Where each agent is both grounded in his agency and a ground of the agency of others, the notion of a ground is robbed of its foundational character. Implicit in this dissipation of grounding is the overcoming of foundationalism in the sense of the "metaphysical thinking" defined by Heidegger. In his words: "Metaphysical thinking rests on the distinction between what truly is and what, measured against this, constitutes all that is not truly in being" ("Who is Nietzsche's Zarathustra?" in *Nietzsche,* II, 230). This can be taken as the distinction between reality and appearance—the former being "what truly is," the latter being everything else that, measured against this, is not truly existent. Taking this distinction as a distinction of agency, the reality can be understood as the cause of the appearance. The reality can exist by itself, the appearance cannot so exist and, hence "is not truly in being." Both sorts of distinctions have been undermined. In the model of receptivity we have put forward, we cannot distinguish between subjective image and objective original (see pages 98, 105). Neither can we draw an unambiguous distinction between receptivity and action. For us, what truly is, in the sense of what truly exercises agency, is nothing less than the whole self-determining plurality of agents and actions that make up a world. This cannot be otherwise, given that receptivity is receptivity to action. Since the very selfhood of the actor is determined by action, this, too, can be considered as received.

§5. *Receptivity as Embodiment.* With this, we may return to our original question: How are we to think of receptivity as prior to space and time? Our answer is that receptivity, understood as the process whereby something comes to be "in" a subject, is an embodiment. It is, first of all, an embodiment of the agency of the being I am receptive to. The agency appears as my perceptual agency. For example, my receptivity to the visual world does not just make the latter present to me as a spatial-temporal world. It also turns me into a perceiver of it. It makes the perceptual syntheses that present this world "my" syntheses. I embody them. Situating the act of perceiving "in" me, receptivity also determines the sense of this being "in." The sense is taken from the perceived world—that is, from its way of unfolding itself in perspectivally arranged patterns of appearances. My coming to embody this act is thus my assuming the spatial-temporal structures of a perceiving self, which are correlated to those of the world I perceive. So understood, receptivity results in the categories of space and time, categories I can apply to myself. On the basis of my embodying these syntheses, I can posit a "here" with a corresponding "out there," and a "now" with a corresponding "earlier" and "later." Yet given other types of synthesis, I need not do so. I need not, because in the model of receptivity we have put forward, space and time are not given beforehand, but are rather set by the being I am receptive to. My embodiment of its agency through my syntheses is also an embodiment of its appearing presence. Embodied by the materials that are successfully synthesized, the being appears. The materials determine the type of its appearing and, hence, determine the "receptacle" in which it is to count as real. For a spatial-temporal object, this is space and time. For a mathematical object, say, a number, the receptacle is the set of conceptual implications (implications, say, of Piano's axioms for a number) that give it its conceptual domain. Such an object is just as "real" (and no more real) than a physical one. Our assertion of the reality of concepts or "ideas" (εἶδη) does not make them, as Plato would have it, into foundational elements. Our dispensing with foundationalism means that what counts as real (or "certain") is set locally.

This point may be put in terms of the dialectic of intention and fulfillment. As inherent in synthesis, the dialectic is that through which a being's embodiment occurs. It is also that which prevents us from taking embodiment as a process creative of its being. Intentions succeed only to the point that they find appropriate material. Material, however, can count as such only in terms of its being material *for* a specific intention. As we said, the causality of both factors is what makes synthesis capable of either success or failure. As such, it is essential to its being receptive to (rather than creative of) its object. The dialectic, we can say, is our way of being open to the agency of the being in its providing us with the material for its presence. Open to the latter, we continually act to adjust the sense of our intention—the sense of what we are intending to see—to fit the changing patterns of evidence. When we are successful, the sense fits the pattern. It becomes the sense that the pattern manifests, the latter being the sense of the actual sensible being. Now, to say that what counts as real is set locally is to assert that the standard of success is set by the particular being in question. Its agency in providing the material determines our agency in attempting to grasp this through an appropriate intention. Thus it provides the material our intending sense must fit. For a sensuous being, this consists of sensuous appearances. Here, I grasp the being when, fitting my intention to such appearances, I see how they fit into the pattern that unfolds the sense of the sensuous being I intend to see. Similarly, my intention directed to a conceptual being is fulfilled when the conceptual implications it implies are actually seen to obtain. This holds for all theoretical (conceptual) projects, including the writing of this book. In each case, the intention I put forward sets the type of evidence (the material) that would fulfill or embody it. It implies the evidence that would cause the being it intends to appear. The intention, however, does not provide this material.[18] It is, in itself, simply part of the search for this. When, through the appropriate adjustments of its own sense, the intention is successful in finding the appropriate material, we can say that the entity bearing this sense has been shown "to be." Success, however, is relative to the type of entity intended. It determines what will count as "real." Given this, "being" has multiple senses. In Aristotle's words, it "can be said in many different ways,"[19] each way having its own manner of evidence and corresponding standard of certainty.[20]

Implicit in the foregoing is the answer to the question we posed about the writing of this book. At the beginning of this chapter, we noted that the incoherence of the Cartesian project arose from its inability to explain the knowing subject—specifically the subject engaged in this project. This is because the categories of being it proposed were inadequate to describe it (see page 173). How do we escape this objection? How do we account for the writing of this book? How does its account account for itself? The key, here, is to see the giving of the account as itself a receptivity to being. As such, it is a receptivity to agency, the very agency that embodies itself in its writing. Thus, if the intention (the "thesis") of the book is successful, the conceptual implications intended are actually seen to obtain. They appear in and through the openness we have as mind. This is an openness to the conceptual as conceptual. Now, according to our account, the embodiment of the book's intention by a suitable conceptual material yields the ontological categories appropriate to it. In other words, its intended sense, when embodied, results in the presence of being with this sense. With this, we have the subject situated and, hence, defined by these ontological categories. Its receptivity to being, thus, becomes its agency as a subject whose being is just such as is required to be receptive to the being in question. As long as the intention is successful, the possibility of ontological conflict—a conflict that makes impossible its writing—is avoided. The account, in other words, accounts for itself.

18. This is why, as Frege says, the definition of a concept is not the creation of the object with the properties it describes. The definition of the concept, "zero," for example, does not mean that there exists a number with these properties. "Only when we have proved that there exists one object and only one with the required property are we in a position to give this object the proper name 'zero'" ("Selections from Grundgesetze, Volume I," in *Translations from the Philosophical Writings of Gottlob Frege,* p. 145). Such a proof, we would say, fills the intention expressed by the concept with the appropriate material.

19. *Metaphysics* 10003a33.

20. Cf. *Nicomachean Ethics* 1094b25.

Taking receptivity as embodiment does not just allow us to dispense with the self-referential inconsistency of modernity. It also allows us to evade two of its characteristic dichotomies. The dichotomy of the real and the apparent is avoided because our position takes appearing as the embodiment of what we intend to see and, hence, takes every appearance as a realization. Thus the elements that fulfill an intention are not to be understood as transporting the image of some original out there. They are rather the material for its reality as a sensible being. The position also dispenses with the dichotomy of freedom and determination—in Kantian terms, autonomy and heteronomy of the will—since it allows me to say that an action that is received is also my own. This is because my receiving this action is my becoming concrete as the place of the action. All my actions insofar as they have objective correlates, yield a centering environment. As such, they result in my being as a central actor. I become concrete, that is, have an objective content, by being situated as the performer of the action. Before the action, there is, then, no objective "me" corresponding to it. Here, we may recall our earlier remark that there is no point in looking beyond or "outside" a person for the agency of the object of thought or desire that prompts a person to action. Determined by such an object, the person is none-the-less the agent because he is the place where the agency of such objects can appear. The person is, thus, both passive and active at the same time. Undergoing the entity's action by virtue of his receptivity, he none-the-less acts on his own. His undergoing such action is, then, his *embodying* its agency. This embodiment or receptivity is his own becoming concrete as the actor of the action.

Having said this, we must observe that in place of this last dichotomy a certain duality or, rather, complementarity still remains. Even though there is no corresponding "me" in an objective sense before some given action, a simple abstract receptivity still remains. Such receptivity prevents the "what" of embodiment, namely, the objectively describable characteristics embodiment entails, from being what I am on the deepest level. This, as we said, is the level where receptivity and anonymity are thought together. It is the level where my lack of objective features is a lack of any limitations regarding what I can receive. Given that such anonymity is also the absence of any term that could function in a causal relation, this level is also that of my complete, if negative, freedom. Such freedom always stands in a complementary relation to the positive state where I freely express what I am in my concreteness through an action I receive from another.

8

Implications

Epistemological Implications

Many of the implications of our postmodern reversal have been previously mentioned. We will, however, review them before considering the reversal's ethical import. The first implication is a certain ontological identity between the self and its world, one that involves the very sense of being as agency. The most basic level to express this is that of temporality. This is because the original agency of the subject is temporal. It is that of the welling up of moments from its central nowness. The unfolding of the subject's action occurs through the departure of such moments. Identity on this level springs from the fact that this original agency is not just the subject's. It springs from the shifting presence of the object. Thus, my agency, qua welling up, is my registering my object's change of presence. How it shifts its presence, its mode or manner in doing this, gives me the mode of my own temporality and, hence, agency. For example, the perspectival unfolding of a spatial-temporal object gives me a corresponding temporality. Registering such an object, I can be said to perceive in the successive time marked out by the pattern of its shifting presence. The agency of my perceiving it becomes a temporal process timed by its presence.

The second implication of the postmodern reversal follows directly from this. If there is an identity between self and object and this identity is primarily temporal, then the fact that different objects display different forms of temporality means that these different forms are also displayed by the self that registers them. The conclusion, then, is that there are as many forms of subjective being (of selfhood) as there are of temporality. Playing music with another person, speaking with him, and undergoing a moment of insight are examples of different forms of temporality and, hence, of selfhood. An implicit premise here is that subjectivity or selfhood begins with that registering of being which is temporality. This registering gives it its initial agency. It, thus, gives it its initial being as an activity or agency. My registering a being's mode of presence determines the form of my temporality. More specifically, my registering how a being shows itself shapes or informs that welling up of moments which is my primitive root as an active center. As we indicated, the form of the object becomes the form of the self. The shaping that occurs when I view a perspectival series is very different from that which arises when I am speaking to another person. In the latter case, I do not remain on the sensuous level, but constantly shift between the sounds, words, and sentences he speaks and the ideas expressed by them. Just as to say, "I see what you mean," implies a very different sense of seeing than that involved in viewing some physical object, so the temporality which expresses the shape of the action of this seeing also differs.

The cognitive performances by which a self grasps an object are, of course, more than the passive registering of its presence. The algorithms such performances instantiate are those of the dialectic between intention and fulfillment. They involve the constant attempt by the self to anticipate the pattern of appearing through which a given object manifests its sense. This anticipation is the self's intending of this sense. It is also, as we noted, a focusing, a picking out of the object from its background (see page 136). The object stands out when we can distinguish its pattern from those of its surroundings. The self, then, "makes sense" of what it registers when it grasps the patterns exhibited in such registering. When the pattern it anticipates actually unfolds, that is, when there is a coincidence of the anticipated and experienced pattern, it can be said to grasp its particular object. What this signifies is that the self isn't just passively timed by the world taken as an undifferentiated assemblage of objects. It times itself according to the object it has picked out. Playing music with someone, I time myself primarily by one aspect of my partner, dancing with a person by another aspect.[1] Reasoning with him, by yet a third. With this, we have a level of

---

1. Concretely, of course, both forms of being timed—by the audible and visual aspects of the other person—are involved in these performances. String players, don't just listen to each other, they watch each other intently. Their body language tells them when to begin after a pause.

ontological identity that links the attending subject to a particular, *attended-to* object.

This account of identity is the reverse of Kant's. For Kant the identity between self and object is founded on the self. To speak more precisely, what we have in Kant is an identity between the appearing self—its categories and concepts—and the appearing object. They are linked by the fact of subjective synthesis. Categories and concepts express the rules for connecting perceptions to synthesize various types of appearing objects. Thus the object that appears through a particular subjective synthesis is inevitably correlated to the concept that expresses the rule for this synthesis. As for the synthesis itself, its ground is the noumenal self or subject. For Kant as we saw, the action of synthesis pertains to this self's very selfhood. It acts to insert the material it receives (the "transcendent affection") into the before and after of time. The result is the appearing, phenomenal subject as well as its appearing objects. It is also their correlation, that is, the match of subjective concepts and categories to objects. Our position, by contrast, places the ground of the correlation in the appearing entity itself. The correlation holds because the entity times the subject. Intending it, we are open to it. The fulfillment of our intention occurs when we register its shifting presence in the pattern we anticipate. This registering it is its timing us.

Kant originally proposed his system as a defense against skepticism and relativism. He also conceived of it as a reversal, a kind of "Copernican Revolution" of what had gone before. "Previously," he writes, "it was assumed that all our knowledge must conform to the object." Objects set the standards for knowing. His reversal is to make objects conform themselves to knowledge—that is, to the subjective conditions by which we know them. Basing ourselves on such conditions, we have "the possibility of an a priori knowledge which would determine something about objects before they are given" (*Kritik der reinen Vernunft,* B xvi). Thus, the judgments that are based on the conditions for the possibility of experiencing an object could never, by definition, be contradicted by experience. The truths they express would have a universal validity—that is, apply without restriction. At a stroke, then, skepticism regarding the possibility of knowledge would vanish. So would relativism, insofar as such truths would hold for every possible empirically experiencing subject.

What happens when we reverse Kant's reversal and make the subjective conditions of knowing dependent on the object? This second reversal can, perhaps, lay better claim to the term "Copernican Revolution," since it does not make the subject the center of reference. Does it, however, return us to the kind of relativism that, abandoning all standards, limits itself

to the claim of "true for me"? Certainly, we do admit a plurality of forms of
objective being and, as determined by this, a corresponding plurality of
types of subjective being, none of which can be said to count as normative. Yet to base an accusation of relativism on this is to misunderstand
"relativism." Relativism, in the classic sense of the term, presupposes a
subject to which things are relative. Its assertion is that different subjects
imply different truths. What is true for me (or for my clan, race, epoch) is
not true for you, for we are differently constituting subjects (or subjective
collectivities). The hidden premise of relativism, thus, seems to be that
there are different a priori systems within us, different rules for constitution which are present as conditions for the givenness of objects. It is a
matter of indifference here what one takes to be the origin of such a priori
systems. It could be linguistic, historical, economic, psychological, or
some other set of given circumstances. The only necessity is that their
rules not be universal, but hold only for one group and not another. Since
this holding affects the very givenness of the objects in question, no debate about them is really possible. If this is relativism, our view is actually
the reverse of this. We do not assume a subject to which things are relative, but rather make the subject relative to the world. In relativism, the
subject is given prior to the world as determining its appearance. We, however, assert that the world is given prior to the subject as determining *its*
appearance. The world determines the forms of activity, that is, the forms
of cognitive performance the subject actually manifests. Where subjects
agree, the focus of their agreement is, then, not on themselves, but rather
on the world.

   This can be contrasted with Kant's understanding of what it means for a
judgment to have "objective validity." In such a judgment, we do not grasp
the object in itself. Rather, "we grasp the object (though it remains unknown as it is in itself) through the universal and necessary connections of
the given perceptions" that result in the object's presence ("Pro-
logomena," §19; IV, 298). This is to base objective validity on the necessary universality of the subjective performance that first results in the type
of object in question. It is, in other words, to say that subjects ultimately
agree with one another, not because of their objects, but because of an a
priori correspondence of the constitutive systems responsible for such objects. Kant can do this because he takes the rules of such systems as those
governing the very possibility of experience. If pressed on the point that
multiple types of experience might very well be possible, their differences
pointing back to different constitutive systems, he would point to the fact
that the ultimately constituting subjects are "causa noumena." As prior to
the world they constitute, they are prior to all the conceptions of being

different that can be drawn from it. Taking them as posterior, we, by contrast, have to base any agreement in their subjective performance on the type of object in question. The latter determines the type of constitutive system the subject manifests. Agreement, then, involves getting others to look, that is, to place themselves in the presence of the same object. It requires, in other words, getting them to allow themselves to be constituted by the object. "True for me" does not, in this context, signify a private subjective claim, but rather one of a certain constitution by the world. Thus if the world does support a plurality of norms of truth, this is because it has a plurality of beings, each of which occasions a different constitution of the subject.

This, of course, is the opposite of the Kantian position, which draws its norms from a single foundation. For it, the subject, not the appearing world, is "the transcendental ground of the necessary lawfulness of the appearances which compose an experience" (*Kritik der reinen Vernunft*, A 127). It gives us a single standard of being and appearing. Epistemological certainty follows, since the conditions for the possibility of knowing are precisely those conditions for the subjective synthesis that result in the object. Our position, by contrast, offers epistemological certainty without any ontological normativity, any single standard for what counts as being. The certainty follows because for us, as for Kant, the subject is always on the level of identity with the object. We also assert the correspondence between conditions for subjective synthesis and those for the object's appearing. Thus, for us as for Kant, the question never arises of how the subject can somehow transcend itself to reach the object as an alien presence. The difference, however, is that now the weight of normativity falls on the object. Its presence is what makes the subject be. It shapes the subject's being on the basic level of its activity (or actuality) as a set of cognitive performances. Because, however, our foundation is plural, we cannot offer any ontological normativity. The plurality of the norms of subjective performance comes from the plurality of the types of being with which it can, in its knowing processes, achieve identity.

This brings us to our final epistemological implication. It, too, has been mentioned by us before. Our basing normativity on being entails the abandonment of any notion of a "true" world over against which an apparent world could be ranged. Traditionally, the "true" world stands as a norm for the apparent. The latter becomes "true" to the point that it follows the norm. Thus, for Plato, the appearing world embodies truth to the point that it manifests some self-identity in its changing presence. The true world is that of the forms (the εἴδη). Unchanging, constantly "the same with themselves according to themselves," they represent the standard for the "truth" (and, indeed, the "being") of the apparent world in its becoming. The same sort of dichotomy appears in Descartes's positioning mathematics as the true world. The truth of the apparent world is in its manifestation of quantifiable relations. This is why its primary qualities are more "true" (and, hence, more "real") than its secondary ones. Compared to the primary, the secondary count as mere appearances. Our position, by contrast, does not base itself on a dichotomy between the true and the apparent. What comes to presence in me, it asserts, is *both* true and apparent. It is apparent in the sense of being a "mere" appearance because it is only a partial perspective. It is one appearance of the world—specifically, the appearance from my here and now—alongside of which other appearances, other perspectives, can be ranged. It is true in the sense that none of these serve as an ontological standard for judging its presence. In each and every case, being comes to appearing presence in and through a self. As a self, I am such a place. Thus, an object's being spatial-temporally present occurs through its timing and spacializing me. This does not mean that I determine its presence, that I serve as a kind of Kantian condition for the possibility of experience. Rather, it determines my presence. Timing me, it sets the conditions for my appearing as a functioning self, a self that allows it to come to presence. The general point here is that my functioning is part of the world's original functioning. It functions through me to makes itself epistemologically present.

To add a general remark, we may note that it is only when we confuse epistemological with mere physical, bodily presence that we can assume that the first can occur elsewhere than ourselves. Apart from selves, bodies, as we observe them, do present themselves to other bodies. Their presence, however, is physical, not epistemological. Given this, we should not confuse the standards for one type of presence with those for another. Thus the universality of a physical standard for bodily presence—whatever this might be—does not imply any corresponding universality on the epistemological level. Our assertion that the weight of epistemological normativity falls on the world concerns, by definition, its epistemological presence. To be open to it is to be open to all its possible aspects.

Ethical Implications

Our survey of our epistemological implications has essentially been a review of positions already stated in our text. We have, however, by and

large, not explored the ethical import of our stance. Its ethical implications spring from the finitude of the embodied self. More precisely, they
spring from the finitude of this self considered as a constituted formation.
To draw them out, we must then begin by recalling what we said about the
foundational character of the self. The self, we said, is built up in layers. It
is, concretely, the continuous process of its own generation, a process in
which one layer serves as a basis for the next. Corresponding to these
layers, we have different types of openness. The openness of the registering of motion as time is different from, yet ultimately foundational for, the
openness of the fully concrete person interacting with others. Corresponding to the foundational character of our openness there is, then, the foundational character of the self as constituted. For us, this is the foundational
character of being human.

We can express this last character in terms of the dialectic of intention
and fulfillment. The syntheses that build up the self from level to level
proceed through this dialectic. The "fulfillment" that brings the self to one
level is, in this process, also the basis for a new intention, one that points
to a fulfillment on the next level. This holds not just for the primitive
levels of constitution—the constitution that moves from the grasp, say, of
temporal unities, to those which unfold themselves in space—it also holds
for our collective intersubjective constitution. Fulfillment in the context of
such constitution signifies a "filling out" of the conception of being human.
The "fullness" which results from such filling out is not, at any level, to be
considered an endpoint. It is rather to be understood in terms of the process itself, that is, in terms of an extended horizon involving intention (or
anticipation) and fulfillment. Thus "fullness" as fulfillment is to be taken as
a provisional term. Its context is the horizon in which human accomplish-
ments are taken, not just as fulfilling the notion of being human, but also as
anticipating further potentialities for being human. According to this conception, we can, for example, say that the accomplishment of human
speech opens up a whole range of further possibilities—civil society, commerce, and so on. Each of these, when actualized (or fulfilled) in some
particular way, points, in anticipation, to further potentialities. The "fullness" that guides this process is a kind of teleological ideal. It is a goal
toward which this layered process of intention and fulfillment tends. It is
also that which brings itself about through our own actions and institutions. These form the material for each stage of its realization as well as the
elements for the intentions, built upon this, for its next stage. As we earlier
noted, the instantiation of the dialectic is the instantiation of our openness
to the action of the goal. Our openness to teleological action comes in the

process of intentions continually arising and seeking appropriate contents. The intentions themselves determine what content is "appropriate," and yet they themselves arise from such content. They base their anticipations on it. Such anticipations may or may not be correct. For example, the anticipations that led in the nineteenth century to the development of communism as part of the ideal of human fullness seem to have largely failed. Based upon the solidarity of workers and the depredations of capitalist industrialization, the intention arose towards what was called the "new socialist man." The actions called forth to bring this about did not succeed. This failure, however, does not imply the failure of the dialectic itself. The possibility of failure is inherent in it insofar as it is an openness.

As this example indicates, the contents required for the advance towards the goal of human fullness are provided through our actions and institutions. Fulfillment, here, means providing the environments that ground the "self" in each of the stages of its development. "Self," in this context, refers to the individual and the collectivity in which it finds itself. The latter is the human community taken as a self-grounding assemblage of actors and actions. The ideal of human fullness corresponding to it is that of a collective actualization of all the possibilities inherent in this assemblage. My finitude as an individual self shows itself in the fact that I can actualize one possibility of my being, that is, engage in a specific course of action, only by neglecting other possibilities. By definition, then, my finitude implies a plurality of subjects when it is placed in a teleological framework pointing to the ideal of human fullness—that is, of the harmonious realization of *all* the possibilities of being human.

To draw the moral implications from this is to speak of tolerance. Tolerance is an openness to the possibilities implied in the ideal of human fullness. This does not mean that it is an openness to every possibility of human behavior regardless of its effect on others. The ideal of human fullness is that of a *synthetic* process, one involving the "placing together," or collective realization, of different forms of selfhood. As such, only those possibilities which do not permanently exclude other possibilities fall within the purview of tolerance. This means that, as a *positive,* practical ideal, it embraces as values to be realized only certain possibilities: those which permit the actualization of further possibilities within the horizon of being human. Those whose actualization results in harm, in the narrowing of the potentiality for humanity in individuals, it forbids as a *negative* command. If it did not forbid them, it would contradict itself. It would include both teleological progression and its opposite. It would be directed to the goal of fullness of human being and, at the same time, embrace actions contrary to this goal's realization. A few common examples will make this clear. Tolerance, understood negatively as a prohibition—ultimately, as a prohibition of intolerance—forbids lying and theft. The first, to the point that it is collectively actualized, undermines the possibility of speech to communicate verifiable information. Thus lying undermines those human possibilities, such as civil society, which presuppose this possibility. Theft, when collectively actualized, has a similar effect on the possibility of possession and, hence, on the possibilities, such as commerce, springing from this. Insofar as lying and theft cut off such possibilities, they narrow human potentialities and are actually acts of intolerance. Tolerance, however, is directed to the expansion of our potentialities. Because of this, it is never a static notion. Within the schema of intention and fulfillment, its structure at any given time is determined by the stage of the advance towards human fullness.

Intolerance can be defined as the opposite of tolerance. It is an attitude that promotes, not progress towards fullness, but rather regress. Intolerance reduces the possibilities actually available to us. Thus, the thief attempts to limit the possibilities of possession to himself, cutting them off from other persons. Of course, a thief cannot literally succeed in this attempt and remain a thief. His action presupposes that others will continue to possess the goods he wants, that the possibilities of possession can always be reinstated. The case is quite different with intolerance in its extreme form. Here, it appears as *radical evil,* the evil that strikes at the *root* of things. The effect of this evil is such that it cannot be made good again; that is to say, its effect is a possibility that is permanently foreclosed to us. Applied to an individual, it has the effect of a permanent loss. Children, for example, subjected to sexual abuse may permanently lose the possibility of normal adult sexual relations. A single parent, to take another example, can permanently foreclose the possibilities of a child's emulating the other, absent parent. All personal access to this individual can be cut off. All physical evidence of this person's presence can be eliminated. If a picture or letter remains hidden among the child's belongings, it can be ferreted out and destroyed. With the young child forbidden to speak of the absent parent, the memory itself will go. Applied to the human community, the same permanent closing off of the possibilities of being human will obtain. Beginning with the destruction of the historical records of a particular society, radical evil, may proceed beyond this and include the permanent suppression of the society's native language. A further expression of it would be the wholesale destruction—the "ethnic cleansing"—of the members of the society. All these actions, as expressions of radical evil, have as their point the elimination of the possibilities of being and behaving exhibited by the members of this group.

As the experience of our century indicates, such exemplary evil exists in a continuum with the more common, everyday forms of intolerance—intolerance expressed as a negative attitude toward some particular ethnic or cultural group. Intolerance of an ethnic group can precede its destruction. It contains the germ of radical evil insofar as it manifests the attitude that other persons who think and act in a certain way are not to be accounted as genuinely human. As such, it also includes racism. Here, its attitude is, perhaps best exemplified in the following piece of dialogue from *Huckleberry Finn* where Huck explains to his aunt Sally, why he is late:

HUCK: It warn't the grounding—that didn't keep us back but a little. We
    blowed out a cylinder head.
AUNT SALLY: Good gracious! anybody hurt?
HUCK: No'm. Killed a nigger.
AUNT SALLY: Well, it's lucky; because sometimes people do get hurt.
(Samuel Clemens, *Huckleberry Finn,* ch. 32; p. 216)

This lack of recognition of the humanity of a group—here, the African Americans—is also a nonrecognition of the goal of human fullness. Intolerance can, accordingly, be defined as an attempt to banish the striving towards this goal. It directs itself against already realized human possibilities or against possibilities that are present as anticipations springing from these. It, thus, typically takes the form of attempting to *narrow* or at least *hold static* the meaning of being human. In the former case, it attempts an actual regress from the ideal of human fullness. In the latter, its attempt is to eliminate the teleological action of this ideal as a goal.

In a century that began with the destruction of Turkish Christian Armenians, whose middle period was marked by the elimination of Eastern European Jewry, and whose end witnessed the attempted "ethnic cleansing" of the Moslems of Bosnia, intolerance becomes a paramount moral question. It is not enough to just condemn it. One must also understand it, which means that one must be able to answer the question of how it is possible. To draw the answer from the implications of our study, we have to say that radical evil is a possibility springing from the status of subjectivity as embodied. Such a status implies our finitude. It is a mark of my finitude that I can permanently close off possibilities for myself. In fact, I must, since, as finite, I can actualize one possibility of being only by neglecting other possibilities. As we said, an individual's recognition of the goal of human fullness implies his recognition of other individuals and their possibilities. Only through others can he play his part in the collective realization of the possibilities of being human. The negative corollary of this is that the denial of the recognition of others also closes oneself off from this goal. Now, the totality of presently given individuals is also finite. As with the individual, its finitude is given by its embodiment. Human subjectivity as such is embodied in a contingently situated, finite set of individuals. This finite embodiment means that the possibilities we presently actualize are not the totality of all that could be actualized. Once again, this finitude shows itself in the fact that humanity can, through its collective actions, permanently foreclose possibilities, possibilities that as a finite totality, it can never regain. *Like the individual,* it can close off possibilities for itself; though, *unlike the individual,* this cannot be made up by an appeal to a greater collectivity—that is, others. This follows because it, itself, is this collectivity. Given that radical evil is this permanent foreclosure of possibilities, the potentiality for such evil is the mark of the collective finitude of humanity.

We can penetrate more deeply into the possibility of radical evil by observing, first of all, that humanity is not its own ground. Were it its own ground it could find within itself the resources to make good the losses that have marked its history. Humanity's embodied finitude implies its contingent situatedness. Its contingency signifies that it does not contain within itself the reason for (the ground for) its being *this* humanity, exemplifying *this* set of possibilities, rather than some other. Not having such a reason, it is not its own ground. In fact, as we have seen, it is grounded by the world. It is the world that gives it its situating environment. Now, the world taken as a ground is not something we can completely control. In fact, as our study implies, the notion of a ground of embodied subjectivity is not such that it can be thought of as a kind of principle whose manipulation would somehow set things aright—that is, restore the losses of the possibilities that humanity suffers. This is because this ground is not any specific thing or agent. As the world, it is the whole assemblage of actors, actions, things, and events. In a situation of individuals determining environments, which in turn determine individuals, there is no first cause, no manipulable ultimate determinant. Here, each agent is both grounded in his agency and a ground of others. Since this is not a systematic structure with clear principles and beginnings, it is not within our ultimate control in any positive sense. We cannot, then, determine it in some unambiguous fashion to restore our losses.

What is in our control is, of course, our ability to destroy it. In an ultimate catastrophe, say that of atomic war or environmental disaster, such
destruction could be total. What makes this catastrophe possible is not just
our finitude. Our intelligence gives us this power. It is the same intelligence that gives us our freedom. By virtue of it, we can do everything.
We are not, as we said in discussing the choral ode from *Antigone,* limited
as the animals are to expressing a given environment. Our receptivity to
the forms of things is a receptivity to what abstracts from a specific environment. It is thus a receptivity or openness to what can be used for
constructive or destructive purposes, depending on the environment in
which it is employed. Now, the fact that this freedom is embodied in a
layered self gives us perhaps the deepest reason for the possibility of radical evil. By virtue of the power given to us by our minds, we can do
everything; and this includes stopping at nothing. On this level of our selfhood, everything is permitted. Yet, because we are embodied, what we
permit can destroy us. The essential point here is that embodiment turns
the abstract freedom of mind into the reality of choice. Although I can
conceive of multiple alternatives, I can, as embodied, only actualize one.
Such actualization is the letting go, the suppression, of the other alternatives as possibilities to be actualized. With this, we have the risk that such
suppression can be permanent. The fact that through freedom one can
suppress oneself, including one's freedom, follows from the layered structure of the self. The freedom which is mind can undermine itself by striking at the conditions (the founding layers) of its embodiment. Once undermined, such freedom is, of course, no longer available as a means for
restoring its conditions.

This discussion of radical evil points to what is distinct in the ethics
implied by our postmodern reversal. This is not some set of ethical rules.
It is not the claim that humanity may be conceived as open to a teleological ideal of the fullness of its being. Such a claim can be found in philosophers as diverse as Hegel and Husserl. It is, rather, its emphasis on the
vulnerability of the self. What the reversal does is give ontological sense to
the fact that actions can have permanent consequences, that they can lead
to an undermining of selfhood that cannot be made good again. The best
way to put this is in terms of the shift it implies in the epistemological
paradigm of modernity. This is a shift from observation to incarnation as
the fundamental mode of knowing. Modernity positions the subject as a
disembodied, Cartesian (or Kantian) spectator. Our reversal gives it the
ontological sense of "flesh." The term signifies that what we are open to
incarnates itself through us. Our openness is our being the place of its

presence. As this place, we know ourselves in knowing what comes to presence through our actions and perceptions. It is not just that our self-knowledge is mediated—namely, that we know ourselves because we know other things. It is that our very selfhood is received. What we know positions it, gives it content. As received, it is, by definition, vulnerable.

The same holds for our freedom. As an incarnate being, I am both free and determined. I can be both because my freedom is not my own but given to me by the world. Deprived of the world, that is, deprived of the teleological action of its goals, my freedom loses all content in a positive sense. As a "freedom for" the world, that is, for acquiring the various goods it might offer, it becomes completely empty. Without the world, I lose my sense of myself as the place where the objects of thought and desire can manifest themselves as such, that is, as animating agents for my behavior. With this, of course, the freedom that springs from the mind, that is, from entertaining objects of thought, also goes. The presence of such objects depends upon the mind's being provided with the material required for its action of grasping unities in multiplicity. Its conceptualization, in other words, depends on the elements of its experience. Deprived of a sufficient range of the latter, the mind can become stunted. Given access only to certain elements, it can be irrationally compulsive in the conclusions it draws. On the most basic level of my freedom, that of the welling up of my activity, my dependence is on the world's timing me. Deprived of the world on this level, activity and selfhood both vanish.

The above examples are sufficient to draw a number of points regarding an ethics based on our reversal. Any such ethics would have to take account of the foundational model of the self we have presented. As founded, the self is vulnerable to being undermined. It would also have to respect the limits imposed by our incarnational model for the self's knowing. If we take the model seriously, we cannot construct an ethics for ourselves apart from the world. The notion of an autonomous agent—as presented, say, by the Kantian system—is not available to us. From this follows the point that the worth of an individual cannot be that of the autonomous agent proposed by this system. If individuals are worthy of respect, it is not because, as Kant thought, they are "rational beings" who count themselves as members of a nonsensuous, nonphysical "intelligible world," acting out of the autonomy that this implies. Moral worth must, rather, be rooted in the self as flesh. If respect is to be given, its object must be the self's status as the place of embodiment. In such a view, one may still value mind or reason more than the senses, but only because they permit a greater range of embodiment, a greater range of the behavior that brings the world to presence.

Implicit in the above is a point bearing on the earth itself. Considered as a place of embodiment, it can also, in a certain extended sense, be accounted flesh. Thus, once we engage in our paradigm shift and take subjectivity as flesh, the earth itself comes to share the moral worth traditionally associated with subjectivity. In the Cartesian tradition, the worth of the earth is that of mere matter. For Kant, it has value only insofar as it serves the purposes of rational autonomous agents. The latter have value in themselves. The earth has value only as a means for their ends. Our reversal, however, undoes the separation of self and world, of agent and the earth, that the modern paradigm demands. The reversal requires that we take the earth as part of ourselves insofar as our selfhood is established through our interactions with it. The establishing of our selfhood is not a matter of our agency alone. It is, we have stressed, a function of the whole assemblage of individuals determining environments determining individuals. To call the totality of environments, individuals, agents, and actions "the earth" is, in fact, to recognize the extended sense in which it is *the* place of embodiment, is "flesh" in a preeminent sense. To recognize it as such is to give it a kind of ultimate moral worth. Thus a further implication of our view is that only those ethical theories which allow the earth to sustain itself as such a place can be considered as valid. The earth, in other words, becomes their verification principle. To ask whether a model for ethical behavior is valid is, of course, to inquire into its impact on the ideal of human fullness. This, however, involves the earth as the place of such fullness. Such fullness, in other words, in not a matter of human conduct alone. Such conduct is no more autonomous than human selves are. Given this, the inquiry must ultimately focus on its impact on the earth itself.

This allows us to make a final point, which is that the same paradigm shift changes the relation between ethics and metaphysics. Traditionally, metaphysics, the science of being qua being, was considered to be the ultimate, verifying science. It provided all other sciences, including the science of ethics, with its justifying ontological ground. From our perspective, the "earth," in the above defined sense, provides this ground. As the ultimate place of embodiment, it determines what can or cannot come to presence. Given this, theories of being must ultimately be based on it. Their basis must include, then, the *conduct* that allows things to come to presence. Devaluing such conduct, they undermine their basis as an account of being, that is, of what can come to presence. Defining ethical conduct as that which safeguards, engenders, and nourishes coming into presence, our position subordinates metaphysics to it. This is because metaphysics depends on such conduct to provide it with its data. Given this, ethics becomes a principle of verification for metaphysics.[2] Only those theories of being which allow of ethical conduct in the above defined sense are to be considered as having a claim to validity. Similarly, only those theories of ethical conduct which allow the "earth" (including its physical presence) to sustain itself can have a like claim. This implies, of course, that our own metaphysical claims—our claims, for example, that time is posterior to being, that the agency of the self is received, that flesh is a primary ontological category, and so on—must all be judged by this standard. They can be considered to be verified to the point that they allow conduct that sustains the "earth" in the sense we have given it.

The general shape of the ethics implied by our reversal should, by now, be clear. According to it, the moral considerations we extend to ourselves we are equally obligated to extend to all other places of coming to presence—this, to the degree that they are such places. This obligation follows from the shift we propose. It is a shift from a morality based on the moral agency of selves considered as autonomous agents, as ultimate foundations, which, as such, are invulnerable. It is a shift to a morality of engenderment, of the self as a place of coming to presence. Love provides a good example of such engenderment. Children left alone, especially infants who are not picked up and held, often suffer emotional damage. Meeting their bare physical needs is not sufficient. Without physical affection, without their parents' returning their gaze, their growth as persons, as individuals who are capable of empathy, may never occur. The engenderment of love can also be illustrated in less dramatic terms. Small children, even when they are playing by themselves, often require a parent's (or adult) gaze. Sensing its absence, they suddenly feel lost. They "find" themselves when the gaze is returned. The gaze is part of their engenderment in the basic sense of giving them a human "here." Having this "here" is more than simply locating oneself at the zero point of one's spatial environment. The "here" that arises from the gaze of the parent is a location out of which the child can return this gaze. Seeing himself through his parents eyes, he is both subject and object: both a seeing subject and an object seen. He, thus, becomes a *located* seeing, one whose relation to the whole has a certain objective sense. Losing this, as when the parent turns away, he becomes lost.

---

2. This relation between ethics and metaphysics was first proposed by Lorna Green in her 1975 Ph.D. dissertation for the University of Toronto's Department of Philosophy. Her basis for it, however, differed from mine.

Carefully regarded, this locating of the child involves a double incarnation. Loving his parent, he takes up the parent's standpoint. He shares in a kind of primitive empathy in, say, his parents seeing him. Incarnating himself through empathy in them, he see himself through them. With this, a second incarnation arises as he permits himself to come to presence through this loving gaze. He sees himself through their seeing him. The child thus *incarnates himself in the world* of things, not as a thing, but *as his parents' child* with all the human content this involves. The same model, we note, applies not just to sight, but also to touch. Touching, for example, his mother, a child touches himself. Her return of his touching allows him to incarnate himself as a located touching. The same may hold for our other senses, such as hearing and smell. If it does, then the result of this double incarnation is the located selfhood of the sensing individual. Deprived of such contact, the child becomes placeless. The emotional damage he suffers is nothing less than a lasting inability to find himself within the human community. He suffers the evil of permanent emotional distress which no autonomy can relieve.

These remarks on love are been a reworking of Hegel's account of mutual recognition in the "Lordship and Bondage" section of his *Phenomenology of Mind.* For Hegel such recognition begins with the fight to the death of two pre-selves. The winner of the fight is the pre-self that is willing to risk everything, including his life. Engaging in the risk, the pre-self shows "that it is fettered to no determinate existence, that is it not bound at all by the particularity everywhere characteristic of existence as such and it is not tied up with life" (p. 232). In short it grasps itself in its absolute autonomy. Such a grasp transforms it into a self. The self that is grasped is, in its autonomy, paradigmatic for modernity. Upon it and its struggles for mutual recognition, struggles that often turn its history into a "slaughterhouse," Hegel builds his account of the advance of society. The working out of the paradigm of mutual recognition through struggle and risk, the forcing of larger and larger sections of humanity to grasp their autonomy, does in broad measure describe the establishment of modernity and the modern state. An account in terms of our paradigm would be the opposite of this, since it places selfhood not in autonomy but in the engenderment of the other. Advance, for us, would not be advance in autonomy but in co-engendering. It would be the engenderment of selves through the environments provided by selves as part of the earth. A successful society would be a web of engenderment through which humanity could advance towards the goal of its fullness. Progress towards this goal would be marked by an increase in the ways in which it could bring to presence the richness that is the "earth" in our defined sense of this term. Unlike Hegel, we cannot point to a concrete realization of what we propose, since its subject is not the modern, but the postmodern, not the present state, but the state to come. The postmodern is an age, concretely, a political system, which will be recognizable through its own special metaphysics and ethics. They will show themselves to be postmodern by satisfying the verifying principle of the earth.

Bibliography

Aquinas, Thomas. *Summa Contra Gentiles.* Trans. James Anderson. Notre Dame, Ind.: Notre Dame University Press, 1975.

Aristotle. *Aristotle's Physics.* Trans. H. G. Apostle. Bloomington, Ind.: Indiana University Press, 1969.

———. *Aristotle's Physics.* Trans. Richard Hope. Lincoln, Neb.: University of Nebraska Press, 1961.

———. *The Basic Works of Aristotle.* Ed. R. McKeon. New York: Random House, 1941.

———. *The Metaphysics,* 2 vols. Trans. H. Tredennick. London: Loeb Classical Library, 1956.

———. *On The Soul.* Trans. W.S. Hett. London: Loeb Classical Library, 1964.

Berkeley, George. *Of the Principles of Human Knowledge.* La Salle, Ill.: Open Court, 1963.

Bohr, Niels. "Light and Life." In *Interrelations: The Biological and Physical Sciences,* ed. R. Backburn. Chicago: Scott, Foresman and Company, 1966.

Brague, Remi. "The Mediaeval Model of Subjectivity, Towards a Rediscovery." In *The Ancients and Moderns.* Ed. Reginald Lilly. Bloomington: Indiana University Press, in press. Citations in notes and text are from the original paper (same title) given at the New School for Social Research in New York as part of the 1991 Hannah Arendt Memorial Symposium.

Cervantes, Miguel de. *Don Quixote.* Trans. S. Putnam. New York: Random House, 1949.

Churchland, P. M. and P. S. Churchland. "Could a Machine Think?" *Scientific American,* January 1990.

Clemens, Samuel. *Huckleberry Finn.* New York: Signet Classics, 1977.

Corish, Denis. "Aristotle's Attempted Derivation of Temporal Order from That of Movement and Space." *Phronesis* 21 (1976).

Darwin, Charles. "The Origin of Species." In *The Origin of Species and the Descent of Man.* New York: Random House, 1967.

De Boer, Theodor. "Zusammenfassung." In *De Ontwikkelingsgang in Het Denken van Husserl.* Assen: Van Gorcum, 1966.

Derrida, Jacques. "Structure, Sign, and Play in the Discourse of the Human Sciences." In *A Postmodern Reader.* Albany: SUNY Press, 1993.

Descartes, René. "Discourse on the Method." In *Philosophical Works of Descartes,* trans. E. Haldane and G. Ross, vol. 1. New York: Dover, 1955.

————. *Meditations on First Philosophy.* Trans. L. LaFleur. New York: Macmillan, 1990.

————. "The Passions of the Soul." In *Philosophical Works of Descartes,* trans. E. Haldane and G. Ross, vol 1. New York: Dover, 1955.

————. "Rules for the Direction of the Mind." In *Philosophical Works of Descartes,* trans. E. Haldane and G. Ross, vol 1. New York: Dover, 1955.

Fichte, J. G. *The Science of Knowledge.* Trans. P. Heath and J. Lachs. Cambridge, Eng.: Cambridge University Press, 1982.

Fitch, Frederic B. "Self-Reference in Philosophy." In *Contemporary Readings in Logical Theory,* eds. I. Copi and J. Gould. New York: Macmillan, 1967.

Frege, Gottlob. *Translations from the Philosophical Writings of Gottlob Frege.* Eds. and Trans. Peter Geach and Max Black. Oxford: Basil Blackwell, 1970.

Freud, Sigmund. *The Future of an Illusion.* Trans. W. D. Scott. Garden City, N.Y.: Doubleday Books, 1964.

————. *A General Introduction to Psychoanalysis.* Trans. J. Riviere. New York: Washington Square Press, 1965.

Galileo. *Two New Sciences.* Trans. S. Drake. Madison, Wis.: University of Wisconsin Press, 1974.

Heidegger, Martin. *The Basic Problems of Phenomenology.* Trans. A. Hofstadter. Rev. ed. Bloomington, Ind.: Indiana University Press, 1988.

————. *The Essence of Reasons.* Bilingual ed. Trans. T. Malick. Evanston, Ill.: Northwestern University Press, 1969.

————. *An Introduction to Metaphysics.* Trans. Ralph Manheim. New Haven, Conn.: Yale University Press, 1975.

————. *Kant and the Problem of Metaphysics.* Trans. James Churchill, Bloomington, Ind.: Indiana University Press, 1965.

————. *Nietzsche.* 4 vols. Trans. David Krell. San Francisco: Harper and Row, 1991.

————. *Sein und Zeit.* Tübingen: Max Niemeyer, 1967.

————. "Vom Wesen des Grundes." In *Wegmarken.* Frankfurt am Main: Vittorio Klostermann, 1967.

————. "Who Is Nietzsche's Zarathustra?" In *Nietzsche.* 4 vols. Trans. David Krell. San Francisco: Harper and Row, 1991.

Hegel, G. W. F. *Phenomenology of Mind.* Trans. J. B. Baillie. London: Allen and Unwin, 1966.

Hume, David. *A Treatise of Human Nature.* Ed. L. A. Selby-Bigge. Oxford: Clarendon Press, 1973.

Husserl. *Cartesianische Meditationen.* Ed. S. Strasser. Husserliana I. The Hague: Martinus Nijhoff, 1963.

————. *Erste Philosophie (1923/24), Erster Teil, Kritische Ideengeschichte.* Ed. R. Boehm. Husserliana VII. The Hague: Martinus Nijhoff, 1956.

————. *Erste Philosophie (1923/24), Zweiter Teil, Theorie der phänomeno-*

logischen Reduktion. Ed. R. Boehm. Husserliana VIII. The Hague: Martinus Nijhoff, 1959.

———. *Die Idee der Phänomenologie.* 2d ed. Husserliana II. The Hague: Martinus Nijhoff, 1973.

———. *Ideen zu einer reinen Phänomenologie und phänomenologischen Philosophie, Erstes Buch.* Ed. W. Biemel. Husserliana II. Cited as *"Ideen I,* Hua II" in notes and parenthetically in the text. The Hague: Martinus Nijhoff, 1950.

———. *Ideen zu einer reinen Phänomenologie und phänomenologischen Philosophie, Erstes Buch.* Ed. R. Schuhmann. Husserliana III. Cited as *"Ideen I,* Hua III" in notes and parenthetically in the text. The Hague: Martinus Nijhoff, 1976.

———. *Die Krisis der europäischen Wissenschaften und die transzendentale Phänomenologie.* Ed. W. Biemel. 2d ed. Husserliana VI. The Hague: Martinus Nijhoff, 1962.

———. *Logische Untersuchungen.* 5th ed. 2 vols. Tübingen: Max Niemeyer, 1968.

———. *Logische Untersuchungen.* Ed. Ursula Panzer. Husserliana XIX. The Hague: Martinus Nijhoff, 1984.

———. *Zur Phänomenologie der Intersubjectivität, Dritter Teil: 1929–1935.* Ed. I Kern. Husserliana XV. The Hague: Martinus Nijhoff, 1973.

———. *Zur Phänomenologie des inneren Zeitbewusstseins.* Ed. R. Boehm. Husserliana X. The Hague: Martinus Nijhoff, 1966.

James, William. "Does Consciousness Exist?" In *The Writings of William James,* ed. J. McDermott. New York: Random House, 1967.

———. "The Notion of Consciousness." In *The Writings of William James,* ed. J. McDermott. New York: Random House, 1967.

———. *Psychology, Briefer Course.* Cleveland: World Publishing Company, 1948.

Kant, Immanuel. "Critique of Practical Reason." In *Kant's Critique of Practical Reason and Other Works on the Theory of Ethics.* 6th ed. London: Longman's, 1963.

———. "Fundamental Principles of the Metaphysics of Morals." In *Kant's Critique of Practical Reason and Other Works on the Theory of Ethics.* 6th ed. Longman's: London, 1963.

———. "Kritik der reinen Vernunft." 1st ed. In *Kants gesammelte Schriften.* Ed. Königliche Preussische Akademie der Wissenschaften, vol. 4, pp. 1–252. Berlin: George Reiner, 1911.

———. "Kritik der reinen Vernunft." 2d ed. In *Kants gesammelte Schriften.* Ed. Königliche Preussische Akademie der Wissenschaften, vol. 3. Berlin: George Reiner, 1911.

———. "Prolegomena." In *Kants gesammelte Schriften.* Ed. Königliche Preussische Akademie der Wissenschaften, vol. 4, pp. 253–383. Berlin: George Reiner, 1911.

Kern, Iso. *Husserl und Kant.* The Hague: Martinus Nijhoff, 1964.

Klein, Jacob. *Greek Mathematical Thought and the Origin of Algebra.* Cambridge, Mass: MIT Press, 1968.

———. *Lectures and Essays.* Eds. R. Williamson and E. Zuckerman. Annapolis, Maryland, 1985.

Kojève, Alexandre. *Introduction to the Reading of Hegel.* Trans. James Nichols Jr. New York: Basic Books, 1969.

Leibniz. "Monadology." In *Basic Writings,* trans. George Montgomery. La Salle, Ill.: Open Court, 1962.

Lind, Richard. "The Priority of Attention: Intentionality for Automata." *The Monist* 69 (1978).

Locke, John. *An Essay Concerning Human Understanding.* 2 vols. London: J. M. Dent and Sons, 1961.

McIntyre, R. "Husserl and the Representational Theory of Mind." *Topoi* 5 (1986).

Mensch, James. "Aristotle and the Overcoming of the Subject-Object Dichotomy." *American Catholic Philosophical Quarterly* (Autumn, 1991).

————. "Between Plato and Descartes—The Mediaeval Transformation in the Ontological Status of the Ideas." *Saint John's Review* 35, no. 2 (Spring, 1984).

————. "Existence and Essence in Thomas and Husserl." In *The Horizons of Continental Philosophy.* Dordrecht: Klewer Press, 1988.

————. *Intersubjectivity and Transcendental Idealism.* Albany: SUNY Press, 1988.

————. "Phenomenology and Artificial Intelligence: Husserl Learns Chinese." *Husserl Studies* 8 (1991).

————. *The Question of Being in Husserl's Logical Investigations.* The Hague: Martinus Nijhoff, 1981.

Montaigne, Michel de. *Selected Essays.* Trans. William Hazlitt. New York: Random House, 1949.

Natoli, Joseph and Linda Hutcheon, eds. *A Postmodern Reader.* New York: SUNY Press, 1993.

Nietzsche, Friedrich. *Beyond Good and Evil.* Trans. R. J. Hollingdale. London, Penguin Books, 1990.

————. *Will to Power.* Trans. W. Kaufmann and R. Hollingdale. New York: Random House, 1968.

Parmenides. "Poem." In *The Presocratic Philosophers,* trans. and eds., G. S. Kirk and J. E. Raven. Cambridge, Eng.: Cambridge University Press, 1966.

Pavlov, Ivan P. *Lectures on Conditioned Reflexes.* Trans. W. Horsley Gantt. New York: International Publishers, 1967.

Plato. "Parmenides." In *The Dialogues of Plato,* vol. 2, trans. B. Jowett. New York: Random House, 1937.

————. *Platonis Opera.* Ed. Burnet. 5 vols. Oxford: Clarendon Press, 1957.

Pylyshyn, Z. W. "Minds, Machines and Phenomenology: Some Reflections on Dreyfus' 'What Computers Can't Do.'" *Cognition* 3, no. 1 (1974–5).

Sacks, Oliver. "To See and Not See." *New Yorker,* May 10, 1993.

Sartre, Jean Paul. *Being and Nothingness.* Trans. Hazel Barnes. New York: Washington Square Press, 1968.

————. "Consciousness of Self and Knowledge of Self," trans. M. Ellen and N. Lawrence. In *Readings in Existential Phenomenology.* Englewood Cliffs, N. J.: Prentice Hall, 1967.

Searle, John. "Is the Brain's Mind a Computer Program?" *Scientific American,* January 1990.

————. "Minds, Brains, and Programs." *The Behavioral and Brain Sciences* (1980).

————. "Reply to Jacquette." *Philosophy and Phenomenological Research* 49 (1989).

Sophocles. "Antigone." In *Sophocles I.* 2d ed. Trans. David Greene. Chicago: University of Chicago Press, 1991.

———. "Oedipus the King." In *Sophocles I.* 2d ed. Trans. David Greene. Chicago: University of Chicago Press, 1991.

Stent, Gunter. "Limits to the Scientific Understanding of Man." *Science* 187 (1974).

Vattimo, Gianni. *The End of Modernity.* Trans. Jon Snyder. Baltimore: John Hopkins University Press, 1988.

Wittgenstein, Ludwig. *On Certainty.* Trans. D. Paul and G. E. M. Anscombe. New York: Harper, 1972.

Index of Names

Index of Subjects

antinomies, 58–59
Anton's syndrome, 159
appearance vs. reality, 2, 7, 8, 30, 34, 77–78, 152–53, 199, 202, 207–8
applicability vs. validity, 108

being
  as being perceived, 31–31, 64
  coextensive with intelligibility, 24, 79
  determined by knowing, 29, 30, 31, 41, 43, 46, 50–51, 62, 63, 74, 82, 180
  determined by time, 6, 73, 83, 85, 123, 180
  determining time, 74, 76, 85–87, 95, 119–20, 125, 167, 174, 176, 185, 187
  as perceiving, 35–37
  pluralization of, 76–77, 98–99, 119, 200–201, 204, 206–7
  as prior to knowing, 29, 74
  as self-identity, 24–26, 27
  as temporal presence, 7, 73, 123, 125, 131, 180
  as at workness (ἐνεργεία), 89–90, 91, 147, 151, 198

causality, 31, 33, 38
  final, 94–96, 98–100, 102, 103, 105, 132, 147–48, 150–51, 160, 161, 170. *See also* teleology
  law of, 17

material, 44, 103, 108–9, 141, 173
and normativity, 61–61
circularity
  of Aristotle's position, 100–101
  of historicism, 82
  of modernity, 64
  of proof of God, 29, 44
  of science, 61, 107–8
clarity and distinctness, 2, 14–15, 18, 19, 28–30, 34, 42, 55, 62, 195
complementarity principle, 193, 195, 196, 197, 202
Copernican revolution, 68–70

Dasein, 76n. 5, 99, 100, 101, 102, 166n. 13
desire, 149–50, 152, 160–61, 165, 167, 202, 215
dialectic of intention and fulfillment, 139–42, 167, 173, 179n. 2, 200, 204, 209–10
discrimination factor, 136, 137, 139, 140
doubt, Cartesian, 2–3, 13–14, 18, 22, 28, 35, 36, 42, 53–54, 144, 178–79, 181, 190, 195
dualism, 22, 24, 36, 39–40, 57–58, 103–4, 105, 106, 169, 170–71

earth, 215–17, 219
embodiment, 17–18, 75, 116–17, 130, 161,